MAKE YOUR OWN KIND OF MAGICK

Witchcraft embraces as many different traditions as there are Witches. If your vision is to create a tradition of your own—one rooted in natural magick, shaped to fit your personal goals and beliefs—*Embracing the Moon* will shine a light on your path.

Embracing the Moon is based on a practicing Witch's personal magickal system. She has already cast the spells, blended the oils, used the invocations, so you know they work. From basic tenets of Witchcraft, to spellcasting, to ritual Shadow Work, this guide opens a whole world of magick to you.

Make your spiritual path as unique as you are. *Embracing the Moon* gives you all the options, expert insights and support you need to work natural magick in a way that's meaningful for you.

About the Author

Yasmine Galenorn (Washington) is a writer and poet. A Priestess of Mielikki and Tapio, Galenorn has been a Witch in the Craft since 1980. Practicing both as a solitary and with others, she is a teacher of magick and Witchcraft who has led numerous public and private rituals. She holds a degree in Theatrical Management and Creative Writing and has a background in the performing arts. She is happily married and lives with her husband and four wonderful cats.

To Write to the Author

If you wish to contact the author or would like more information about this book, please write to the author in care of Llewellyn Worldwide and we will forward your request. Both the author and the publisher appreciate hearing from you and learning of your enjoyment of this book and how it has helped you. Llewellyn Worldwide cannot guarantee that every letter written to the author can be answered, but all will be forwarded. Please write to:

Yasmine Galenorn
c/o Llewellyn Worldwide
P.O. Box 64383, Dept. 304-2
St. Paul, MN 55164-0383, U.S.A.

Please enclose a self-addressed, stamped envelope for reply, or $1.00 to cover costs. If outside U.S.A., enclose international postal reply coupon.

EMBRACING THE MOON

A Witch's Guide to Ritual
Spellcraft and Shadow Work

Yasmine Galenorn

1998
Llewellyn Publications
St. Paul, Minnesota 55164-0383

FIRST EDITION
Second Printing, 1998

Cover design by Anne Marie Garrison
Book editing and design by Astrid Sandell

Library of Congress Cataloging-in-Publication Data
Galenorn, Yasmine, 1961-
    Embracing the moon : a witch's guide to ritual spellcraft &
shadow work / Yasmine Galenorn
      p.   cm.
    Includes bibliographical references and index.
    ISBN 1-56718-304-2 (pbk.)
    1. Witchcraft. I. Title.
    BF1571.G25   1998
    133.4"4—dc21   97-49901
                                         CIP

Printed in the United States of America

Llewellyn Publications
A Division of Llewellyn Worldwide, Ltd.
P.O. Box 64383, Dept. K304-2, St. Paul, MN 55164-0383

DEDICATION

I dedicate this book to all of the Witches, Shamans, Priestesses, Medicine Men, Wise Women, Druids, Midwives, Wolves, Bears, Panthers, Snakes and all others slaughtered in the name of religion, domination and economics.

We do remember.

Also by Yasmine Galenorn

Trancing the Witch's Wheel: A Guide to Magickal Meditation

Forthcoming

Kissing the Sun: Pagan Holidays and Celebrations for the Whole Year

ACKNOWLEDGMENTS

I would like to acknowledge all of those who helped me with this book, especially:

James "Thunderhande" Staples, Priest of Thor

Daniela Staples, Priestess of Freya

Kay Ridgway, Dancer of Many Paths

Allwynd, Painter of Dreams

Phillip Christophers, Prince of Horses

Samwise Galenorn, my Beloved Husband and Computer Guru

Pakhit, Luna, Meerclar, and Tara, my Furry Children

and, of course

Mielikki, Goddess of Fey, Mistress of the Hunt, my Lady of the Forest

Tapio, Lord of the Forest, Pack-Master, Dark-Bearded One, my Lord of the Wolves

and

Madame Pele, Mistress of Kilauea, honored guest in my home, my heart and my life

You have all brought magick and wonder to my life

Thank you

CONTENTS

Introduction

My journey into magick and Witchcraft officially began on February 29, 1980. For several years I had been casting around, testing different spiritual paths to find the one right for me. I looked into Buddhism, Agnosticism, and the New Age movement, but still nothing seemed right. I had heard of Witchcraft, and while I no longer connected it with Satanism, I believed it was for those who felt powerless to control their own lives. I had never heard of the Goddess as most Witches see Her, and while I felt the wild pull of the Moon, I never paid it much attention.

Then, on February 29, 1980 (Leap Year Day, of all days), my life changed, inexorably and forever.

I was attending The Evergreen State College, had recently turned 19 years old and was in my junior year. I'd obtained my A.A. degree at age seventeen, and by the time I was nineteen, there had been many changes in my life. I'd hitch-hiked to California to live with my sister, gotten engaged, and broke the engagement just as quickly. I returned to Washington State and enrolled at Eastern Washington University but decided I didn't like it there. I went home for a brief time and that didn't work out, either.

So I decided to move to Olympia, Washington to attend Evergreen. From the moment I arrived in September 1979, I knew that

I had made the right decision. Situated in Western Washington along Budd Inlet, the Evergreen State College sits on one thousand acres of land, most of which is relatively undeveloped. While I found some of the academics lacking, I quickly fell in love with the environment and knew that I could never again move inland, away from the coast with its rolling oceans.

Back then, it still seemed safe to walk alone at night and I often took off after midnight to wander through the mist that rose along the soccer fields through the trees.

It reminded me of the Faerie-land I heard of in childhood—mystical and ancient—and when the mist clouded the sidewalks I felt as if I were slipping between worlds. Were dragons hiding around the corner? Might I be about to stumble on a group of trolls in the shadows of the woods? I longed for something new, something different to show me the realities that I suspected were out there.

Then, in early 1980, I had two experiences that would forever change my life.

The first was in late January, shortly after my nineteenth birthday. I was meandering along a particular path that I walked during the day and wanted to see by moonlight.

A good friend of mine during this time wanted to come with me. It was around two in the morning and we were walking along, talking quietly, when we both suddenly stopped, arrested by a glowing light in the trees no more than ten feet away.

There, glowing white and brilliant, stood a unicorn. The little horned horse couldn't have been more than three feet high and everything around it shimmered with an ethereal light.

Cautiously, I looked around to see if it might be some kind of reflection. I could see the moon clearly through the trees; it was shining, but the moonbeams were obviously not the source of the vision before us.

There was no one near us. The only movement was the slight quiver of a breeze gently blowing against the cedar and fir boughs.

"Do you see what I see?" I whispered to my friend.

She nodded and I could tell she was afraid. "I think so," she said. "What do you see?"

"It looks like a unicorn," I answered.

"I think so, too," she said.

We looked at the unicorn and it stared back at us with its dark and compelling eyes—and we watched each other for at least thirty seconds.

Half a minute may not seem like much time, but it can be an eternity when you're gazing into the eyes of what is supposed to be a mythological creature. It flicked its tail gently once or twice, shifted its head—this was no statue—and, as abruptly as it had appeared, the unicorn vanished.

I immediately ran to the place it had stood. There were too many shadows to look for tracks, but I proved to myself that it had not been a balloon, statue, or piece of metal reflecting in the moonlight.

I searched for all possibilities, I went crashing around in the nearby woods dragging my friend behind me, searching for anyone else who might have been there, but the trail and forest surrounding it were quiet and empty.

Finally we gave up and returned to our dormitory. My friend remained frightened, even when we woke up another friend to tell what had happened. It didn't help that she thought we were both stoned and told us to go away.

I accepted what I had seen. The next day I went back out to search, but the unicorn had been standing in a thick pile of wet leaves and there were no tracks anywhere.

I'm sure that an entire police force wouldn't have found anything. I believe that we'd slipped through into another dimension, or, more likely, that the unicorn had slipped through into ours.

It didn't matter. I had seen a unicorn and was thoroughly enchanted. My friend, however, didn't want to talk about it. Not long after our experience she refused to discuss it, and several years later when I tried to bring it up again, she insisted she didn't remember that night. I let it drop. Some people are not meant to follow the path leading to unicorns.

So, when I went out walking about a month later on Leap Year night, I felt expectant. I suppose I hoped to see the unicorn again but I was in no way prepared for what was about to happen.

The moon hung huge, glowing, and silver in the sky. I was walking up the road when I felt something near my foot—a cat, trying to get my attention. Mangy, lonely, and probably hungry, the cat reached up and pawed at my hand. I bent to pet it and it promptly ran off into the bushes.

A while later I crossed the campus commons and heard a mew. It was the same cat, running out from under a bench. Again, I petted it and again it purred, then ran off.

I had been wandering for about two hours, enjoying the crisp night air, when I began across the soccer field. There was no mist that night, the field was clear, the sky shining with stars. A third time I heard a cry, and for a third time the same cat came running out of the trees, demanding attention. I began to suspect there might be more going on than coincidence.

As the cat ran away I turned from where I stood and looked up at the moon. Suddenly, all sound stopped; the frogs stopped croaking, traffic fell silent, and in the core of my being it felt like time itself had dropped away.

I stared up at the moon, totally enthralled, and heard a woman's voice echo around me. Ancient beyond old, it seemed to reverberate from every direction.

"Do you know who I am?" She said, and without being told, without ever hearing of Her, I knew who She was.

The Goddess. The Goddess of all things and all creatures, the Moon Goddess, the Earth Goddess . . . this voice contained all of Her power.

"Yes. Oh yes, Lady," I whispered.

"You know what you are."

And then I knew—just as I knew it was the Goddess with whom I was speaking—that I have been before and always will be, a Witch.

"I am a Witch," I said, wondering at the revelation.

"Are you ready to come home to me? Are you ready to reclaim your heritage?" She asked.

This was it. If I said no, I felt I might lose my chance forever. I also understood with perfect clarity that this was the path I had been waiting for, had been searching for. I leapt into the abyss.

"I'm ready," I said. "I want to be Yours."

"You must find your way back to me," the Goddess said. "It will be difficult, but you must persevere. You are mine, remember this."

The world around me sprang back to life. The frogs began to croak, cars swept by, the Moon was once again just the Moon, but now it was so much more. And I . . . I have never looked back.

When I realized how much there was to learn, I immediately ensconced myself in the library. I was surprised by how little seemed to be written about Witchcraft. Though there must have been more available, at the time all I could find were books discussing the history of the Salem Witch Trials. I read them but knew that, somewhere, there had to be information on modern Witches and Witchcraft. Someone else had to know about the Goddess.

About a year later, I found two books in the library. One was Starhawk's book *Dreaming the Dark*. Shortly after, I discovered Margot Adler's book *Drawing Down the Moon*. Using these two books, I began my first excursions into magick and ritual.

Later I would discover Starhawk's *The Spiral Dance* and still later, Z Budapest's book *The Holy Book of Women's Mysteries* and Sybil Leek's *Diary of a Witch*. In early 1985, I also managed to get hold of a copy of *Circle Network News* and *The Beltane Papers*, two periodicals.

In 1985, I reached another turning point. Starhawk came to The Evergreen State College campus and hosted a one-day workshop on magick and ritual. I scrimped and saved to pay the nominal cost. There must have been sixty or more people there—townsfolk, housewives, students—I hadn't had the faintest idea how many people were interested in the Craft. It blew my mind that there were actually enough people to fill the room. While I didn't make any lasting contacts, it encouraged me to continue my studies. I knew that I wasn't alone even though it often seemed like it.

Most of my magick and ritual for the first eight or nine years came through experimentation—trial and error. As Witchcraft and Wicca became increasingly popular, I added to my library. In late 1987, I began working with a friend whose magick, while different than my own, was similar enough at the time to allow us a lot of fun and results, and it filled that gap I felt so keenly as a solitary Witch.

In 1991, I started to link up with other people. I began to lead rituals at CUUPs (Covenant of Unitarian Universalist Pagans) and became well known in the Pagan community that was quickly growing in the area. Working with a study group and pseudo-coven, I came to realize that experimenting had taken me places that books never could. My rituals and magick worked.

I also realized that I could not call myself Wiccan. While there are many more similarities than differences between my beliefs and the Wiccan creed, the differences are there. I call myself Wiccan on hospital forms, surveys, and the like, simply because it can be used as a blanket term for many Pagan branches of Witchcraft; but I don't consider myself Wiccan when it comes to technicalities.

I am a Witch. This book is a compendium of my magick, rituals, and beliefs. I have used just about every spell in this book with results varying from fair to excellent. The others I have designed, with good results, for people who needed help.

Be aware that some of my spells call for a few drops of your own blood and some seem a little harsh. There are reasons for including these.

I have worked intensely with the Dark Mother over the years. She is a Goddess of blood and lust and strength. Her compassion is just, her mercy saved for those who truly deserve it. There are evil people in the world and it is my firm belief that love will not cure them. These people—the child abusers and molesters, the rapists and murderers, those who prey on the innocent and unsuspecting— they do not change. All the white light in the world isn't going to change them.

The concept of karma is well and good, but sometimes one must be willing to be an instrument of karma. We have police officers and prisons in the mundane world, and we need a little of this on the spiritual level as well. My friends and I like to think of it as being "karmic facilitators."

I have helped a number of women whose children have been molested. I do healing spells for the children, "justice spells" for the court system, and rituals that offer the offender up to the Dark Mother for Her justice. If the person is truly guilty—the Goddess will know—I ask that true justice be meted out on the spiritual level. It works.

As far as blood ritual goes, our blood carries the very essence of who we are—it carries our life-force. Occasionally we will want to bind a spell solely to ourselves and the strength of our desire. While hair and fingernail clippings can be substituted, I've had my best luck using a few drops of my own blood.

I never use the blood of any person or any creature who cannot agree to the practice. All animals are sacred to the Goddess and, while I do eat meat, I never involve an animal in my magick who doesn't show an interest in being in circle with me. I never use animal blood in my rituals, it would go against the grain of my magick.

If I need a drop of someone's blood for a spell I'm casting for them, I tactfully ask how they feel about this. If they show any discomfort I drop the issue and ask for a lock of their hair instead.

Use your common sense. Use your humanity. The use of magick and ritual brings with it a great responsibility. You must have foresight and compassion to be an effective Witch.

Magick, Witchcraft, the Goddess . . . my life would be empty without them. It may not be the path for you, but only you can make that decision.

About This Book

This book is intended for the serious practitioner of magick and Witchcraft. While all spells and rituals can be performed "as is" with good results, the more advanced student should experiment, alter the spells as needed, substitute when necessary—in other words, get to know the magick first, then don't be afraid to play with it.

Using the word "play" is not to suggest in any manner that magick is anything less than serious and difficult work. But you should enjoy your magick, too. There are times for the energy to be solemn, when the magick should, by necessity, be somber and even grim. But working magick frees the soul to touch upon a side of life few people ever experience. Natural Magick uses the forces and elements around us, in cooperation with the Gods, to alter our lives for the better.

A simple explanation, but a very complex process.

What Magick Can Do for You

Magick can draw the right relationship to you, it can increase your prosperity, it can protect you on psychic and sometimes physical levels. Magick can aid in unlocking your creative abilities, open the door to your psychic strengths and gifts, and guide you in understanding and attuning to the cycles of the Earth.

Magick can mean the difference in a successful job interview, or can be the deciding factor when you are up for a promotion.

Effective magick is a lot of hard work but it can also offer a creative and fun outlet for your energy and time.

WHAT MAGICK CAN'T DO FOR YOU

Magick can't guarantee that you're going to win the lottery. It's not designed to gain control over people or to make someone infatuated with your personal charms. Magick won't take the place of a good lock on the door, it won't do your job for you, or take the place of practice on the piano. It's not a quick fix or a jump-start into stardom.

Magick isn't about controlling the forces around you, it isn't a substitute for calling the police about an abusive partner. You probably won't learn to fly (in-body) or to levitate a table.

Magick isn't here to grant you three wishes, no holds barred. If you expect it to do the work for you, you're probably going to be disappointed.

HOW SHOULD I START?

If you are a beginner, perform the spells and rituals as written until you get the feel for the magick. Study the chapters and practice the exercises presented in Part One. Just because you carve runes on a candle, say a few words to the Gods, and stare at the flame, it doesn't mean you are casting a spell.

You must understand the nature of magick before you can work with it effectively. Each magickal system works with a slightly different variant of universal energy and what works in one system may not work for another.

If you have been studying Cabalistic Magick, Ceremonial Magick, or anything other than Natural Magick, you're not going to understand the differences until you do the exercises and spend the time training yourself under my system.

While most people can learn to practice Natural Magick and Witchcraft, I also know that my particular practices may not be right for everyone. Many of my students jumped in and enjoyed the process, but there were a few for whom my teaching just didn't work.

Sometimes the student wasn't willing to devote the time and energy it takes to learn. In other cases, my views of magick didn't resonate with their individual reality bases.

I encourage you to devote at least three months of daily practice to the exercises presented in Part One. Of course, you can jump ahead and cast the spells, but without the ability to focus the energy that comes through practice, your results may not be as strong as when you are thoroughly grounded in the energy.

If you are an intermediate or advanced student, you can either cast the spells and do the rituals as they are written or, using my guidelines and what you have gleaned through your own experience and other reading, you can make the necessary adjustments and substitutions.

Even though I have been in the Craft since 1980, I am always picking up new ideas from the books I read. I fully subscribe to the idea that you can learn something from every experience, even if it only shows you what you don't want to do.

Being an advanced student of the Craft has its own pitfalls. It's easy to get lazy, to fall into a rut, and simply go about the motions. Sometimes we need to rekindle the spark that drew us to magick in the first place. Sometimes all it takes is a nudge—a new spell or talking with another Pagan. Other times, we need to explore new dimensions of our magickal selves—a reason so many Witches have studied the Cabala and Ceremonial Magick. While I am not drawn to these two subjects, I am thoroughly fascinated by the Egyptians, Shamanism, and Hawaiian Magick.

If you are suffering from a lull, start exploring the myriad avenues open to us in the metaphysical field. Who knows, you might discover a whole new love.

USING THIS BOOK

This book is divided into three parts and also includes a Resource Guide, Glossary, Bibliography, and an Index.

Part One is designed to prepare you for work in Spellcraft and Ritual. It includes chapters on visualization, magick and ritual procedure, creating sacred space, elements and deities, magickal tools, and chants, rune charts, and symbols. With proper study, these chapters will prepare you to practice the more advanced aspects of the magickal system presented in this book.

Part Two includes spellcraft designed to improve your life. Included are the basics of herbal and candle magick, spells for prosperity, love, lust, beauty, glamour, protection, purification, healing, and creativity. There are also ideas for making your household more magickal.

Part Three delves into the shadow magick of ritual—the magick of Nature and the magick of the Gods. Since I am pledged to a Woodland Goddess, I work intensively with Faerie Magick and have included some rituals and spells designed to increase your connection with those realms. In this section, you will also find chapters devoted to animal magick (to increase your connection with other species and with your totems), Goddess invocations, God invocations, and rituals designed to help heal the damage being done to our planet—including an endangered species ritual.

Once you have read through Part One and practiced the exercises, skip through and try the spells as you like. Again I suggest reading the whole book—you might find something that you don't expect. I recommend keeping a journal regarding your efforts. Don't forget to date the entries (see Book of Shadows, chapter eight).

Too often, books of spells and rituals are too simple for my taste. There is a time and place for quick, simple spells, and I include some of those in this volume. But on these pages you will also find more complex spells that take longer than half an hour to cast.

I love magick and Witchcraft, not just for what it offers in a tangible sense, but for its very nature. The Universe is so vast and fascinating; magickal work is one way to explore some of its paths. Bright Blessings and may your connection to the Lady never waver.

Part One

Ritual Preparation

1

VISUALIZATION

In its simplest terms, visualization is the process of forming a mental image, of visualizing some object or event. Magickal visualization, however, involves much more than that.

Before we begin, one point must be clarified. Some people simply can't seem to visualize no matter how hard they try. Perhaps they aren't visually oriented or they might block themselves through fear, through trying too hard or not really understanding the mechanics of visualization.

Subconscious motives are often hard to discern. If you are one of these people, then the system of magick in this book will be difficult for you to use because much of it rests on the foundation of intense visualization and the ability to sense and manipulate the energy that surrounds us.

However, I have found that with practice most people can learn how to visualize and their capacity increases as they devote more time to it.

If you find it difficult to form mental images at will or on command, keep practicing and see if it gets better after a few months. Sometimes a little discipline is all it takes to retrain your mind after months or years of apathy. Remember, you can't become a concert violinist without putting in thousands of hours playing the scales. Magick is no different.

If you can use your imagination, you can learn to visualize.

You are sitting in your favorite chair and a song comes on the radio. It is the song that you heard the night you met your best friend. Every time you hear the song you slip into a light trance, remembering what happened that night—who told what jokes, who tripped and spilled their drink, who started the argument that actually got you two talking—it doesn't matter what the events were. What is important is that you relive them through your memory. In reliving those events, you are visualizing.

To use visualization in magick, you simply learn how to "remember" in reverse.

Yet many people have difficulty at first.

In our society, daydreaming is often discouraged. People expect you to be constantly on the go. If you sit down and let your mind wander for even a few minutes someone is going to come up and say, "What's wrong? Do you need something to do?"

While visualization is not the same as daydreaming, the two are similar. If you have difficulty visualizing, you might be confronting some guilt issues. Giving yourself time to focus on what you want isn't always socially acceptable. You also might find that you don't really know what you want—this can make your visualization unclear, as well.

Remember that you must know what you want in order to get it. If you can't visualize something, it probably means that you don't have a clear idea of what you truly desire. Perhaps your subconscious might be warning you that what you think you want is not what you really need.

Exercises in Simple Visualization

The following exercises are designed to help you develop primary abilities in visualization. Even if you have been using visualization for a while, I encourage you to try them. A refresher course can't hurt. Once you are proficient and the exercises become easy, move on to the advanced exercises and work with them. Be patient, give yourself plenty of time.

EXERCISE ONE: THE PICTURE

We begin with a memory-visualization exercise. Find a painting or poster that you like and are familiar with. It shouldn't be too big or crowded with different elements.

> Hold the painting and look at it for five minutes. Examine it thoroughly, make mental notes about its composition, the colors, and all of the other elements. When five minutes have passed, turn the painting face down. Sit back, get comfortable and close your eyes. Re-create the painting in your mind. How many elements can you remember? Don't simply list them off, instead actually see them. Can you see the painting as a whole? Or do you just see bits of it to start with? Linger over the different images that float through your mind. Spend five minutes visualizing the painting.

> As above, examine the painting for five minutes. Then put it away and go about your daily business. Wait for two or three hours before you try to re-create the picture mentally. With this exercise you begin to create distance between the subject of your visualization and yourself.

> For the last part of this exercise, sit down in a comfortable position. Take a few minutes to think about several different pictures you have seen in the past. Choose one of your favorites. Close your eyes and visualize it with as much detail as you can.

This exercise helps to develop your sense of sight. The next exercise involves three-dimensional visualization and includes not only sight but touch, taste, and scent.

EXERCISE TWO: A PIECE OF FRUIT

For this exercise, you will need a good, ripe piece of solid fruit, like a pear, apple, or peach.

> Relax, sit back, and look at the piece of fruit you've chosen. Turn it over, feel it in your hands. Look at the color, see where one shade blends into another. Lift it to your nose and inhale deeply. Let its aroma fill your lungs. Close your eyes.

For five minutes let your fingers examine its indentations and curves. Now take a bite of it. Allow the flavor to linger on your tongue. How does the flesh feel between your teeth? Swallow. Now, put it down and rinse your mouth out with water.

After a ten-minute break sit down, relax, and close your eyes. Re-create the experience in your mind. Spend five minutes visualizing the fruit.

Several days after you performed this exercise, sit in a chair, relax, and close your eyes. Choose one of the fruits you practiced with. Relive the experience, make it as vivid as you can. Feel it in your hands and on your tongue. Smell the aroma and taste the fruit.

This exercise involves four of your five physical senses: touch, sight, taste, and smell. Each of these is important in visualization, as is your fifth sense, hearing. To work with that sense, practice the next exercise.

EXERCISE THREE: THE SONG

You will need a cassette recorder or compact disc player and a recording of one of your favorite songs. It should have lyrics and they should be understandable.

Play the song several times. Close your eyes and listen to it. Don't try to memorize it, just let the music filter through your mind. If you notice that your thoughts are drifting, gently direct them back to the song. Notice how your body reacts to the music, pay attention to the sensations that the song brings up.

Now turn off the music and give yourself a five-minute break. Then sit down, close your eyes, and play the song in your mind. Let your body hear the music. Do you feel like swaying to the music? Keep your eyes closed, stand, and respond to the music. Don't strain yourself if you can't hear all the lyrics in your mind. If your thoughts start to wander, bring them back to the song. Pay attention to the different instruments and how they sound.

After you have practiced this exercise several times, sit down, relax, and replay the song in your mind without listening to it first. Try to re-create all of your body's reactions to the music.

EXERCISE FOUR: IMPORTANT EVENT

This exercise will guide you in learning to re-create what you've already experienced and will begin to teach you how to alter events in your life. It is a good preparation for the more advanced exercises.

Think of an important event in your life, one that was a good experience for you. Try to recall as many of the details as you can. Relive the experience, feel the joy, the excitement . . . recapture your feelings from that time and let yourself experience them again. Don't embellish what happened, you want to be as accurate as possible.

Next, choose an event that was not as happy—not a major trauma but something that didn't turn out quite the way you wanted. Again, faithfully re-create the experience.

For this part of the exercise, use the disappointing event you recalled. Instead of visualizing the actual ending, revise it. See the experience as you wanted it to play out. Re-create the ending as a happy, but realistic, possibility.

This exercise has two purposes. It gives you practice visualizing that which has not yet manifested and it is a good way to clear up lingering disappointments about things that didn't go the way we'd hoped. Its purpose is not to deny the past, but rather to give us experience should we someday be faced with a similar situation.

ADVANCED VISUALIZATION EXERCISES

Once you feel you have become proficient with the basic elements of visualization, you can proceed to these more advanced exercises.

For beginners, I suggest that you practice the basic exercises at least three weeks before tackling this next section, but only you can judge your progress. Do not rush, learning magick isn't a race.

EXERCISE FIVE: THE JOB INTERVIEW

This exercise involves one of the most dreaded social situations in America: the job interview. I've known many people who were petrified of going to job interviews. In these cases, magick and visualization can really help.

If you are currently happy in your job or career and have no plans for leaving, you might want to try one of the other advanced exercises instead, but remember—if you ever expect to be up for promotion this can come in handy.

> Find a time when you are not rushed. Make yourself comfortable, sit back, and close your eyes. Imagine that you have a job interview soon. Think of a job or promotion that you would like to attain. Now imagine that it is the morning of the interview.

> See yourself get out of bed—bright and alert. You look in the mirror and say, "I know I'm going to get that job or a better one because I am the right person for the position." Take a shower, put on your deodorant and, if you wear it, perfume or powder. Brush your teeth.

> Envision yourself dressing for the interview—everything you wear has been neatly pressed the night before so you don't have to worry. When you are dressed, look in the mirror and see how good you look—perfect for the position you're interviewing for.

> Now, see yourself gathering your résumé and personal history together. You look at the clock, you have plenty of time to get to the interview. You drive, walk, or take the bus and arrive at the interviewer's office fifteen minutes early.

> The person who will interview you greets you and takes your résumé. They seem happy to see you and when they ask you questions, you have ready answers and reply easily and confidently. They might ask you questions such as:

> "Why are you the right person for the job?"

"Why do you want to work for our company?"

"Tell me about your strengths and your weaknesses."

Each time they ask you a difficult question you have no trouble in answering. Now see the interviewer write something down on your résumé and then stand up, smiling. You know you have made a good impression. Shake hands and leave the office.

See yourself back in your home. The phone rings and it is the interviewer, offering you the job.

As an alternative ending for this exercise, follow the visualization until you arrive back in your home. Now imagine that you get a call from the interviewer. The person says, "We don't think you're right for this position, but we have an opening that we think would suit you much better." Practice reacting to this until you are comfortable with the possibility.

EXERCISE SIX: OTHER SCENARIOS

There are many scenarios you can use in place of the job interview presented in exercise five. With each of the following suggestions, your future or happiness should not be dependent on a single outcome. You should practice each one with at least two possible endings that would be satisfactory. Sometimes what we think we want isn't what we actually need. Give the universe some help—allow it more than one chance to make you happy.

The Party: This is a good scenario for those who are uncomfortable meeting strangers. See yourself mingling freely and happily with people you've never met. You are witty, charming, and interesting.

The Confrontation: Imagine a time when you have to confront someone on an uncomfortable issue. See the two of you discussing it calmly and coming to a mutually agreeable compromise. If you have truly been wronged, you can visualize the other person apologizing for their behavior. Just remember, it usually takes two to create a problem.

Buying a Car: This is a good exercise for those who have difficulty protecting their rights when making major purchases with negotiable pricing. See yourself researching the material (and then actually follow through); then see yourself walking into the dealer and calmly stating what you want. Envision the dealer being fair, and you may also envision yourself sticking to a price that you will not go above and see yourself paying just that price for the car.

Goal-Setting: See yourself setting a particular goal then following through until the goal is accomplished. This exercise can be very telling—if you cannot see yourself finishing the goal, then perhaps it is not one you should be pursuing. Envision yourself reaching the goal in a variety of ways.

Visualization is a powerful tool on its own, but when coupled with magick, it can produce incredible results.

2

Magick and Ritual Procedure

There are many definitions for the word *magick*. *The American Heritage Dictionary*, Second College Edition, states that magick is:

> 1. The art that purports to control or forecast natural events, effects, or forces by invoking the supernatural. 2.a. The practice of using charms, spells, or rituals to attempt to produce supernatural effects or to control events in nature. b. The charms, spells, and rituals so used.

This is a good answer, as far as it goes.

If you ask ten Witches to define magick you will get ten variations of the above answer. Below I offer my definition, as applied in this book and in my magickal practice. If you want to pursue the study of different systems, by all means, do. It's a fascinating subject.

Yasmine's Definition of Magick

I propose that magick as we know and use it is the use of natural and supernatural forces and elements surrounding us to alter reality and promote change within our lives and environments.

Magick comes from the four elements: Earth, Air, Fire, and Water. It comes from the Deities that we work with, from our own bodies and auras, from beings who inhabit other planes of existence, and from the force connecting everything throughout the universe. It is that primal force of creation and it cannot be destroyed, only changed.

Energy, as I define it, is the force or current used in magick.

The cornerstone of any spell or ritual is the ability to focus and direct energy, to channel it to the desired end through the use of tools, visualization, and will.

Raising Energy

This exercise is the cornerstone for my magickal system. You must master this exercise in order for your magick to have the kick you desire. The good news is that the majority of people I have taught learned it within five minutes. Then it was just a matter of practice for them to become proficient at it.

It helps to have another person with you when you learn this exercise but it's not a necessity. I first learned it several years before I became a Witch with a few of my friends from a drama class. We were using it to raise energy before putting on a show. When I became a Witch I realized that this simple little exercise was going to make my spellcraft stronger and easier.

If you are working with another person, sit on the floor or on chairs facing each other, about twenty inches apart (your knees should not be touching). If you are learning this alone, pick a quiet place where you will not be rushed or interrupted.

Remove jewelry and watches. Do not listen to music or watch television while practicing this, at least not to begin with. You will need your full concentration. I suggest removing your glasses.

Hold your hands in front of you, palms facing each other. Your elbows should be bent so that your hands are turned inward. Bring your hands together and rub vigorously for a few seconds.

Now very slowly begin to separate your hands, keeping them level with one another. You should feel a tingling sensation—some people notice a magnetic sensation, as if your hands are trying to pull together or push apart.

Still moving slowly, separate them a little more until your hands are about two inches apart.

Now slowly bring them together again, not touching but very close. Feel the prickles between your hands.

Once again, begin to separate them.

Continue this back-and-forth movement until your hands are separated at least five or six inches. If you are very kinesthetic you should be able to still feel the connection when they are over a foot apart.

The energy that you feel between your hands is the energy that I call magick.

If you are working with another person, have one partner slowly lower one hand, palm facing sideways, between the other person's hands during this exercise. Do not touch hands. Both people should be able to feel the flux of the energy as another element comes into play. Then switch places and try again from the beginning.

TIPS FOR RAISING ENERGY

- Practice this exercise daily for a month to get a good grasp on it. You may notice that the energy varies in strength depending on your physical state of being, the weather, whether or not you just had a fight with your mate, or for any other number of reasons.

- If at first you don't succeed, try again. I have only known one person who hasn't been able to master this. However, he had serious personal blocks and shouldn't be practicing magick anyway.

- This is not a game. It is very real energy, so be careful how you use it.

- After you have practiced this for a week or so, try to raise the energy without rubbing your hands together first. I hardly ever have to do that step anymore—I just place my palms together, settle into a quiet trance state, slowly pull them apart and there it is!

- Once you are comfortable with raising energy, start playing with it and shaping it. It is easy to use your hands to shape it into a ball or to pull it out (using bent fingers to stretch it) like taffy.

- You may find that it takes a lot of focus to keep the energy together at first. If it keeps dispersing, leave it alone for the day and try again later.

- Once you are comfortable with shaping the energy, start focusing it. You can slowly turn your hands so they are facing a plant or a stone (or a rune or a candle) and let the energy pour out into the selected object. This is called charging an item and it means that you are filling the item with energy. You can charge places on your body that ache or are tired and see an immediate lift in energy or reduction in pain. (Do not use this as a replacement for medical therapy—see chapter twelve).

THE CONE OF POWER

Once you are working in circle, whether it be for ritual or spellcraft, you will want to do what is known as building the cone of power.

This simply means that you increase the energy (as a solitary practitioner or in a group) until it peaks. When it peaks you will release it into the universe to go do its work. It is known as cone of power because the energy seems to take that shape as it is rising.

You can tell when the cone is peaking because your body will tremble, like when you're just about to sneeze or have an orgasm; it builds up a thick pressure in the solar plexus and crown chakras.

To release it, mentally or psychically let go, as if you were expelling breath from your lungs with a sharp gasp. Then immediately jerk your focus away so that you can't rein the energy in and it will fly out of your body and the circle to the pre-determined destination.

There are several ways to raise the cone of power: raising energy (as explained above), chanting, drumming, or dancing all work as methods of building energy.

The important thing to remember is that you must focus on your intent while raising the cone, then release when the time is appropriate. If you try to hold the energy still when it's ready to go it will begin to disintegrate.

When working with other people it is the usual practice for one person to monitor the energy and focus it through themselves so that the power doesn't disperse and everyone works at about the same rate.

In many groups or covens this person is often referred to as the Priestess or Priest and the ability to monitor energy comes only with practice and natural talent.

COLORS, PHASES OF THE MOON, AND DAYS OF THE WEEK

Often you will hear Witches talking about what phase the moon is in or on what day they are planning to begin a spell. Timing affects spellcraft but there is no absolute rule. If you desperately need a jolt of prosperity or an increase in luck, you may not be able to wait until the Waxing or Full Moon. I have compensated for this with the use of Moon Water (see chapter four).

MOON PHASES

Waxing Moon: Waxing to Full is the time to cast invoking spells that draw situations to you.

Full Moon: The Full Moon is the time to focus on the culmination of spells cast during the Waxing phase; it provides the strongest power for invocations.

Blue Moon: Any time a single month has two full moons in it, the second full moon is referred to as a Blue Moon. This moon is considered stronger than a regular full moon.

Waning Moon: Waning to New is the time to banish and release things from your life and to devoke (to take apart or let go of).

New Moon: The New Moon is the time to examine hidden issues; to plan for new beginnings and ferret out secrets.

Black Moon: Any time two new moons occur during a single month, the second new moon is referred to as a Black Moon and is considered to be stronger than the regular new moon.

There are some Witches who will not do any magick during the New Moon. However, I have had excellent success working on the New Moon, especially with Dark Mother Rituals and with spells to discover new information about certain situations. It is also an excellent time to scry.

Days of the Week

Certain days of the week have been, over the years, invested with certain attributes. The following list shares not only their most common associations, but also their planetary correspondences.

Sunday: (the Sun) success, power, swift change, God ritual

Monday: (the Moon) psychic work, Goddess ritual, Faerie magick

Tuesday: (Mars) protection, victory, courage, athletics

Wednesday: (Mercury) communications, intellectual pursuits, flexibility

Thursday: (Jupiter) business, group pursuits, joy, laughter, expansion

Friday: (Venus) love, friendship, nature, beauty, arts and crafts

Saturday: (Saturn) crystallization, hidden or obscured matters, limitations and boundaries

Colors

Working with color, much like selecting appropriate timing, is an important part of spellcraft. Each of us has our own associations with certain colors, and if they differ from those in the following color chart listing commonly held color connotations, then listen to your intuition and use what is right for you. For example, red is most often associated with love but to me green represents love and caring and I often use it instead of red when casting love spells.

Black: banishing, hexing, cleansing, scrying into hidden issues

Blue, Dark: joy, creativity, group efforts, peace, communications

Blue, Light: devotion, inspiration, peace, tranquility

Brown: money, business, home-hunting, earth rituals

Gold: success, sun, God rituals, fortune, good luck

Green: prosperity, fertility, good fortune, renewal, earth rituals

Indigo: deep meditation, karma work, opening psychic powers

Magenta: swift changes, beauty

Orange: power, healing, stimulation, success, Sun rituals

Pink: love, platonic love, friendship, kindness, emotional healing

Purple: wisdom, contact with spirits, opening psychic powers

Red: passion, love, sex, courage, vitality, force of will, victory

Silver: Moon rituals, Goddess rituals, fortune, good luck

White: purification, healing, can substitute for any color, lunar rituals

Yellow: communications, intellect, healing, swift changes

INVOKING AND DEVOKING PENTAGRAMS

The pentagram is a symbol used by many Witches, Wiccans, and Pagans. It has a long history and continues to frighten some people because the Christian church did such a good job of equating it with Satanism. Unfortunately, many Wiccans and Witches are reluctant to use it or wear it (in the form of a pentacle) precisely because of this reason. But I feel it is important for us to reclaim the symbol and return it to its proper place of honor and power in our religion and Craft.

At the same time, I become irate when I see someone wearing a pentacle who does not follow the Old Religion—I wouldn't wear a crucifix because I am not Christian. I expect the same respect from people of other religions or no religion. Just calling yourself a Witch doesn't mean you truly are one.

When used as a symbol, a pentagram will either attract or repel energy. You will see directions in many of my spells to draw an invoking or devoking pentagram during the ritual (by draw, I usually mean using a ritual tool or your hand to outline the symbol).

There are several ways to draw this symbol. Here, I present the most common for invoking. The devoking pentagram I use is different than that used by many covens. I use this method because I believe that when you devoke, or take down, a symbol, energy, or force, you should begin the devocation at the place you finished invoking. I have included diagrams that illustrate both this devoking method and the more traditional method.

Invoking, Devoking, and Traditional Devoking Pentagrams

In teaching my students to draw an invoking pentagram, I ask them to stand and draw the pentagram in the air using the following phrases as a guide:

> *Start at the top,*
> *draw down to the left point*
> *then over to the right side.*
> *Draw straight across to the left side.*
> *Draw down to the right point.*
> *Now sweep up to the top.*

A devoking pentagram can be drawn with these spoken instructions:

> *Start at the top.*
> *Draw down to the right point*
> *then over to the left side.*
> *Draw straight across to the right side*
> *now down to the left point*
> *and sweep up to the top.*

Once you have memorized the invoking and devoking pentagrams, practice raising energy and focusing it into the lines of the pentagrams as you invoke and devoke them.

PREPARATION FOR RITUAL AND MAGICK

Before you plan a spell or ritual, you must first decide if you really need to perform it. Can you achieve your goal through easier means? Have you done everything on the physical plane that you can? Magick is not easy nor is it a quick-fix. All the protection charms in the world won't do you any good unless you remember to lock your doors and keep your checkbook in a safe place.

I REALLY NEED TO CAST THIS SPELL!

If you decide that you truly need to cast a spell, spells can be done in a pinch no matter where you are or what you have with you. Once you are ready, follow these directions.

First, prepare your ritual space by physically cleaning it to get rid of the clutter and dirt. This is very important because clutter attracts scattered energy. If you have the time, clean the cobwebs out of the ceiling corners, vacuum and tidy up the area. Remember that while spells can be accomplished without divine help, most ritual involves some form of divine invocation. You don't want to insult the Gods by calling Them into a space that is dirty just because you just didn't feel like cleaning.

You might also wish to smudge the area you will use for ritual with sage or cedar, or asperge the area using sage or cedar water.

Smudging is the process of using smoke from incense and burning herbs to cleanse the energy of a space or person. You can buy a smudge stick or use a stick of incense or ground herbs on charcoal (see chapter five).

Asperging uses herbed or blessed water to cleanse an area. The usual practice is to fill a bowl with spring or New Moon water and to use a branch off a sacred tree to scatter droplets over the area or people involved. Some people don't appreciate getting wet, so inform them of what you are doing before scattering the water. Asperging is a good substitute for smudging if you or those you are working with are allergic or sensitive to smoke and incense.

Prepare any food or drink you'll need ahead of time. Gather all spell components in advance. You don't want to interrupt your workings by running around searching for the matches or incense once you've begun. On occasion, you will forget something. It happens to everybody. Don't worry about it—just try to be as organized as possible.

To prepare yourself for ritual, take a ritual bath using an herbal wash or bath oils. If there isn't time for this, at least try to wash your hands and face before ritual and spend a few minutes in solitary meditation to prepare yourself to enter sacred space.

If your body can handle it, you might wish to fast for a day before major rituals and workings or use magickal tinctures as an enhancement for your psyche. Pay attention to your health; for example, I have borderline hypoglycemia (low blood sugar), so I usually do this only if I'm involved in a very special ritual.

STANDARD RITUAL PROCEDURE

There is not only one method and one method only that you should follow for your ritual and spellcraft. However, some common denominators run throughout most of the rituals I've participated in. I present these commonalities here, and have found that the following Order of Service works well.

ORDER OF SERVICE

- clean and prepare ritual space

- prepare self

- set up altar

- cast circle (or create sacred space)

- invoke the elements

- invoke deities

- magickal workings or main ritual

- cakes and wine

- thank deities

- devoke the elements

- open circle or sacred space

We've already discussed ritual preparation of space and self. The next step is to set up your altar. To do this, you'll need your tools, spell components, and desired altar dressings. These accouterments can be anything that suggests the nature of your spell or ritual to you. For example, if your ritual is based on the element of Water, you might have seashells, starfish, amethyst, lapis lazuli, coral, blue glitter confetti, blue, purple and green altar cloth, water collected from a special stream, river, or lake—the list is infinite. Your altar is limited only by your imagination. The following suggestions can help get you started on your ritual altars.

SUGGESTED ALTAR DRESSINGS

fresh flowers	broom	deity candles
seashells	horns or antlers	coins or money
scarves	confetti	pictures
glitter	ivy, vines, moss	beads or necklaces
cauldron	winding ribbons	crystals
God images	Goddess images	

Consult chapter five for more information on the use of some of these tools.

Casting the Circle

Casting the circle, or creating sacred space, is discussed thoroughly in chapter three. You don't always have to cast a circle of power but you should do something to create sacred space—whether it be with visualization, smudging, or just firmly declaring your intent.

Invoking the Elements

Invoking the elements involves requesting that the elements of Earth, Air, Fire, and Water join your rites. There are several ways of doing this (see chapter four) and many people also like to invoke each one in connection with a particular direction. Invoking the elements is an easy way to add power and dignity to your workings.

Invoking the Deities

Not all Witches call on the Gods to aid them, but They are an integral part of my system. I go into this practice at length in chapters four, fifteen, and sixteen. I firmly believe in the Gods, I am a pledged Priestess to Mielikki and Tapio (Finnish Deities) and also work intimately with Pele, the Hawaiian Volcano Goddess.

I find my work enhanced and strengthened by my willingness to listen to these Gods.

When we invoke Deities for ritual or magick, we are asking Their aid and participation in our rites and life. It behooves us to pay Them the respect They deserve. More than once I have seen a student refer to a God or Goddess as an "archetype" and lightheartedly invoke Him or Her only to find their lives in chaos and turmoil because they didn't have enough respect or attention for what they were doing.

For example, a student of mine, Jim, was doing quite well in class but thought that because he had been in the New Age movement for some time that he had magick all figured out. He knew the Gods were archetypes—symbols that we could direct any way we so chose. Jim wanted change in his life—a "total change without trauma," as he put it. He decided to invoke Kali-Ma, the Hindu Goddess of destruction. I warned him not to unless he was prepared to accept the consequences, but Jim insisted that he knew what he was doing.

Less than a month after he began invoking Kali, Jim bounced a number of checks and lost control of his bank account. His relationship, which had been strong for several years, teetered on the verge of collapse. He began acting out an extremely powerful surge of repressed anger that he didn't even know he had. His job went from bad to worse. It took him a long time to play out the scenario that he had set in motion.

Kali-Ma was not the appropriate choice for peaceful change, but Jim wouldn't put his ego aside and accept that the Gods were more than just names in a book—until his life fell apart. He became very humble with respect to the Gods after that and I doubt if he will ever make such a stupid mistake again.

Sometimes you have to burn your fingers to learn a lesson. Remember this if you find yourself in the midst of a shake-up because you didn't think through what you were doing.

I, too, can speak of this from experience. I was once a young and foolish Witch who had to get her fingers burned. Years ago I believed that change and chaos were the same thing. I come from a dysfunctional family, where chaos is normal. I didn't know the difference.

I believed that if I wanted to change my life, then chaos should naturally follow. So, to invoke change when things got dull or unbearable I began invoking Loki, the Norse God of mayhem and chaos. Within three days of invoking Him, a major upheaval would happen in my life, accompanied by major chaos.

I finally learned my lesson—I could have change without trauma if I wanted but I couldn't do it while invoking Loki. In 1992 when I pledged myself to Mielikki and Tapio, They came to me in a vision and firmly instructed me that I was never to invoke Mr. L. again. I will never break my promise.

MAGICKAL WORKINGS

Magickal workings include the spells and rituals you intend to work with. These depend on your intent. Sometimes you will find that simply creating sacred space, calling the elements and deities, and then drumming and dancing is ritual enough. Other times, you will want a more elaborate ritual. Still other times you will have a very specific magickal intent in mind, such as casting a prosperity spell or a protection rite.

CAKES AND WINE

A full ritual usually includes cakes and wine. This pagan rite has a very long history and is the origin of the Christian communion.

When this step is used in group rituals, one member usually pours the wine while another passes out the cakes, making certain to work in a deosil, or clockwise, fashion. Before the wine and cakes are passed around, the two "servers" should bless them in the name of the Goddess and the God.

A simple blessing for the consecration of the cakes and wine is:

> *Bless these cakes in the name of the Great Mother who provides sustenance that we might live. In the name of the Maiden, Mother and Crone, these cakes are blessed.*

Draw an invoking pentagram over cakes with athame or hand.

> *Bless this wine in the name of the Horned God, whose blood is the fruit of the vine. In the name of the Green Man, Horned One, and Lord of the Dead, this wine is blessed.*

Draw an invoking pentagram over wine with athame or hand.

Serve the cakes and wine. Each member of the group should have a glass or chalice into which the wine can be poured. This keeps cold germs and the like from being passed by use of a group chalice. A traditional greeting for this part of the ritual is:

May you never hunger.
(if you are passing out cakes)

May you never thirst.
(if you are pouring the wine)

The response of the participants may be anything from:

Goddess (or God) *bless* to *And may you never hunger* (or thirst).

The first toast should be made after everyone has been served and it is offered up to the God and Goddess. After that, people can offer further toasts or drink in silence.

The cakes are considered the body of the Goddess and the wine is considered the blood of the God. If you cannot drink alcohol, a sparkling cider is a good substitute for wine. Specific holidays may use other liquids (for example—creamy milk makes a wonderful 'wine' for Imbolc).

The cakes can be anything from cookies to chunks of hearty bread. Cookies are usually shaped in rounds or crescents to mirror the image of the moon. This is an easy recipe for crescent cakes:

Crescent Cakes

¼ cup butter
½ cup powdered sugar
1 egg
1 teaspoon vanilla
   or lemon extract

¼ cup milk
1 cup ground almonds
1 cup all-purpose flour
1 teaspoon baking powder
¼ teaspoon salt

Preheat your oven to 350 degrees. Grease cookie sheet. Cream butter and sugar. Add egg and vanilla, beat well. Add milk. Stir in ground almonds. Sift flour, baking powder, and salt together. Beat these ingredients in to the butter mixture. The dough may be stiff; gently knead it on a floured board four or five times and then roll out the dough. Cut into crescent shapes or full moon shapes. Bake 8–10 minutes, until very lightly browned. Yield: 15–24 cakes.

The cakes and wine ceremony is a good time to reflect on the ritual—talking about general subjects should be discouraged because you are still in sacred space. Until the circle is devoked, that energy should be maintained.

If you are working solitary, bless the cakes and wine yourself and then offer up whatever toasts you choose.

It is good form to keep one cookie and a little wine to put outside after the circle is opened, as a libation to the Gods.

THANKING THE DEITIES

Many Witches refer to this part of the ritual as "dismissing" the deities but I don't think that sounds respectful.

When you have finished cakes and wine, all participants should stand and join hands. Thank the Gods and Goddesses you have invoked for participating in the ceremony with you. A simple devocation is:

> Lord and Lady, we thank you for participating in our rites tonight. As we open the circle and go about our daily lives, remain in our hearts, watch over us and guide our feet along the paths that are best for us. Blessèd be.

This short devocation is respectful yet clearly states that the ritual is over and that you no longer require Their presence.

DEVOKING THE ELEMENTS

This part of the ritual is discussed thoroughly in chapter four. Keep in mind that the elements are not just mindless energies. There are powerful beings associated with each element and you don't want to make them angry.

OPENING THE CIRCLE

Opening the circle, which is explained in chapter three, refers to letting go of the focus that you have used to keep the ritual guarded and the energy condensed. After a powerful ritual it can be like stepping out of a hot room into a cool breeze. If you are working in a group it is traditional, when the circle is opened, for everyone to hold hands and say, "Merry meet, merry part, and merry meet again!" Then everyone cheers. After the circle is open one person or the whole group can go outside to leave the wine and cake for the Gods.

NEGATIVE MAGICK

Unlike those who consider themselves Wiccan, I hold with the opinion that hexing is sometimes appropriate. I believe that on rare occasions it becomes necessary but I seldom take that route; only when it's imperative to stop someone from inflicting harm on myself or others do I cast dark spells.

I do warn you that, if you intend harm to someone with magick when other methods will take care of the problem, you always run the risk of the spell backfiring onto you or some innocent person.

Be very cautious. I have been in the Craft for almost twenty years and I consider myself quite experienced; but I hesitate to touch this area of magick because of its unpredictable and volatile nature, which usually leads to chaos. There's already enough of that in this world as it is.

For more information on hexing see chapters twelve and fifteen.

3

CREATING SACRED SPACE

When you cast a circle of sacred space, you are focusing both energy and your will to create a space charged with magick that is conducive to spellcraft and ritual.

There are many ways to cast a circle, providing many options to experiment with to find the method that works best for you. The way you cast the circle may vary from one time to another depending on your magickal goal.

Sometimes I do not cast a circle before spellcraft, especially if I want the magick to affect my whole household. Casting a circle can seem to separate my magickal life from my daily life. Since magick pervades my every breath and vision, I often choose to expend a little more energy to keep the spell focused, yet open to my whole life.

Having said that, I still defend casting a circle. First, when you are a newcomer to the Craft, casting a circle can help to protect you from wayward energies that a more experienced Witch can usually deflect.

Second, some rituals are very personal. I choose to keep those focused on me and me alone. Therefore a circle is useful in securing the spell or ritual for personal use.

Third, a circle of power concentrates the energy and can make spellcraft more likely to succeed.

On those occasions when you don't have time for a full ritual but have a great need to do something magickal, you will make do just like our ancestors did.

It may not be a popular opinion among the general Pagan community, but the truth is that we don't know if our ancestors cast circles. There is little evidence to suggest this practice among most traditions. The concept of creating sacred space, however, dates back thousands of years.

There are many ways to create sacred space. In this chapter we will explore several, including circle casting, and I will present suggestions on how to create methods specifically tailored to your personal needs.

Grounding and Centering

Before you attempt to cast a circle you should ground and center yourself first. This is the process of calming yourself as you get into the right frame of mind and body to work with magick.

There are several ways to ground and center, ranging from elaborate meditations (see my book *Trancing the Witch's Wheel* for a good guided meditation on grounding) to simple Tai Chi exercises.

METHOD ONE

Everyone involved in the ritual should stand in a circle. Spread your arms wide. You should not be touching anyone else. One person should memorize and lead the following meditation, pausing at the appropriate areas (marked with a *Pause*) for a count of ten. Or that person can ground themselves first, privately, and then read the meditation for everyone else.

Close your eyes and feel your feet grounded firmly on the floor.

Pause

You are solid, your weight rests comfortably and evenly on your hips, legs, and feet. Feel the weight of the day, the weight of your body settle firmly in your legs, feet, and hips.

Pause

Now feel roots begin to grow out of the bottom of your feet. They push through the floor and grow down into the soil.

Pause

These root tendrils push through rock and stone, through dirt and crystal, through cavern and underground stream.

Pause

Feel the roots from your feet plunge deep into the Earth, they are traveling fast, growing, writhing, searching as they burrow through the soil.

Pause

Feel the roots from your feet as they break through into the core of the Earth. The core of the Earth is glowing magma, hot and healing, and the roots from your feet plunge into the lava.

Pause

The lava begins to rush up the roots, pouring through the tendrils, up through rock and stone, up through dirt and crystal, through cavern and underground stream.

Pause

The lava travels up the roots through the floor into the bottoms of your feet and fills you with a glowing warmth.

Pause

Now feel the lava pour up, filling your ankles and calves, welling into your hips and thighs, warm and embracing.

Pause

The lava fills your stomach and wraps around your heart. It travels down your arms, into your hands and fingers and loosens the tension from your shoulders.

Pause

Now it wells up into your head, releasing old pains and tensions from your neck.

Pause

Your arms begin to rise over your head and the glowing lava from the core of the Earth pours out your fingertips and through your crown chakra to fountain up.

Pause

Now the lava fountains from your fingers and head, pouring in glowing showers to the Earth again, and you feel this cycle connect you and ground you. You are rooted and filled with Earth's energy.

Pause

Reach down and touch your fingers to the floor, feel the connection between you and the Earth below you.

Pause

When you are ready, stand up and open your eyes.

METHOD TWO

This method of grounding takes less time but may not induce as deep a centering as the first method. However, it is satisfactory for most ritual and spellwork.

Stand with your feet firmly on the ground, separated to about shoulder level. You may close your eyes if you wish. Raise energy between your hands (see chapter two). When the energy is firm between your hands, reach out and sweep your hands down to the floor. Gather up energy from the Earth. It should feel like you're sweeping up a gust of warm air.

Bring the energy against your stomach as you slowly stand up. Pause a moment, then, palms facing inward, push the energy up to your heart. Pause a moment, then push the energy up over your head and let it cascade out of your hands. Then sweep down again and repeat. Perform this exercise about four or five times until you have built up the energy. It is easier to do than it sounds.

METHOD THREE

If you are confined to a chair or bed, this exercise can still effectively ground and center you. This method involves using a large bowl of clean soil or a large, thriving house plant.

Sit facing the dirt or plant. Close your eyes and raise energy between your hands. Turn your palms so that they are facing the plant or touching the soil. Feel the soil or energy of the plant beneath your hands as you listen to the following meditation.

Feel the pulse of Earth's energy beneath your hands. It coils up like the tendrils of a plant to touch your fingertips.

Pause

The energy enters your fingertips, you can feel the warmth of the soil, the cool touch of the plant enter your body as it begins to spread.

Pause

Feel the strength of Earth as it races up your arms, filling your chest and lungs with the breath of the Mother. Take three deep breaths, and with each breath you will drink in the energy of the Earth.

Pause

The cool green fire of the forest pours through your limbs into your lower torso, filling your legs and feet with its strength and healing powers.

Pause

The green fire enters your mind, clearing away any tension held in your neck, shoulders and brow. Let the life-blood of the forest calm you.

Pause

The energy from the Earth pours up through your crown chakra, fountaining down to embrace you in a cocoon of green, healing light. As it circles around your body, feel your connection with the Mother grow and strengthen.

Pause

When you are ready, you may open your eyes.

CIRCLE CASTING

It is a basic tradition in modern Witchcraft to cast a circle of power within which to confine and focus the energy we raise during ritual and spellwork. You need nothing more than yourself and your will to cast a circle; however, the use of ritual tools can aid through their own magickal energies and through the symbolic energy they represent.

I cast most circles with my athame, my ritual dagger. It has a carbon steel double-edged blade and an elk antler handle, which I oil regularly with magickal oils in order to keep it energized. I did not make the dagger nor was it a gift. It has neither a black or white handle like many traditions insist upon.

The day I discovered it was the third day of a regional Pagan festival—September 23, 1994. Until then I had been using another dagger that was almost, but not quite, right. I knew that I would find the right one eventually, but didn't know when or where.

I was looking through the vendors' stalls when I came upon a knife and sword vendor. The dagger was sitting there in front and I was immediately pulled to it.

The significance of the day was not lost on me—September 23 is Mielikki's Day and I am a pledged Priestess of Mielikki. One of Her animals is the stag, so finding an antler-handled dagger on Her day seemed most appropriate. I bought the dagger and we've been happy together ever since.

While I use a ritual dagger to cast my circles, I also know people who use sacred feathers, crystals, magickal wands, and even hammers (particularly Norse Pagans) to create their sacred space. On many occasions, I have simply used my hand to cast the circle. One reason the dagger, or athame, is so commonly used is because the sweep of the blade through the air symbolically cuts a circle to separate the mundane and magickal worlds. The double-edged blade also reflects the dual nature of energy—as we reflect magick out, so our magick is reflected back onto us.

In casting the magickal circle, most Witches start from the East (commonly associated with the element of Air). However, I always start from the North (associated with Earth) because I like to ground my circles before I do anything else and for me, casting from the North does that.

To draw the ring of power, you must first become a conduit for energy, which is accomplished by grounding and centering, then raising energy and letting it flow through you, down into your arms, then out through your fingertips. If you are using a magickal tool, you will direct the energy through your body and into the tool. It will flow out from there.

When the energy is flowing, turn in the direction you wish to start. If you are working in a small space, you may stand (or sit, if need be) in the center of the area that is to be the circle and simply turn around. In a larger space, you may choose to 'walk the circle' as you cast it. Whichever method you choose, begin to circle deosil, letting the energy pour through you to create the sacred space.

On the following pages, I have included several rituals and chants to use while casting a circle. Use them as they are written, or select bits and pieces and create your own.

Whatever you choose to do, be certain it reflects your own nature and path. If the thought of handling a dagger is unsettling then your concentration will waver when you try to use one. If the very thought of using a feather to cast the circle sets you laughing then, your focus won't be as strong as it needs to be. In other words, find what works for you.

TRIPLE GODDESS CHANT AND CIRCLE

This is a beautiful way to cast a circle and it raises the energy in a secure and comforting manner. The chant may be spoken, however, it makes a lovely song. If you use this chant in a group situation, give everyone a copy of the chant before the ritual so that they may memorize and practice it. When you have a group of ten or eleven people singing the chant over and over again (as in Method Two) it quickly assumes a hypnotic, haunting atmosphere.

Each of the following three ritual methods uses this chant. While the first two versions work well for groups, the third is ideal for solitary use or with only one other participant.

TRIPLE GODDESS CHANT

Maiden, cast Your circle white
Weave a web of glowing light
Stag and bear, hawk and wolf,
Bind us to thee.

Mother, cast Your circle red
Weave the strands of glowing threads
Earth and Air, Fire, Water,
Bind us to thee.

Old Crone, cast Your circle black
Weave the wisdom that we lack
Sunlight, moonlight, starlight's shimmer
Bind us to thee.

METHOD ONE

This method works best with a larger group and everyone should memorize the chant before the ritual.

Gather the participants in a circle and have them join hands. The Priestess stands in the center of the circle with an athame or ritual tool. One person, selected before the beginning of the ritual, should start the chant. Everyone joins in, chanting in unison, except the Priestess who begins to cast the circle, turning deosil in the center of the group. She should focus on using the power raised by the group through chanting as her source of energy.

The Priestess must time her movements so that she makes one complete turn for each of the three verses. When the third circle is complete the group gently disengages hands and proceeds to invoking the elements.

METHOD TWO

As above, the group should memorize the chant. To begin, all participants, including the Priestess, gather in a circle holding hands. The Priestess begins the chant and the rest join in. Sing the chant several times as power is raised (it usually takes five or six repetitions). Each person must focus on the energy, and visualize it stretching out to create a harmonious circle of sacred space around the group.

The Priestess must pay attention to the rising energy. Though you want it to peak, you do not want it to release as it does in the cone of power. The chant should stop just before that point.

If all or most participants are experienced, the need for the Priestess to monitor the energy is greatly reduced. Experienced Witches can usually tell where the energy is and how much more needs to be built.

When the chanting is over, release hands and proceed to calling the Elements.

METHOD THREE

This method will be effective with only one other participant or if you work as a solitary.

One person, usually the more grounded, stands in the center of what will be the circle. This person then holds the hand of the other participant, who wields the ritual tool and walks the edge of the circle as the chant is sung. In this manner, both participants focus the energy and take part in creation of the sacred space.

An alternative method is for one or both participants to sing the chant over and over, as in Method Two, until just before the power peaks. Then proceed to calling the elements as usual.

If working solitary, simply cast the circle thrice round, one verse per turn, using whatever ritual tool you desire.

FOUR-PERSON CIRCLE CHANT

This chant and circle casting are especially useful when you are working with a small, even number of people. Energy changes when you are working with even or odd numbers. It is also useful when leading large public rituals where monitoring energy can be difficult.

FOUR-PERSON CHANT

Cast the circle, feel it grow
Feel the pulse of ebb and flow
Energies of old arise
As of our will, this ring's comprised.

A web of love, a web of light
To weave our ritual tonight
A ring of Earth, light from the Moon
Runic rhymes and ritual tunes.

Within this circle we shall call
Elements comprising All
That none may enter here within
Who has not been made welcome.

Within this circle, hand to hand
Between the worlds we now stand
Circle, circle, now be cast
As so we join, from first to last.

Four people are needed for this chant and each person should be prepared to invoke one of the four elements directly after the casting. If you are leading a large ritual, all other participants should form a circle, holding hands, around the central four people. Each ritualist will stand at one of the compass points, facing out toward the group.

If there are only four people participating, then each person should stand at one of the compass points facing in toward the others.

Whether a public or private ritual, all four should ground and center first, raising the energy but not letting it drop back to the Earth. Working from North to West (or from East to North, if you prefer to begin your circle there), each participant in turn focuses the energy they've raised to connect with the power coming from the participant before them, building the circle as they go. Each sings one verse of the chant (see diagram on page 51).

After completing their stanza, the ritualist should visualize the energy sweeping from their compass point to the next—where again, it will be picked up and focused.

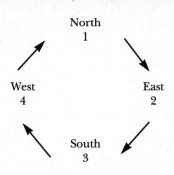

Four-Person Circle Chant: Energy Moving Deosil

I recommend that you pair this with the Four Part Calling of the Elements (chapter four). They work especially well in combination for large public rituals.

SOLITARY CIRCLE CASTING

Sometimes when casting a circle by myself, I choose to cast it in silence. Other times, I use the Triple Goddess Chant I presented earlier. Still other times I want something different, something new.

Presented here are two different ways for solitary circle casting. One is a chant; the other simply a statement of intent.

SOLITARY CIRCLE CHANT

Three times 'round I cast my blade
That this circle shall be made.
First, white crescent from the Maiden's Brow,
Her strength and independence, be here now.
Second, red blood from the Mother's Womb,
As I weave my life on Her starlight loom.
Third, black shadow from the Crone's Abyss
Teaches me wisdom with Her Underworld Kiss.
Sacred Space within this circle now lies
Protected from unwelcome eyes
Let no one enter here within
Who has not been made welcome.
So Mote It Be.

CALLING THE CIRCLE

I cast this circle with my blade of power.
I cast this circle once in the name of the Maiden and the Green
Man, that Their youth and vitality embrace my rites this night.
I cast this circle twice in the name of the Mother and the Horned
Lord, that Their strength and passion empower my rites this night.
I cast this circle thrice in the name of the Crone and the Lord of
Death, that Their wisdom and shadows balance my rites this night.
In the name of the Lord and Lady, this circle is cast.
Let nothing unwelcome enter within.
By my will, so mote it be.

OPENING THE CIRCLE

A besom, a magickal broom, is traditionally used to open the circle.
With all ritual participants holding hands, the priestess sweeps the
circle thrice 'round, widdershins (counterclockwise), saying:

The circle is open but unbroken.
Merry meet, Merry Part, and Merry Meet again!

OTHER WAYS OF CREATING
SACRED SPACE

It is not always necessary, or desirable, to cast a circle for your magick. However, you will often want to create some type of sacred
space. The following techniques describe several ways to do this.

SMUDGING

As explained in chapter two, smudging is the art of using smoke to
clear a space of negative vibrations. To do this, buy a smudge stick—
a bundle of sage, cedar, or herbs tightly bound together—or make
one if you are so inclined. When you light one end on fire, the
flames quickly go out and smoke billows up from the burning herbs.

Smudge sticks are easy to use and produce volumes of smoke. You can also use incense, either stick or powdered, to smudge your ritual space.

You will need:

1 smudge stick (I like sage, cedar, and lavender), or 1 stick of
    incense, or powdered herbs, incense, and charcoal
matches
a large shell or bowl filled with salt

If you have smoke detectors, you may want to disconnect them if there is a chance they will go off while you are smudging. Just remember to reconnect them as soon as you are done.

Light the incense or smudge stick with the matches. If you are using charcoal and powdered incense, you will need to light the charcoal tablet first and let it smolder to get hot before you use it. Only use charcoal specifically meant for incense—the briquettes used for outdoor cooking can kill you if you use them indoors.

Once the flames have gone out and the incense or smudge stick is smoking, raise energy and focus on the thought that you are clearing the space of any negative energies. Thoroughly permeate the area with smoke. You may have to light the smudge stick several times—they have a tendency to burn out quickly.

If you wish to say something at this time, you can. A simple invocation like the following is easy and effective:

*With this sacred smoke, I cleanse and purify this space, making it
ready for magick and ritual. With this sacred smoke, all negative
energies are scattered and dismissed and this space is made sacred
and holy for our rites.*

When the ritual area is full of smoke, plunge the end of the smudge stick into the salt and set it in a safe area for it to cool. If you don't want to burn the rest of the incense, you can put it out in the same way. Charcoal can be covered with cold water and left in a heat-proof bowl in the sink.

If you want to smudge a person, instruct them to stand with their arms out to their sides and their legs spread. Carefully, so as not to get any sparks on their clothing or hair, blow the smoke from the incense or smudge stick so that it thoroughly engulfs them. Smudge both the back and front of the person. You can smudge yourself by waving the smoke around your body.

After you are finished, you might want to open the windows to let the smoke carry away any negative energy it might have picked up. Again, remember to reconnect your smoke detectors when you have finished.

ASPERGING

Asperging is useful when you or a member of your group is allergic or sensitive to incense, or when it is not desirable to fill the room with smoke. Asperging uses water droplets that have been charged with energy and sacred herbs to scatter protective and cleansing energy in a given area.

You will need a small bough from a sacred tree—cedar is one of the best, although a rowan branch or other sacred bough will do.

Fill a bowl with water—you can use water from a special lake or stream, or Full Moon Water or New Moon Water (see chapter four), or bottled spring water. Place the bough into the water and let it sit for at least an hour, if possible. You can also raise energy and charge the water by focusing the energy into the bowl.

When it is time to cleanse the area, take hold of the bough and begin to scatter water droplets around the ritual space. Be respectful—watch for artwork or fabrics that shouldn't be water-stained.

You might want to say something like:

> *By sacred herb and blessed water I consecrate and purify this space.*
> *All negative energies depart and scatter, you are not welcome here.*
> *Each drop of water carries with it the strength and power of the*
> *cedar* (or rowan, etc.) *to cleanse and protect. Blessèd be.*

TONING

This is most effective when used by a group, although I have practiced it alone with success. Everyone should stand or sit in a circle, close their eyes, and join hands. One person begins to hum, finding a frequency that feels right. Others will then join in. It might take several tries to find the right vibration for your voice (you will feel your chest vibrate around your heart chakra), but that's okay. The tone you are using may abruptly change, you might need to raise or lower the volume—the whole key to toning is to tune into everyone else so that the notes blend as a whole and create an intense wave of energy.

During this time you will want to focus on the concept of creating sacred space, of pushing away negative energy, and on clearing out psychic clutter.

If the group is in sync, the volume will rise and drop several times, finally reaching a peak. At this point it will abruptly release without anyone trying to force it. You might want to practice as a group several times before using it to create sacred space.

At times during toning you may feel that your head is vibrating so much that your teeth rattle—it can also feel like you're in an airplane just about ready to take off.

Toning is a fun way to raise energy.

PHYSICAL METHODS OF CREATING SACRED SPACE

While most methods of creating sacred space involve more active participation, you can enhance the energy of the space in other ways. Physically create the circle out of tree boughs to bring the tree's energy into play. Try to find boughs that have been blown off of the trees rather than cutting, though. You can also create the circle using a ring of salt. While this will keep slugs out of your circle, it tends to be impractical on a carpet and it certainly isn't good for the Earth.

Placing crystals around the space sets up a certain resonance.

Bundles or bowls of herbs will add to the energy field, as well.

Pictures can alter the mood for the ritual.

A circle created out of Yule lights reminds one of faerie lights and magick.

For one ritual years ago, two of us used yards and yards of crepe paper ribbons in blue, green, and lavender to fill the living room. We tacked the ends to the ceiling and the walls and tied them around furniture and created a tangled web of ribbon that represented the sea and seaweed. Needless to say, we were very careful that the candle flames were nowhere near the lowest ribbons and kept a close eye on the burning tapers so that no disaster happened. We were preparing for a Water Element and Siren ritual. The ribbons created the beautiful illusion of actually being under the ocean.

Don't forget the effect music can have on ritual. In the Appendix, I include a list of music that I've found especially effective in any number of rituals.

ISN'T ALL SPACE SACRED?

Some people claim that all space is sacred but I have sadly realized that with the energy running through most cities today, and with the tensions daily life brings, we really need to create special, sacred space for our magick and rituals into which the outer world will not intrude. While some of my spells don't call for this—precisely because they are meant to touch the world around us in a profound way—I urge you to practice creating sacred space and casting circles whenever you have the time. It's worth it.

4

ELEMENTS AND DEITIES

All life is made up of four elements: Earth, Air, Fire, and Water. When we talk about the elements in magick we are not only speaking of their physical nature but examining what they represent—their psychic or spiritual meanings. When we invoke them during our rituals and spellcraft we are invoking their essence to join us and infuse our work.

Perhaps each element is self-explanatory; our ancestors must have noticed the strength and seeming solidity of the mountains; the sustenance that comes from the Earth—fruit trees and berries and grains. They knew that when the winds altered direction a change in weather was sure to follow. They looked at the immensity of the sky and saw how clear, how pure it seemed to be.

When fire struck the Earth, the flames changed and transmuted forests and prairies, altering everything it touched—softened vegetables and meat with its heat, gave warmth, consumed acreage when out of control. There were certain plants and trees that would grow only after a wildfire had passed through. And water—water cleansed the body and sustained life, it hid its inhabitants, be they dangerous or friendly. Tides ebbed and flowed with the phases of the moon.

Gradually, a system of beliefs about each element grew to be incorporated into different shamanic practices.

Today when we work with the elements we work with concepts not too different than those outlined above. While there are generally accepted attributes for each element, many cultures have little differences that can substantially alter the meanings.

For example, many traditions start their focus on the elements in the east—traditionally associated with Air. I start mine in the north, Earth, because I like to ground and solidify the ritual first.

I have good friends who are Norse Pagans—they associate the east with Earth and the north with Ice (the opposite of Fire and an important concept in Norse Paganism) instead of Air. When they explain why—to the north lies cold ice and snow, to the east (in the northern hemisphere, at least) lies the fertile farmlands—it makes perfect sense. Therefore, they invoke Ice instead of Air.

Native Americans have a different way of looking at the elements; the Celts did, too. The point is that for everyone this will be a little different. As you experiment, you will begin to understand the elements as they exist for you. For the most part, I have even ceased calling directions; now I prefer just to invoke the raw element itself.

Below, I have listed four tables of correspondences—one for each element, which are based on generally accepted principles. Along with enumerating the correspondences that go with the each element, I have included a number of exercises you can do to forge and explore your relationship with each element.

THE ELEMENT OF AIR

Direction: east

Rules: the mind; all mental, intellectual and some psychic work; knowledge; abstract thought; theory; mountain tops; prairie open to the wind; wind; breath; clouds, vapor and mist; storms; purification; removal of stagnation; new beginnings; change

Time: dawn

Season: spring

Colors: white, yellow, lavender, pale blue, gray

Zodiac: Gemini, Libra, Aquarius

Tools: censer, incense, athame, sword

Oils: frankincense; violet, lavender, lemon, rosemary

Faeries: Sylphs

Animals: all birds

Goddesses: Aradia, Arianrhod, Nuit, Urania, Athena

Gods: Mercury, Hermes, Shu, Thoth, Khephera

AIR EXERCISES

- Go outside on a breezy or windy day and face the wind. Let it rush past you and open yourself to its influence.

- Play with feathers of different birds and attune with the energy of each. (Be aware that it is illegal to possess certain feathers.)

- Listen to and play wind chimes, xylophones, bells, or recorders and other wind instruments.

- Play with the difference between hot and cold air. Stand in front of a fan, then in front of an oven that's hot and cracked open. Focus on what the differences are besides just temperature.

- Line up a number of different granular incenses. Light a piece of incense charcoal. Drop just a pinch of incense on the coal, one at a time, and see what the different smells do to your psyche.

- Play with your breath—make different sounds, first vowels and then consonants. See where the sounds resonate in your body.

- Pay attention to your breath. Vary the rate at which you breathe. First breathe through your nose (one nostril at a time, then both), then through your mouth. Be careful not to hyperventilate with this exercise.

- Exhaust your mind by reading for a long time, or focusing on some idea for a long time, then take a hot bath and let your thoughts wander. See where they lead you.

A SPELL TO GREET THE DAWN

When you have made your connection with the Air Element, consult your calendar. For three days, beginning on the day of the next New Moon, spend fifteen minutes of each day focusing on a project you want to begin or on something in your life that has become stagnant. Then, on the fourth morning, wake up before dawn and go outside, preferably into a field or large yard if you can. Greet the dawn and ask the element of Air to help you clear the way for this change that you want to make.

Repeat the following chant until the energy rises, then raise your hands to the sky and let the spell go.

Blow wind blow, let my mind flow
Change come in, stagnation go!

Stay outside until the sun rises while you contemplate the nature of Air.

THE ELEMENT OF FIRE

Direction: south

Rules: creativity, passion, energy, blood, healing, destruction, temper, faerie fire, phosphorescence and Will o' the Wisps (see chapter thirteen), volcanoes, flame, lava, bonfires, deserts, the sun

Time: noon

Season: summer

Colors: red, orange, gold, crimson, white, peridot

Zodiac: Sagittarius, Aries, Leo

Tools: wand, candle

Oils: lime, orange, neroli, citronella

Faeries: Flame Dancers, Phoenix

Animals: Salamander, Lizard, Snake

Goddesses: Pele, Freya, Vesta, Hestia, Brid

Gods: Vulcan, Horus, Ra, Agni, Hephaestus

FIRE EXERCISES

- Spend time out in the noon sun (wear sunscreen to protect your skin).

- Visit a desert or rocky place, observe and attune yourself to the arid landscape.

- If you have the opportunity to visit a volcano or old lava flows, I encourage you to do so. The time I spent visiting Pele was one of the most intense periods of my life.

- Dance around a bonfire.

- Light a candle and sit in a darkened room. Look a few inches above the flame (do not look directly at the flame or you will get eyestrain) and spend some time in meditation on the element of Fire.

- During a summer night, try to visit a beach or shoreline during the times when the phosphorescence is high in the waters.

- Attend a Fire-Walk if one is in your area. Make sure it is led by a competent teacher and if you have any qualms about participating, just observe.

CREATING FIRE POWDER

You will need to be in an area where you can safely have a bonfire, though you can probably substitute a good-sized grill for the bonfire (just break the wood into small pieces).

Cast a circle.

With a non-toxic marker or a carving tool, if you have the skill, write or carve words and runes for fire on a piece of wood—preferably rowan or ash (see chapter six for rune charts). Raise energy on the wood and focus on the transformative power of fire.

Light your bonfire, taking care to observe all safety precautions. Once it is burning brightly, put your piece of wood into the flames in a position where you can see it.

While the wood is burning, prepare your herbs. You will need the following:

¼ ounce chamomile
¼ ounce lemon balm
¼ ounce powdered ginger root
¼ ounce galangal

Using a mortar and pestle, powder and break up the herbs as much as possible. Galangal is a hard herb, you may need to shave it with a knife or, before you begin the spell, run it through a food processor. Once the herbs are finely ground, add a sprinkle of red and gold glitter.

When the wood has burned to charcoal, rake it out of the fire and allow it to cool. Break off a piece and grind it to make ¼ cup of powdered charcoal. Stir this into the herb mixture (this is messy work, don't wear good clothes unless they are easy to clean).

To this powdered mixture, add:

11 drops dragon's blood oil
11 drops lime oil
11 drops orange oil

Mix well, then raise energy and focus it into the mixture while chanting the following:

Fire, Fire, burning higher,
  Bring to me what I desire.
Fire, Fire, burning bright,
  Bring to me your strength and might!

You can use this powder in charm bags (a bag worn around your neck brings vitality and inner strength); you can roll an oil-anointed candle in it when practicing candle magick; you can keep some in a heart-shaped charm bag near your bed for virility and passion. Just don't eat it, and remember that the charcoal can stain cloth.

THE ELEMENT OF WATER

Direction: west

Rules: emotions, feelings, love, sorrow, intuition, the subconscious and unconscious minds, the womb, fertility, menstruation, cleansing, purification, oceans, lakes, tide pools, rain, springs and wells

Time: twilight

Season: autumn

Colors: blue, blue-green, gray, aquamarine, indigo, white

Zodiac: Cancer, Pisces, Scorpio

Tools: chalice

Oils: lemon, lily of the valley, camphor

Faeries: Undines, Sirens, Naiads,

Animals: all fish and marine life

Goddesses: Aphrodite, Isis, Mari, Tiamat, Vellamo, Ran, Kupala

Gods: Ahto, Osiris, Manannan, Neptune, Poseidon, Varuna

WATER EXERCISES

- Go swimming, wading, or walking in the rain.

- Take a ritual shower or bath.

- Sit on the edge of a stream and listen to the sound of the water rush by.

- Skip stones across the water and watch the ripples. Can you apply what you observe to your life?

- Collect water from many sources, such as different streams, oceans, Full Moon Water, and New Moon Water (see below). In a quiet trance state, dip your fingers into each bowl, one at a time, and attune yourself to the differences in texture, energy, and temperature.

- Play with sea shells, sand dollars, or other objects with a close connection to water. Try to get the feel for each creature's energy pattern that might be imprinted in the shell, as well as the energy of the place from which it came.

MAKING FULL MOON WATER, NEW MOON WATER, AND SUN WATER

Full Moon Water is used in a number of spells throughout this book. I use it when I need to do an invoking spell during the Waning Moon. Fill a glass jar with water. Add a moonstone and tightly cap the jar. Three days before the full moon, set the jar outside at night where it can capture the moon's rays (it doesn't matter if it is overcast). Bring it inside the following morning. Repeat this for the next two nights. After this, replenish the water each month by adding water to the jar and setting it outside the night before the full moon to capture the moonlight.

New Moon Water is used when I need to do a banishing spell during the Waxing Moon. Fill a glass jar with water. Add a piece of black onyx to the jar and cap. Follow directions as given for Full Moon Water, except you must set the jar outside during the new moon (and two days before it), instead of the full moon.

I use Sun Water when I am working with solar spells and healing rituals. Fill a glass jar with water, add a piece of carnelian or citrine to the jar and cap. Set the jar outside, where it can catch the sun's ray, at sunrise on a clear day. Repeat this for the next two days. Replenish as necessary.

THE ELEMENT OF EARTH

Direction: north

Rules: the body, growth, nature, sustenance, material gain, prosperity, money, death, caverns, fields, meadows, plants, trees, animals, rocks, crystals, manifestation, materialization

Time: midnight

Season: winter

Colors: black, brown, green, gold, mustard

Zodiac: Capricorn, Taurus, Virgo

Tools: pentacle, salt

Oils: pine, cypress, cedar, sage, vetiver

Faeries: Gnomes, dwarfs

Animals: all four-footed animals

Goddesses: Ceres, Demeter, Gaia, Persephone, Kore, Rhea, Epona, Cerridwen, Mielikki

Gods: Cernunnos, Herne, Dionysus, Marduk, Pan, Tammuz, Attis, Thor, Tapio

EARTH EXERCISES

- Take a walk in the woods.

- Talk to your plants and listen, meditate on them.

- Work in your garden, focus on each plant in turn to see if you can attune to their individual essences and their needs.

- Make herbal charms for yourself.

- Take a class in herbalism.

- Go on a berry picking expedition. Stay in the patch at least one hour, working in silence. The berry devas are very strong and readily make themselves known.

- Begin collecting interesting stones that catch your eye.

- Lie in the grass and observe the activity going on around you in the insect world.

A NOTE ABOUT CRYSTALS

Over the years I have acquired a number of beautiful and rare crystals. I always treat them with respect and use them in magick. But until I was talking to some friends one day it never occurred to me that most crystals are procured in ways deleterious to the Earth: strip mining, dynamiting, tearing the Earth apart while building roads through the jungles, gouging great holes in the mountainsides. I rarely buy crystals anymore because I choose not to support an industry that so severely harms our Mother.

Now, some people may not acquire their crystals in this way—there are places, I understand, where quartz is just sitting around waiting on top of the ground. But if I don't know where something comes from I'm not going to take a chance purchasing it.

You must make the choice for yourself.

As I said, I use the crystals I have purchased over the years—now that I have them I'm not going to toss them out. That would be the ultimate disrespect for the Earth and her beauty. These crystals have become like members of my family.

ATTUNING TO THE EARTH

Keep a nature diary. Pick a spot near your home that you can visit at least once a week—ideally daily. In your journal, record the weather, the temperature, the different plants and growth cycles you observe in this spot, animals and insects, when the seasons change. Record how the plants change—which ones go dormant?

Which retain their vitality? Is there snow during the winter? How much is there and what plants survive the cold? Keep your journal for one year. You will have a detailed and intimate knowledge of the life-cycle of your special place.

INVOKING THE ELEMENTS

When we invoke the elements during ritual, we call them in to our circle and our rites, and ask for their help and guidance. There are many invocations you can use. These are some of the invocations I prefer. As you work with them, feel free to change the wording to suit your needs—in other words, experiment.

There are many ways to invoke the elements. You can invoke them silently; you can have a candle on the altar for each direction and light it as you call the element; you can use musical instruments while you invoke them. (If you choose the latter, I suggest that you use a drum for Earth; a flute or recorder for Air; a lyre or stringed instrument for Fire; and a rainstick or bells for the Water.)

After you have cast your circle, turn and face the North.

Raise your hands or athame in greeting and say:

Spirits of the North, Spirits of the Earth,
You who are stone and rock, bone and crystal,
You who are tree and root and branch,
You, whose soil is the body of the Goddess
And whose grass is the green of Her hair,
Spirit of Earth, come to me!
Spirit of the Wolf, Spirit of the Gnome,
I call upon thee.
You who rule from the blackest caverns below
To the highest mountain tops,
Hear me.
Bring to these rites your spirit of prosperity,
Of stability and manifestation.

Begin turning deosil (clockwise), focusing a line of Earth energy through your hand or athame. Make one full sweep, saying:

With a ring of stone and bone and crystal,
I encircle this sacred space and all within.
Let nothing enter unwelcome.

Draw an invoking pentagram in the air, facing north.

Spirits of the Earth, welcome and blesséd be!

Turn and face the east. Raise your hand or athame and say:

Spirits of the East, Spirits of the Air,
You who are mist and vapor and cloud,
You who are fresh breeze and wild hurricane,
Webweaver at the edge of Dawn
Sweeping out stagnation to weave the new day,
Come to me.
Spirit of the Hawk, Spirit of the Sylph,
Hear me.
Bring into these rites purification and clarity,
Sweep through and remove stagnation.

Begin to turn deosil, focusing a line of Air energy through your athame or hand. Make one full circle, saying:

With a ring of mist and vapor and fog
I encircle this sacred space and all within
Let nothing enter unwelcome.

Facing East, draw an invoking pentagram in the air.

Spirits of the Air, welcome and blesséd be!

Turn and face the south. Raise your hands or athame into the air and say:

Spirits of the South, Spirits of the Flame and Faerie Fire
You who are the crackle of bonfires
You who are the golden sun and glowing lava,
You who are the heat of the desert, and the
Sparkle of phosphorescence on the shore and
In the water,
Come to me.
Spirit of the Phoenix, Spirit of the Flame Dancers

Hear me.
Bring into these rites your spirit of creativity
And passion,
Your ability to transmute and rise new from the
Ashes.

Begin to turn deosil, focusing a line of Fire energy through your hand or athame. Make one full circle, saying:

With a ring of sunlight and lava, I encircle this
Sacred space and all within
Let nothing enter unwelcome.

Face the south, draw an invoking pentagram in the air.

Spirits of the Flame, welcome and blesséd be!

Turn and face the west. Raise your hands or athame into the air and say:

Spirits of the West, Spirits of the Water
You who are the Moon Mother,
You who are the Undines of the Rivers
And the Sirens of the crashing ocean breakers
You who are the Naiads of the Grottos,
Come to me.
Spirit of the Shark,
Hear me.
Bring to these rites your deepest intuition
And truest emotions,
Teach me to be flexible, to adapt and flow
Like your waters.

Begin to turn deosil, focusing a line of Water energy through your hand or athame. Make one full circle, saying:

With a ring of wave and rain and tears
I encircle this sacred space and all within
Let nothing enter unwelcome.

Face the west. Draw an invoking pentagram in the air.

Spirits of the Water, welcome and blesséd be!

FOUR-PART CALLING OF THE ELEMENTS

This invocation is meant for use in conjunction with the Four-Person Circle Casting introduced in chapter three or as part of a four-day ritual to attune yourself with the elements.

If you choose to use it as a ritual, focus on one element each of the four days. As you chant, try to feel the power of that element sweep through your body. If you can, call Earth while in a garden, Air while on a hilltop, Fire in the noonday sun and Water while standing in a pond or at the ocean shore. Spend an hour or so after the Calling focusing on the different aspects of each particular element, what part it plays in your life, and how it affects your body.

THE CALLING OF THE FOREST AND MOUNTAIN

Mountains rising to the sky
Fir and cedar, oak and thorn
Ravines deep-green in forest's night
Dusty path old and worn
Powers of earth rise up in me
Powers of earth rise up in me

Caverns dark and crystals bright
Meadows filled with wildflowers
Maple willow bracken ash
Fern-shaded passion's bowers
Powers of earth rise up in me
Powers of earth rise up in me

Here amidst the foliage wild
Where ancient Powers run
I call to me my destiny
Between the moon and sun

Ancient ones of green and gold
Of dirt and root and bone
Grant me your powers that I've seen
Mysteries carved in stone

Knowledge of the powers of Earth
I beseech the Goddess, give
Guide me to their mysteries
And let my magick live.

THE CALLING OF THE WIND AND GALE

Rising wind and cool night breeze
Hurricane and vaporous clouds
The tingling hint of dawn's first light
Mist boiling in a milky shroud
Powers of air rise up in me
Powers of air rise up in me

The first squall of autumn's gale
The gentle zephyr of spring's new breeze
The chill blast of winter's breath
The whispering heard through summer trees
Powers of air rise up in me
Powers of air rise up in me

Here before the waking dawn
Where ancient powers fly
I call to me my destiny
Between the stars and sky

Ancient ones of blue and white
Of breeze and calm and storm
Grant me your powers I've seen
Mysteries without form

Knowledge of the powers of Air,
I beseech the Goddess, give
Guide me to their mysteries
And let my magick live.

THE CALLING OF THE FLAME AND FAERIE FIRE

Sparkles of the faeries' flame
Will o' the Wisps on summer nights
The golden glow of forest green
Glimmering in the sunlight
Powers of flame rise up in me
Powers of flame rise up in me

Balefire crackling on the hill
The flickering light of candle's flame
Passion drumming in the night
Lava flows, wild, untamed
Powers of flame rise up in me
Powers of flame rise up in me

Here before the flickering flame
Where ancient powers reign
I call to me my destiny
Ecstasy unchained

Ancient ones of red and gold
Of sparkle, crackle, trance
Grant to me your powers I've seen
The mystery of the dance

Knowledge of the powers of Flame
I beseech the Goddess, give
Guide me to their mysteries
And let my magick live.

THE CALLING OF THE SEA AND OCEAN

Raging river running wild
Grotto's pool of deepest green
Ocean crashing on the shore
Its hidden depths yet to be seen
Powers of water rise up in me
Powers of water rise up in me

Azure lake with flashing fish
The trail of a single tear
Raindrops splashing to the earth
The perfect scrying mirror
Powers of water rise up in me
Powers of water rise up in me

Here within the foaming sea
Where ancient powers dwell
I call to me my destiny
Where roaring waves do swell

Ancient ones of blue and green
Of snow and rain and sleet
Grant to me your powers I've seen
Mysteries of the deep.

Knowledge of the powers of Water
I beseech the Goddess, give
Guide me to their mysteries
And let my magick live.

BEYOND THE ELEMENTS: INVOKING THE ANCESTORS

Often during my rituals I also like invoking the spirit of my (spiritual) ancestors. I am one-quarter Cherokee and three-quarters Irish, pledged to Finnish Gods and heavily involved with Hawaiian legends and Pele's fire. So I have a mixture of energies that I work with.

While I believe that for certain things you shouldn't mix or blend too many energies (especially with deities: see the next section for more information on this), I also believe that with enough experimentation, you can find a comfortable way to work with all of the energies in your chosen path.

Sometimes to enhance my rites, I invoke the spirits of those who have, over the eons, worked with the magick of nature and the powers of the Earth. The following invocation is one of my favorite ways to do this.

DRUMMING IN THE ANCESTORS

I usually only do this if I am in circle, because I generally don't like inviting spirits into my home unless I call them into a defined area.

After casting the circle and invoking the elements I pick up one of my drums (you can drum on just about anything. In the past I have used a wooden tabletop and a two-liter soda bottle half-filled with water. If you don't have a drum, improvise).

I begin a slow, steady beat. When the pattern is set and I am in a light trance state I chant the following in a slow, rhythmic voice:

Ancestors
I call you
Ancestors
Witches
Shamans
Healers
Wise Women
Medicine Men
Shape Changers
Ancestors
I call you
Join us in this circle
You who are of welcome intent
Be with us
Work with us
Hear us
Speak to us
Share with us
Gather 'round
You who have gone before
You who have lived before
You who have worked the magick before
Ancestors
We are calling you
Join us tonight
Ancestors

ELEMENTS AND DEITIES   75

ANGELS, GHOSTS AND OTHER ASTRAL ENTITIES

Beware! Far too many New Agers and Pagans new to the Craft have an idealized view of the astral plane. Before you decide to work with entities on these levels, think your plans through and take the following information into consideration.

- Angels are part of the Christian religion. If you read the Bible, you'll realize that they don't resemble anything like the cute little cherubs on the angel cards and angel decks and other angel paraphernalia. While some Witches call Archangels at each direction, it seems a holdover from Christian tradition and I don't believe it has a place in natural magick. Angels are very powerful beings that exist on another plane. They are basically Jehovah's henchmen, and we have no real proof they have our best intentions at heart.

- Ghosts, spirits, and the like should, for the most part, be left alone. Just because someone is dead doesn't mean they're nice or helpful, and it doesn't mean that they won't lie to you. Too many people accept channeled information at face value. Get rid of your Ouija board. Your best guidance comes from within. When you invoke the spirits without good reason, you can interfere with their ability to transcend their connection to this plane, and they may not be able to go on to their next incarnation. It is difficult to say goodbye when a loved one dies, but séances usually cause more harm than good.

- Astral entities are not necessarily evil, nor are they necessarily good. Until you are highly proficient with magick and your psychic powers, I urge you to leave them alone. They have caused havoc for a number of inexperienced Pagans who decided that they could handle or control these beings and their experiments got out of hand. I've cleaned up more than one psychic mess caused by somebody who thought that reading a book about magick and using a Ouija board rendered them invulnerable.

I am not trying to scare you away from psychic work or development. On the contrary, by avoiding obvious trouble you learn and grow. It isn't productive to invite negative or potentially negative energy into your space. A scary encounter with an astral being has frightened a number of people away from the Craft.

There are very real spiritual guides that we can learn from, but you must be cautious about accepting everything you hear. If you believe you have met a helpful spiritual guide, be sure to question the advice you are getting; make certain that it resonates true. Just like we shouldn't blindly follow religious leaders in the physical world, we also must use common sense and maintain tight boundaries when it comes to the spirit realm.

THE GOD AND GODDESS IN ALL THEIR ASPECTS

The role of the God and Goddess is perhaps the most controversial subject in the Craft today. Some people say the God and Goddess, in fact, all the Gods, are archetypal—subconscious projections of our own human attributes and experiences.

I disagree. There are a number of books on the subject, so I'm not going to present the various arguments here. Instead, I will share my beliefs, what I work with in my magick, and encourage you to do your own research.

I believe in the Gods. I have seen physical manifestations of them, whether among the branches of a tree (Pan); looming over me (the Horned God); or in outline against the night sky (what I only call the Queen of Stars).

I view the Gods as a force that connects everything and everyone in the universe. I see this force as genderless, nameless...pure energy that we can draw from.

I believe that every planet, every star, has an essence, a consciousness.

The Earth's living essence is known by several names, but most Pagans just call Her the Great Mother, or the Earth Goddess. She is eternal, Maiden, Mother, and Crone all in one. Though She moves through the seasons She does not die. Everything on this planet exists within the Goddess, yet everything is also separate.

The scientific community has come around to a similar point of view with the emergence of the Gaia Theory, which presents the Earth as a complex living organism made up of many cells (species).

There is also a male force in the planet, which most Pagans call the Horned God. He is stag of the forest, the fruit of the vine, and His life is cyclic, waxing and waning throughout the Wheel of the Year. He lives, grows, dies, and is reborn. He is lover, son, and companion to the Goddess.

Thus, we have the Goddess and the God.

Next we come to the individual, named deities. I take issue with the concept that humans created these Gods. I think we named them and gave them identity, but I believe that the finite Gods and Goddesses are avatars, or aspects, of the energies that They embody.

For example, we have Poseidon, a Greek God of the waters. While the Greeks named Him, the energy that is Poseidon existed long before humankind as part of the elemental energy of Water.

Another example is Venus, the Roman Goddess of love. The Romans gave Her that name but She existed as part of the elemental energy of Love before we ever walked on this planet.

I go a step further, however, and separate those Gods who are avatars of the Earth from those who rule the more human-oriented realms. I believe that the more shamanistic cultures (some would call them primitive) worshiped the Gods and Goddesses of the Earth more than the Westernized, "civilized" cultures. I suppose one could call these Earth avatars Elemental or Primal Gods and Goddesses.

Pele is a good example of this. The Hawaiian Volcano Goddess is very real. The moment I set foot on the Big Island, She surrounded me. She exists in our realm, in our plane of existence. While Pele resides in the volcano and we can physically make contact with Her home, Aphrodite, Greek Goddess of love, may seem more removed. Her home, Olympus, is on another plane, much like Tapiola of the Finns and the Norse Valhalla.

WORKING WITH DEITIES IN RITUAL AND MAGICK

Working with the Gods can be both a wonderful and cautionary experience. The Gods are quite real. Do not lightly invoke any God or Goddess. Do careful research before you go into circle and summon a Goddess of destruction. (If you haven't done so, read the section on invoking deities in chapter two.) You could get your hand slapped, or far worse karmic kickback, if you don't.

Respect the power these deities wield. Even though They are finite, limited, it doesn't mean that you, as mortal and human, are going to be able to control or deflect everything They send your way.

Another consideration that you must attend to is this: Never, ever invoke two deities who are at odds with each other!

Your common sense and knowledge gained through research must come into play here. If you know through legend and lore that two deities don't like each other, then don't invoke Them together!

By the same token, don't invoke someone gentle (for example, Kuan Yin) along with someone harsh (Kali-Ma). Not only a stupid thing to do, it's potentially dangerous.

Fire and water deities probably won't get along. It's not the best idea to invoke a Goddess of motherhood along with a Goddess of death. Use logic and common sense, and do your homework. Some nations were constantly at war with one another; don't invoke their Gods simultaneously or you might find that same war continuing in your living room.

As I have said, I work frequently with Pele. Pele's eternal rival is Her sister, Na maka o Kaha'i, the Hawaiian Goddess of the Ocean. I have been to the coast of Hawai'i where the lava from Pele's craters pours into the sea and I have felt Their battle. The lava and the water become Pele and Na maka's weapons as They fight. When we were headed down the Chain of Craters Road and I saw the plumes of steam rising from the ocean, the pit of my stomach tied itself in knots, and I knew the Goddesses were reenacting Their eternal struggle.

I would never, ever invoke Na maka into my rituals, let alone my home, since Pele plays such an important part in my life. My house would probably burn down.

Along the same vein, I am pledged as Priestess to Mielikki, the Finnish forest Goddess. Through both inner guidance and direct orders, I was told that while I can work with Pele, and while Pele is an honored guest in my home, anything that belongs to Pele (like my Pele pendant, the Pele pictures I have painted, the Hawaiian red salt I use in my rituals) must stay outside of the ritual room, which is dedicated to Mielikki and Tapio.

During my sixteenth anniversary of entering into the Craft we drew Mielikki down into Daniela, one of my close friends who is a Priestess of Freya. When Daniela was deep in trance, with Mielikki coming through loud and clear, I asked Her how She felt about my working with Pele.

"You can work with Her, you can have fun with Her, but remember, you belong to me," She said.

I then asked if She would be upset if I ever moved to Hawai'i. Mielikki said no. My final question on the subject was about having anything of Pele's in the ritual room.

Mielikki put it this way: "What is Pele's—is Hers, what is yours is *mine.*"

I am very careful, and when I slip up Mielikki lets me know.

WHY INVOKE THE GODS?

There are many answers to this question. The Gods have been integral to my magick and have provided me with guidance, encouragement, and inspiration. What follows is only a glimpse into what the Gods can do for you and your magickal work if treated with respect and integrity.

- The Gods can help you learn valuable lessons.

- The Gods can influence your magick.

- The Gods can give you a boost in knowledge and inner strength.

- The Gods can provide a shoulder to cry on, an ear to listen with, and help when we need it the most but expect it the least.

- The Gods are incredibly ancient and awesome beings. They deserve respect for what They have done and can do.

- Working with the Divine brings us closer to our own Higher Selves, to those parts of ourselves that transcend the mundane.

- Invoking the Gods is a continuation of ancient tradition and forces us to look beyond ourselves, beyond the human world we have created, especially when working with the Earth-oriented Gods and Goddesses who remind us of the incredible responsibility we have in taking care of this planet. We broke it—we have to fix it.

- The Gods force us to take responsibility for our actions—most Gods won't accept excuses for inexcusable behavior and if we don't stick to our ethics, They remind us in subtle—and not so subtle—ways that we aren't being the best that we can.

- The Gods show us the balance—light and dark, life and death, clarity and shadow.

- Working with the Gods can be just plain fun—a rowdy bunch of Norse Gods invoked during a toasting ritual can be a great group to spend an evening with.

Of course, there are Gods who aren't ethical, who work against Their own realms, as well as our world. Chaos has its place in the universe. But if you choose to follow a God of that nature, you should probably just toss this book. It's not written with chaos magicians or havoc-mongers in mind.

5

MAGICKAL TOOLS

The tools used in magick are as varied as the practitioners. However, there are some basic items common to most Witches practicing natural magick, and those will be covered in this chapter.

There are several misconceptions and myths about magickal tools that continually make the rounds. One of the most pervasive is that you shouldn't buy your own, a myth particularly prevalent with regard to Tarot decks. There are several good reasons for buying your tools new. First, new tools won't have any residue of energy or impressions left on them by the previous owner. There are ways of cleansing your tools and a few are presented in this chapter, but sometimes it can be difficult to completely exorcise energy out of an object.

Second, and most important, is that you will get exactly what you want if you select your tools yourself. I've received a number of Tarot decks over the years as gifts from one acquaintance or another; some I've liked and kept. Others I've given or traded away because I knew that I probably would not use them and I don't like things collecting dust when they could be helping someone else.

Another common myth is that someone will give you a tool when you are ready for it. The reality is that if you need a tool you should do what you can to procure it—in an ethical manner, of course—because the Gods help those who help themselves.

An alternative to buying your own tools is to tell or show friends exactly what you want a few weeks before your birthday, Yule, or other gift-giving occasion, and hint broadly about how much you'd like to have it. It's an effective method and saves your friends from having to figure out what to give you!

Like the idea of not buying your own tools, you'll probably come across a number of "rules" about your magickal tools during your reading on the Craft. My belief is that you question every supposed rule or regulation and ask yourself if it makes sense, why it makes sense, and if it applies to you and your particular path.

For example, some books on Witchcraft insist that you have a black-handled knife as your athame that, it is said, should never cut anything other than a handfasting cake and especially should never draw blood. These books usually urge you to own a white-handled knife or *bolline*, which is used for all the mundane cutting during spellcraft.

This is a "rule" that I do not accept. My athame has an elk handle (neither black nor white), and if I need to cut something during a ritual I don't hesitate to use my dagger if there's nothing else easily available. I haven't compromised my athame's ability to conduct energy nor have I incurred the Gods' wrath. I make sure to take good care of the dagger and we get along just fine.

Tarot cards are a more delicate matter. Because they are oracular tools, they should be kept out of sight—if only to make sure that no one plays with them without your permission. I use them in magick and have been known to buy a deck just for one or two cards that I particularly like. Since they are divinatory tools and must be kept clear—I read not only for myself but for others on a professional basis—I make sure that they aren't left out where just anybody can pick them up.

My tools and private altars are kept in one room set aside for ritual, but not everybody has the space to do this. Keeping them together in a single space "congeals" the energy and allows it to build up. However, more often than not, I find myself casting my spells on the dining room table. Go figure.

My husband and I also have a seasonal altar set up in the living room which we change six times a year (to represent Spring, Beltane, Summer, Autumn, Samhain, and Winter). We make a ritual out of the seasonal transitions and I change the pictures on the wall so they match the mood of the season.

You'll probably come across a number of "rules" about your magickal tools during your reading. My rule is that you ask yourself what you need; that, however you procure it, you treat the tool with respect; and that you question every supposed rule or regulation and ask, "does it make sense?"—"why?"—and—"does it apply to me?"

Learning to Let Go When It's Time

It seems hard, at first, to give up something, especially when it represents a specific period or person in our lives, but on occasion it's necessary. When we learn that letting go doesn't mean loss but instead means opening space for something new, then we don't cling so tightly to ideas and things that prevent us from evolving in our life-paths.

Of course, not everything old has to go—I still have the porcelain kitty statue that I traded a necklace for in first grade. Her name is Miss Kitty and she's my office mascot. I love her dearly and she's moved with me everywhere I've gone—even when I was living in a converted school bus after giving up nearly everything I owned.

Miss Kitty is my buddy; she's thirty years old (or older, I don't know how long she'd been around when I first got her) and we've grown up together. Every time I move, I panic because I'm afraid she'll get broken even though I wrap her in tons of paper and bubble wrap. It would be foolish of me to give her up. I still need her.

When it comes to assembling your collection of ritual tools, you'll probably spend several years finding just what works for you. Since 1980, I have had three different athames (before the first, I used a butcher knife from the kitchen), four or five incense burners, at least five chalices (currently I'm using a wine goblet because I haven't found the chalice I want), numerous candle holders for my God and Goddess candles—in other words, something that works now may not work later.

Don't hold on to a specific tool—or idea for that matter—just because it worked for you originally. People change, life changes. Without change, we stagnate and decay. It's okay if you find yourself looking at your athame after a year or two and saying, "It just isn't *me* anymore."

Growth involves letting go of outworn ideas and objects. We must create a void if we want something new to enter our lives. This is true on many levels.

My first pentacle was silver with moonstone. I remember the day I got rid of it. I was standing on the beach and the Goddess was there, whispering in my ear. She said that the pentacle had to go because it represented a period in my life that was over. It was time to move on. I took off the pentacle and threw it in the ocean. Since then, I've had five other pentacles, none of which felt just right. Finally, two years ago, I bought a little gold pentacle with peridot in the center. It was close but still too small and delicate for my nature.

My friend Lori came over and I took one look at her and knew that the pentacle was hers. I offered it to her and she happily accepted. That year for Yule, she had a pentacle made for me that was exactly what I wanted—a bronze crescent moon with Goddess, which sits atop a silver pentacle. Lori knows that I love peridot and she had a cabochon of the gem affixed in the center of the pentacle.

I am content now and expect to wear this pentacle until the day it no longer suits me, which may be a year, two years or never. I tell you this story for one reason: to assure you that if you let go of things when they need to go, when they don't feel like yours anymore, something better will come along to fill the void.

Cleansing Your Tools

There are many reasons for cleansing a tool. You might have bought it used, it might come as a gift, you might find it in a pile of junk in the attic. Even if you buy a tool brand new, it is still a good idea to cleanse it before you consecrate it.

Cleansing a tool requires more than just polishing the sides of a censer or buffing up a blade. When you cleanse a tool you remove or exorcise the old energies that other people have wittingly or unwittingly impressed upon it. Depending on the nature of the tool, there are a number of ways to cleanse it.

Crystals like quartz, amethyst, and citrine can be cleaned easily by soaking them in a lukewarm bath into which you have tossed a couple of pinches of salt (negative energy doesn't like salt), then rinse them with clear water. Make sure that your crystal isn't too cold or too hot and that the water is lukewarm, or the crystal might crack. I use a mild dishwashing liquid solution and a nail brush to scrub my big amethyst cluster. This will usually take care of any psychic residue. I wash my crystals about three times a year.

You can also set your crystals out in the sunlight for a day. That will usually clear up any psychic turbulence.

Athames can be cleansed first by removing any physical dirt and rust spots (rust takes elbow grease to remove, or a non-abrasive liquid detergent). After you have polished it on the physical realm there are several methods you can use to clear out the psychic gunk. You can plunge the dagger into the Earth next to a cedar tree or sage plant (both are highly purifying) and leave it for a few hours. If you choose this method, make sure that no one else is going to happen by the area and steal your dagger while you aren't looking; better yet, sit outside with it and read a good book.

You can also smudge the dagger with sage, cedar, or lavender smoke to clear the energy or lay the dagger on a large cluster of amethyst—a great purifier—overnight.

I do not recommend using salt water solutions to cleanse your athame. This treatment will promote rust and could weaken the knife's hilt.

Magick mirrors are best cleansed both physically and psychically by a mixture of mugwort and cider-vinegar. (Let the mugwort steep in the vinegar for a few days, then strain.) This will thoroughly clean the glass and take care of any psychic goo. You can also smudge the mirror.

Other tools, particularly drums and rattles, are probably most easily cleansed by the use of smudging. Chalices can be soaked in a saltwater solution like that used to cleanse crystals.

Another technique is to use your broom, or besom. The very purpose of the magickal broom is to cleanse space and I occasionally "sweep" my friends and altar by raising energy, then focusing it through the broom as I sweep the aura of the person or object. However, it is easy to break delicate objects this way, so be careful.

CONSECRATING A NEW TOOL

Once you have cleansed your tools, you will want to consecrate them. This involves "pledging" them to magickal service to make them sacred. I usually consecrate an object by use of the four elements. On your altar (whether inside or outside) you will want incense, a red candle in a sturdy holder, a small bowl of Full Moon Water (bottled spring water can substitute), a bowl of salt, and the tool you are planning to consecrate. For this example, an athame will be consecrated.

Cast a circle, then invoke the elements and whichever Gods or Goddesses you choose. Light the incense (frankincense is good for this purpose) and your altar candle. Relax and enter a light trance state.

Hold the dagger up to the North. Say:

> *By the powers of Earth, by the powers of salt,*
> *I consecrate and bless this dagger*
> *For use in my rituals and rites.*
> *Empower it with the ability to manifest*
> *And stabilize my magick.*
> *Spirits of Earth, I call upon you*
> *To bless this dagger now!*

Plunge the dagger into the bowl of salt and draw an invoking pentagram over the dagger with your hand.

> *Spirits of Earth, blessèd be.*

Hold the dagger up to the east. Say:

> *By the powers of Air, by the powers of smoke,*
> *I consecrate and bless this dagger*

For use in my rituals and rites.
Empower it with the ability to cleanse
And clarify my magick.
Spirits of Air, I call upon you
To bless this dagger now!

Hold the dagger in the smoke wafting up from the incense and draw an invoking pentagram over the dagger with your hand.

Spirits of Air, blesséd be.

Hold the dagger up to the south. Say:

By the powers of Fire, by the powers of flame,
I consecrate and bless this dagger
For use in my rituals and rites.
Empower it with the ability to energize
And strengthen my magick.
Spirits of Fire, I call upon you
To bless this dagger now!

Plunge the tip of the dagger in the candle flame (if your tool can catch on fire, hold it well above the flame instead of in it) and draw an invoking pentagram over the hilt with your hand.

Spirits of Fire, blesséd be.

Hold the dagger up to the west. Say:

By the powers of the Sea, by the power of Water,
I consecrate and bless this dagger
For use in my rituals and rites.
Empower it with the ability to bring intuition
And understanding to my magick.
Spirits of Water, I call upon you
To bless this dagger now!

Plunge the tip of the dagger into the bowl of water and draw an invoking pentagram over the hilt with your free hand.

Spirits of Water, blesséd be.

Hold the dagger up in the air above your head. Say:

I ask the Lord and Lady
To consecrate and bless this dagger
For use in my rituals and rites.
Great Mother and Horned God, I call upon you
To bless this dagger now!

Draw an invoking pentagram in the air with your dagger.

Lord and Lady, blessèd be.

You can, of course, consecrate several tools during a single consecration ritual. Just be sure to do a separate chant for each one.

COMMON MAGICKAL TOOLS

Below, you will find a list of some of the most common magickal tools, along with brief descriptions of their use.

Athame: A ritual dagger, traditionally double-edged, used to direct energy. It can have any type of hilt you want. It represents both the God's phallus and the element of Air.

Broom: Usually with natural bristles and a natural wood handle. Used to sweep away stagnant energy and negative vibrations.

Candles: Tapers, votives, and other unusual shapes in all colors are used in candle magick and as altar decoration.

Cauldron: An iron or brass vessel used, primarily, as a symbol. Of all magickal systems, use of the cauldron seems most common among those practicing Celtic Magick.

Censer: Used to hold burning incense. Incense burners can be made of anything from wood to brass and iron. Should be heat-proof.

Chalice: A ritual goblet made of glass, wood, ceramic, or metal. Represents the element of Water and the Womb of the Goddess.

Crown: A circlet or headdress worn by a Priestess or Priest. This can be made from metal, wood, or anything else that can be molded to the shape of your head. My crown has two snakes holding a pentagram on their heads, while some Priestesses like to wear the Triple Goddess symbol (the moon bordered by two crescents on either side).

Crystals: Used for invoking power, depending on what type of crystal involved. Also commonly used in scrying.

Drums: Used in ritual for trance work, ecstatic dancing, healing, and journey-work.

Hammer: Used primarily by Norse Pagans. It is sacred to Thor, the Norse God of Thunder and Agriculture.

Herbs: Used in various spell components.

Incense: Invokes the element of Air. Used for smudging and invoking various energies depending on what type is used.

Mortar and Pestle: Used to grind and powder herbs.

Mirror: Used for scrying and beauty magick.

Oils: Essential oils and blends are charged with magickal energy and used to invoke various powers, depending on which energy the herb possesses.

Pentacle: The altar pentacle represents the element of Earth. The pentacle necklace or earrings are worn by Witches, Pagans, and Wiccans to symbolize their religion. Represents the five elements (Earth, Air, Fire, Water, and Spirit), the human body (the head, two outstretched arms and two outstretched legs), and is a symbol of protection.

Rattle: Used in ritual dance, for cleansing, and for raising power.

Robes: Many Witches like to have special clothing, often referred to as robes, for their rituals. It can help alter mood. Whatever you choose to wear for ritual (if anything), it should be easy to move around in, comfortable, and the sleeves shouldn't fall into the candle flames.

Statues: Statues of deities are placed on the altar to represent the Gods.

Sword: Used much like the athame.

Wand: Magickal wands can be made of wood, metal, or crystal and are used to invoke various powers depending on what the wands are created for. Represents the element of Fire.

Water: Full Moon and New Moon waters are used for various spells. Other herbal waters may also be used for spellcraft.

An altar is also a very important part of magickal ritual. Aside from being a surface to hold your tools, it can serve as a medium for expressing the nature of your magick or the specific ritual you are working with. Creating an altar is an art form and is limited only by your imagination. I have acquired a good supply of beautiful cloths and scarves over the years for the altar tables but that's just the beginning. Crepe paper, ribbons, glitter confetti, long strings of beads, candles shaped like animals, plants—even money and coins if you are casting a prosperity spell. Don't be limited by what people tell you should be on an altar. Be daring, be willing to take a chance on finding your own path in the Pagan world.

This list represents only the basic tools of magick. There are so many other things I have used in ritual and magick over the years that it would be impossible to list them all.

6

CHANTS, RUNE CHARTS, AND SYMBOLS

The power of the word is of utmost importance during magickal work. Whether you are invoking the Gods or Elements in front of a group or sitting quietly, performing candle magick and carving your spell into the fragile wax, the symbols and words you select carry your magickal intent. What I offer here are some chants I've created, a guide to the Norse and Celtic Rune systems most common in magick, and a set of symbols and runes that are either unique to my system or are so universal in their accepted use that nearly everyone uses them.

CHANTING

Chanting is an important part of magick. The repetition of words quickly builds energy, focuses the mind, and it is one of the easiest ways to raise the cone of power. Many people I have encountered do not know how to chant properly. Whether the words are sung or spoken doesn't matter. Instead, it's important that the chant be kept up long enough to slip into trance.

I've attended several rituals during which we were encouraged to join in a chant. It was repeated three or four times and just when the energy was starting to flow, it was stopped so abruptly that the energy fell without ever having peaked. Because those leading the rituals didn't seem to notice that no cone of power had been built and no energy had been released, my friends and I questioned the proficiency of these people. We were diplomatic, but the experiences led us to decline further rituals with these particular groups.

To avoid that type of problem when you decide to include a chant in your group-oriented ritual, make sure that everyone gets a copy of the words. It is distracting for the participants to try to follow along with an unfamiliar chant. It disperses the energy and can lead to an unsettled, disgruntled feeling.

There is no fool-proof way to tell how long you should keep a chant going. I've seen some chants peak after twenty repetitions, I've seen a few go on for five minutes or more and still be building power. You must practice and pay attention to the changes in energy the chant produces.

This is easier to achieve when you are chanting alone, although the strength of numbers will not be there. When you are chanting alone, you're never in danger of someone else ending it before you're ready. And if you mess up the words, no one else is going to know.

There is always the question of how long a chant should be and when it turns into a song. There are short chants and then there are long ones. Short chants will usually run no more than four lines and are much easier to work with in groups of more than three people.

Songs can be worked with in magick, however, and long chants can be managed quite easily by two people who work together and have both memorized the words.

I've collected many chants over the years and I doubt if I've even scratched the surface of what's out there. I've also written my own, and it is those chants that I share here.

It is easy to make up your own chants and this can be a fun group project. When you begin to write your own chants, remember that the words must be easy to pronounce, the chant should not be complex (especially if you're expecting seventeen people to keep in rhythm), and the chant must mean something to you.

The Chants

Though I have composed tunes to these chants (in my head only, so please don't write asking me for a copy of the music—I can't give it to you), they can be spoken just as effectively. Or you can make up your own tune if you like. In addition to those chants appearing on the next few pages, many chapters of this book contain different chants given as part of different spells or rituals. If you don't find what you want in this chapter, then glance through the others for something to suit your needs.

This first chant is useful for God rituals, Sabbat festivals (especially Lughnasadh and Mabon), and prosperity spells:

Lord of the Forest, Lord of the Vine
Lord of Magick, Lord of Wine
Come in the night, come in the day
Teach me to love, teach me to play

Use this chant for scrying and general spellcraft:

Queen of Faerie, Lady of the Sidhe
Open my eyes that I may see
Water and earth, air and fire
Magick create all I desire

This chant is useful as a binding chant for any spell:

Bind to me by star and sea
By flame and stone,
The strength of will, the steady flow
From creation's quill, from muse's song
From starlight dance and shaman's trance
The power of mind, strengthen my
Quicksilver thought,
Magick, magick, elude me not
By Horned One's axe and Lady's blade
So mote it be, this spell is made.

Use these next two chants when you are working with faerie magick or shape-shifting:

Nightwing, slithering
Creep through sylvan bough
Horned Lord, Queen of Stars
Let us go a-prowl

We are the creatures of the Night
Dancing under wild starlight!

This chant is good for a general blessing:

May you weave by starlight
May you glow in the golden sun
Flow with the waters, grow in the forest
Ancient, ever-young

Use this when you are generating energy for a new project or idea:

Seed!
Bud!
Blossom!
Grow!

A God chant:

Horned One, Lord of the Sun
Lover of the Goddess
Green Man, Lord of the Wild,
We ask for You to bless us

A Goddess chant:

Ancient Lady, Ancient Moon
Rising now above us
We gather in Your sacred Grove
Asking that You bless us

A good affirmation chant to use daily:

Everything in my life works out
More exquisitely than I plan it

A good elemental chant:

Earth, earth, come to me
Ground now my body
Air, air, hear my cry
Let my mind soar and fly
Fire, fire, in my thighs
Let me dance until sunrise
Water, water, soothe my soul
Balance me and make me whole

A Goddess chant to be used before scrying:

Golden Lady, silver boughs
Sparkling crescent at Her brow
Lady Moon, Mother Sun
Tell me now what's to be done

RUNES AND MAGICKAL SYMBOLS

A rune is a symbol that represents a certain meaning or concept. It is the energy of that concept frozen—in stasis. By concentrating on the rune, by drawing it out and 'feeding it' (with energy, with oils, or other materials), we release its power to work in our magick.

The Norse and Celtic people had two of the most commonly known runic alphabet systems. There are many good books on both of these systems that examine their backgrounds, mythological basis, and deeper meanings. If you choose to work extensively with the runes, I suggest that you study them carefully—the Bibliography at the end of this book has suggestions for good resources for learning more about runes.

THE NORSE RUNES

As far as we can tell the Norse developed a system of magickal pictographs before the second century B.C.E. Later, these glyphs began to represent their language. The runes were considered to be alive, in a sense, and just by drawing them energy was invoked.

In that sense, whenever you use the Norse runes you should 'feed' them—rub them with oil, or magickal powders, or a drop of your own blood (though only in spells pertaining to yourself).

There are many excellent books on the history of rune-lore, and what follows here are very basic meanings for their use in a magickal sense. Their divinitory meanings differ from the magickal uses, so if you want to create your own set of runes for divination, be sure to get a good guide on the subject.

The Norse runic alphabet is known as the Elder FUTHARK (based on the first six letters of this alphabet), and are grouped into three divisions: Freya's Eight, Heimdall's Eight, and Tir's Eight.

Be aware that there are different spellings and pronunciations for these runes, based on the tradition and culture you are coming from. There are many traditions surrounding the Norse runes regarding color and creation, numerology and the order in which they are carved. These traditions should not be ignored. Be sure to study their usage.

With the name of each rune, I have included the letter or letters that it represents in contemporary English.

Freya's Eight

Fehu (F): Increase of wealth and possessions, protection of valuables. Used to send energy on its way, fire in its uncontrolled, primal state.

Uruz (U,V): Used to create change, healing, vitality, strength, to boost energy of magickal work.

Thurisaz (Th): Beginning new projects, luck—the hand of fate helping you, protection, the hammer of Thor, opening gateways.

Ansuz (A): Communications, wisdom and clarity, to attract others to your cause, increase magickal energy.

Raido (R): Safe travel, movement, obtaining justice in an issue, used to keep a situation from stagnating.

 Kenaz (K): The hearth fire, artistic pursuits, healing, love and passion, creativity, strength.

 Gebo (G): Gifts, partnerships on all realms, sex magick, balance, integration of energies.

 Wunjo (W,V): Joy, happiness, love, fulfillment in career and home life, the icing on the cake.

Heimdall's Eight

 Hagall (H): Slow, steady pace, no disruptions, asking for a hand from fate within a situation you do not control.

 Neid (N): Need, desire, fulfilling those needs, love and sex magick, motivation created by distress.

Isa (I): Cessation of energy, freezing an issue where it stands, cooling relationships, separation, division.

Jera (J, Y): Harvesting tangible results from efforts already sown, fertility, culmination of events, abundance.

Eihwaz (I): Banishing magick, removal of obstacles and delays, invoking foresight, clearing up hidden issues and situations.

 Perdhro (P): Unexpected gains, hidden secrets coming to light, discovering that which has been lost, spiritual evolution.

Algiz (Z): Protection, fortunate influences, fate on your side, victory and success, good luck and personal strength.

 Sigel (S, Z): Victory, power, strength, health, the rune of the sun, vitality, drive to work and produce.

Tir's Eight

Tir (T): Victory, leadership, success over other competitors, increase in finances, virility and passion (especially for men).

Berkana (B): Growth, abundance, fertility, Mother Earth, protection, the zenith of an idea or situation.

Ehwaz (E): Abrupt changes, moving into new home and environment, travel, swift change in situation.

Mannaz (M): Cooperation, teamwork, collaboration, help and aid from others, beginning new projects, especially with others.

Lagaz (L): Intuition, imagination, success in studies, creativity, vitality and passion (especially for women).

 Ing (NG): Fertility, successful conclusion to issue or situation, ending one cycle and beginning another.

 Daeg (D): Increase and expansion, prosperity, growth, major turning points in life, turning in new directions.

 Othel (O): Material possessions and protection of those possessions, inheritance (can be genetic traits inherited from elders).

The Celtic Runes

The Celtic runic system is know as the Ogham Alphabet, or the Tree Alphabet. It was based on the sacred trees and forces found in nature.

While the Norse Runes were divided into three groups of eight, the Ogham is divided into five groups of five. There is some debate over whether the last group of five runes truly belongs to the Ogham alphabet because it was added later on, but many students of the system find that these runes add to the whole concept of the Tree Alphabet.

The Ogham runes should always be written on a vertical line as opposed to a horizontal line. Again, if you intend to use this system on a regular basis, I suggest an in-depth study of the material available.

Because little was written down in Celtic society, you may not be able to find as much information on Ogham as there exists about the Norse runes.

Each of the Ogham runes presented here is accompanied by its magickal meaning as well as with the letter(s) and tree it corresponds with.

First Quintet

Beith (B, birch): New beginnings, unseen forces at work bringing change, birth of new ideas, general good fortune.

Luis (L, rowan): Protection, control of senses, the strength to turn away negativity, vitality, healing, magick.

Fearn (F, alder): Prophecy, divination, scrying, intuition, remaining true to your ethics, music, poetry.

Saille (S, willow): Feminine energy, fertility, psychic powers, intuition, cunning, new forces flowing, enchantment.

Nuin (N, ash): As above—so below, fate, divine process, connections to the world, spiritual inspiration, take action.

Second Quintet

Huathe (H, hawthorne): Protection, purification, learning through adversity, sexuality, self-imposed isolation, self-sacrifice.

Duir (D, oak): Strength, endurance, opening new doors, new paths, vigor, power to endure, protection, leadership.

Tinne (T, holly): Balance, integrity, justice, tests and ordeals, courage, mastery over self, legal or money matters, growth.

Coll (C, hazel): Creativity, poetry, intuition, the powers of divination, perception, inspiration, arbitration.

Quert (Q, apple): Choosing that which is beneficial, love affairs, beauty, healing, nourishment, living fully.

Third Quintet

Muin (M, vine): Psychic senses, harvest, visionary states, patience, releasing logic and reason, examine life's lessons.

Gort (G, ivy): Follow the spiral of life, explore personal paths, transformation in self, career and education.

Ngetal (N, reed): Awareness of environment, creating order from chaos, progress through vigilance, harmony of will, action.

Straif (Ss, blackthorn): Fate, wheel of fortune, trials and tribulations lead to change, true liberation, rebirth is possible.

Ruis (R, elder): Passing of old cycles, looking ahead, change and renewal, new residence, career, health.

Fourth Quintet

 Ailim (A, silver fir): Clear vision, foresight, being grounded in the present, nurture new projects, gathering insight.

 Ohn (O, gorse): Increase of material possessions, synthesizing information, sexual energy, repelling negative energy.

Ur (U, heather): World of spirit, healing, personal success, well-being, fertility, prosperity, Faerie magick, romance.

Eadha (E, white poplar): Overcoming fear and doubt, inner guidance, determination, rebirth, omens and signs, creative solutions.

Ioho (I, Y, yew): Death, rebirth, reincarnation, destiny, accepting the inevitable, new starts, contact with past.

Fifth Quintet

 Koad (K, grove): Woodland sanctuary, Faerie magick, cohesion of elements, faith, the unexpected surprise that delights.

Oir (Th, spindle): Joy through process, stretching limits, accepting responsibility, use of will, direct action.

 Uilleand (Pe, honeysuckle): Inner vision distinguishes truth from lies, hidden treasure, defeat confusion, mastering inner forces.

 Phagos (Ph, beech): Wisdom from the past, thirst for knowledge, written communication, truth, law, justice, elders' advice.

 Mor (Xi-z, sea): The Goddess, hidden depths, travel, primal wisdom, bounty, full moon, high tides, childhood issues.

MAGICKAL SYMBOLS

These are some general magickal symbols and their accepted meanings that I use in my magick. They can be carved on candles (see chapter seven) or drawn on paper and burned to release their energy. They can be sewn onto charm bags, written on the body before ritual, carved in a cake of soap for ritual baths—use your imagination, they have many applications. Some of the spells presented in Part Two of this book will give you directions on how and when to use runes to increase the energy.

MAGICKAL RUNES

 Barrenness: Fallow time, rest, recuperation, inward focus, hidden knowledge, stagnation, letting go.

 Bars: To bar someone from doing harm, to keep prying eyes away, to halt a situation where it stands.

 **Caduceus:** Health, strength, vitality, swearing of sacred oaths, healing, legal matters, judicial system.

 Chalice: Compassion, intuition, blessings pouring into your life, success, good fortune, abundance, ecstasy.

 Clasped Hands: Renewing old friendships, new friendships, cozy atmosphere at home, parties, celebrations.

Dark Moon: Hidden knowledge, winter, scrying, dormancy, retreat, rest, banishing magick, recuperation.

 Deosil: To invoke a situation, to tighten and bind a spell, full moon magick, to strengthen work already underway.

 Flame: Transformation, destruction leading to creation, healing, radiance, passion, sexuality.

 Forest: Faerie magick, woodland magick, animal magick, connection with the wild forest energy, solitude.

 Full Moon: Commitment, nurturance, dedication, culmination, strength, summer, protective energy.

 God Rune: Used to represent the Horned God, masculine power and strength, the wild forest.

 Goddess Rune: Used to represent the three faces of the Triple Goddess, feminine force and power.

 **Heart:** Love, romantic alliance, harmony between partners, sparking interest in others, flirtations.

Heart and Phallus: Sex, lust, inner drive, strength, passion, radiance, attraction, vigor, fertility.

 House: Finding a new home, discovery of the country, county, or city in which you are destined to live.

Initiation: Commitment to project or cause, dedication, accepting your place in life, rites of passage.

Money: Prosperity, increase in material possessions, career advancement, success.

Moon: Cyclic issues, lunar magick, feminine magick, menstrual issues, scrying, delving into hidden issues.

Mountains: Stability, strength, manifestation, security, prosperity, Earth, abundance, grounded energy.

Ocean: All-embracing womb, stern strength, psychic vision, emotions, female beauty, inward reflection.

Pentacle: Pure magickal energy, asking for omens and oracles, protection, opening to psychic work.

Quill: Inspiration, creative projects, art, writing, music, protection of finished work, wisdom.

Rainbow: Messages, omens, serendipity, observation, understanding others, clear communications.

Scales: Justice, karma, truth, clarity, higher forces at work, the Eternal Return, the Wheel of Life.

Sickle: Death, loss, sadness, letting go of people or concepts, final stage of a cycle, transformation.

Spiral: Fate, fortune, finding true path in life, inner guidance, destiny, spirituality.

 Sun: Radiance, healing energy, masculine magick, opening pathways, success magick, expansion and growth.

 Waning Crescent: Wisdom, releasing, inner vision, autumn, compassion without illusion, self-focused action.

 Waxing Crescent: New beginnings, spring, enthusiasm, joy, playfulness; spontaneous action, youth.

 Web: Change, weaving new situations into your life, accepting movement, transformation.

 Weeping Eye: Pain, destruction of old plans, growth through hardship, sorrow, strength through difficulty.

 Widdershins: To unravel or unwind a situation, dark moon magick, banishing magick, to tear apart a spell already begun.

Wind: Independence, clear perceptions, innovation, flexibility, education, cleansing, logic, intellect.

There are many other symbols that you can use in magick; you just need to know what they represent to you and to focus on that energy as you are drawing or carving them.

Part Two

SPELLCRAFT

7

MAGICKAL LIVING

There are many ways to incorporate magick into your daily life. Simple rituals and charms can enhance your life. Quiet, reflective magick can have profound influences on your future as well as your present situation. In this chapter, and those that follow in this section, these concepts will be explored, helping you learn to integrate magick into your everyday life.

Some of the more common magickal workings include candle magick, herbal magick, psychic healing, elemental magick, ritual drama, ecstatic dance, guided meditations and journeys, and drumming and chanting. You can combine a few or all of the above to create everything from the most simplistic ritual to an elaborately choreographed experience. You can use all of the tools discussed in chapter five, or none of them. You can work skyclad (naked) or fully clothed. But remember, for all the tools and color coordination and timing with the moon it really comes down to how much you want to work magick, how much energy and focus you are willing to give it, and how much patience you have. If you aren't ready for hard work, then I suggest you drop the idea of becoming a Witch.

In this chapter, we will explore the basics of candle magick, herbal magick, household magick, and different ways to incorporate magickal acts into your everyday life.

BASICS OF CANDLE MAGICK

Candle magick is one of the quickest, most effective forms of magick and many Witches use it frequently because of this. The basics of candle magick include: type of candle, how to dress and carve the candle, and burning the candle.

TYPES OF CANDLES

There are many types of candles that you can use for spellcraft. I do not recommend using candles that are partially burnt unless the spell includes specific instructions for this—any energy that had been in the candle before your ritual will now come into your spell and interfere with the magick you are doing. This energy interference encourages chaos, and it is best to start with a clean slate—a new candle. If you don't have a clean candle then use a different form of magick to help you to attain your goals.

Seven Knobbed Candle: Candle molded into seven knobs. Usually, one knob is burned each day for seven days in a row.

Figure Candles: Also known as image candles, these are shaped into a a specific form such as a male, female, animal, or skull, and are used in sympathetic and natural magick.

Taper Candles: Usually seven to ten inches long and made of either paraffin or beeswax. They can be dipped, in which case the color will only be on the outside, or colored all the way through.

Votive Candles: Small, fat candles, usually two or three inches high, made of beeswax or paraffin and often heavily scented.

A SIMPLE CANDLE RITUAL

The following is an easy, efficient procedure for candle magick. It can be adapted as necessary for your desired magickal intent.

Choose what color candle you will need (see color chart in chapter two) based on your intent.

Decide what kind of candle you will use: taper, votive, image, or other type. A votive candle is good for when you have less time to spend in ritual. Once you've chosen your candle, set up your altar according to the nature of your spell.

Carve your candle. A push-pin thumbtack is perfect to use for this. However, you may wish to use a special carving tool. A friend made a wonderful carving tool out of an antler tip and a nail for me.

Consult your rune charts and decide which ones fit your spell. Don't worry if the wax flakes a little, just concentrate on each rune and each letter as you carve your intent into the wax.

Choose an appropriate oil (if available) and anoint the candle. Start at the middle and rub up toward the wick then return to the middle and rub down toward the bottom. When you begin from the middle point, you balance the energy of the candle.

If you wish, anoint the candle with a drop or two of your blood (do this only if the spell is for you). If you prefer, or if the spell is for someone else, you can stick a few strands of the spell recipient's hair or fingernail clippings to the candle with wax from a candle adapter.

If you desire, roll the candle in powdered herbs or spell powders.

Raise energy and charge the candle with your intent.

Firmly set the candle in a holder and put it on your altar until you are ready to cast the spell. Wax candle adapters are available in most craft stores and they make it easy to fit a candle into a holder that's a little too big.

When preparing your candle, you can do so in circle if you wish, but it isn't necessary.

THINGS TO REMEMBER DURING CANDLE MAGICK

- Let the candle burn itself out if at all possible, unless you are doing a multi-day spell. If you have to extinguish it for any reason, focus on closing the energy down for the day, not on eliminating it. Then, as soon as you can, burn the rest of the candle.

- If you are worried about leaving a candle burning, do what many Witches do: start the spell in circle, then when you have to stop, put the candle in the bathtub in a heat-resistant dish that rests a few inches above the porcelain of the tub. Make sure that all towels, shower curtains, and other flammable bath paraphernalia are well out of reach. Then close the door so animals and children can't wander in and get hurt.

- There are varying opinions on to how to extinguish the candles on an altar. One theory is that by blowing it out you're blowing away the energy. Another says that by pinching it out, you're pinching off the energy. I usually wet my fingers and pinch out the flame, but my suggestion is that you buy a candle snuffer. They are safe, effective, and you're not really using much of your own energy to put out the flame.

- Refer to your rune charts, color charts, and timing charts to coordinate your spell if you are not using one that has been pre-designed.

- Chanting while a candle is burning is very effective. Again, make sure the chant matches the intent of your spell.

- Wash candle holders between spells.

- You can make your own candles, if so inclined, and add oils and herbs directly to them during their creation.

- If you are working out of phase with the moon, pour a little Moon Water (either new or full) into the bottom of a stainless steel pan and place the candle holder in the center of the water. Make sure the water doesn't pour over the top of the holder. This will surround the candle with the energy of the proper moon phase for your spell. You can float spell powders and herbs on top of the water.

BASICS OF HERBAL MAGICK

Herbal magick uses the natural power of herbs to create needed changes in the world around you. I find that it works more slowly, but more steadily, than candle magick. It is also very portable—it is much easier to take a sachet with you than to carry a burning candle.

Each herb resonates with a certain level of energy. It is by using the right herbs for the right situations that we release this energy to cause the desired transformation.

Herbal magick is not difficult; there are several good books on the market that list a multitude of herbs and their properties. Spend time outside in the forest or in your garden attuning yourself with the plants that you find there. Sometimes they are the best source for telling you what you need to use.

TO GATHER OR TO BUY?

Gathering your own herbs is, of course, the preferable route. If the world was perfect, we would have access to organic fields where we could gather our herbs at the proper phase of the moon, proper hour of the day, and at the right time of the year. But the world doesn't work like that.

Some herbs only grow in certain countries or regions. Others are under threat of extinction and shouldn't be touched. Few of us can travel to the Orient, few of us can roam through the deserts or mountains during the growing seasons. Even if we had that luxury, how many herbs could we readily identify?

Buying herbs has become a definite boon to the Craft. No, they won't necessarily be gathered at just the right time, and no, they won't always be fresh, but I have used store-bought, dried herbs for years with wonderful results. This testifies that the power resides within the heart of the herb, not within our limited view of how things work in this universe.

If you buy herbs, bring them home as soon as possible, transfer them to dark glass jars, and label and date them. (Don't forget the labels—I don't know how many herbs I've had to toss because I forgot to stick a label on it. When you have forty jars in a cupboard, you're bound to forget which one is which.)

If you wish, bless the herbs in circle before you store them and keep them in a ceremonial area to ensure their sacredness.

But let's say you have decided to gather your own herbs. You have found a nice patch of chamomile and you want to harvest some.

First, there are several things you should consider before you begin to cut. Be aware of the energy of the land you are working on. Is it pleasant? Does it feel angry? If the land isn't happy, chances are the energies of the plants won't be either.

Okay, so you've determined that the land feels fine—sort of neutral. Good going, so far. Now remember that the phase of the moon will govern what you gather. During the waxing moon the energy rises into the leaves, flowers, stalks, and seeds. During the waning moon it descends into the roots. For example, we use the flowers and leaves of chamomile so you will want to gather the herb during the waxing moon.

Don't harvest the herb in full sun—dawn is a good time, while the dew is still on the plant. Herbal powers tend to recede during full sunlight so anytime from early evening until dawn is fine.

Draw a circle on the ground with a stick or your herb knife, surrounding the plant. Be cautious carrying your athame in public—some states have laws against wearing or carrying a double-edged dagger.

Sit for a moment next to the plant and attune to its energy. Ask permission to gather from it—remember, these are living beings you're about to chop up!

When you feel you've received permission, then cut a few sprigs. Never take more than a quarter of the original plant or you will retard its growth, perhaps even kill it.

After you've finished cutting, leave an offering—a few pennies, a crystal, a piece of fruit—buried near the plant.

If you are gathering roots, you will probably destroy the entire plant. In this case, bring something to replace it—if not a new plant, then food to nourish the Earth.

Always thank the plant, the Earth, and the Goddess for what you've taken and always respect what you've taken. Remember, never, ever take an endangered plant!

DRYING HERBS

Discard all leaves that are brown or insect-eaten. Wash all cuttings then pat them dry with paper towels. You can spread them in a single layer on dry paper towels or a clean paper bag, or you can bundle them and hang them from a thread. Either way, store them in a dark, warm, well-ventilated area and check them every few days. When they are crisp, strip them, pick out the seeds, stems, and other detritus, and store them in appropriately labeled dark glass containers.

To dry seeds or seed heads (sunflowers, for example), gently bundle the cuttings together at the stem ends if the seed-heads or plants are thin enough, and place in a paper sack. Cinch the opening around the seed heads and, high on the sides of the sack, cut a few holes for ventilation. When they are dry, shake them and work with your hands to remove the seeds from the heads.

Roots can take a year or more to dry. Hang them in a well-ventilated, dark spot.

Replace herbs at least once per year.

HERBAL GLOSSARY AND USAGES

Herbs: Plants, usually dried, used to make magickal and aromatic charms, sachets, potpourri, and the like.

Oils: The essential or synthetic base of a plant, in liquid form. Used for anointing and aromatherapy. Making an oil blend is simple; follow these directions:

Start with a base of ¼ ounce of olive or almond oil. To this base, add appropriate essential oils with an eye dropper, one drop at a time. Most of the oil blends I give formulas for in this book also specify herbs and gems. To incorporate these into your mixture, add a few pieces of the herb and a crystal chip to the vial. These ingredients help to add energy and help the oils blend when I shake them. After mixing your blend, raise energy and charge the oil with your intent.

Never take oils internally unless they have been specified safe.

Tinctures: Can be used internally or externally. These herbal infusions can be put to a variety of uses. For direction, consult a good herbal text to discover the various medicinal and magickal properties of herbs. For example, a mugwort tincture can help with scrying, while a chamomile tincture can act as a sleep aid. Tinctures are derived by soaking the plant in alcohol—I find vodka works best, because it has no taste and its strong alcohol content draws out the plant's essence very effectively, allowing your tincture to be purer. To make a tincture, follow the following instructions. While this example illustrates making a chamomile tincture, it can be adapted for any herb you choose.

Start with a clear quart jar. Say you want to make chamomile tincture. Fill the jar about ½ full with cleaned chamomile. Then cover this to the rim with vodka. Cap tightly and set in a dark cupboard for 3 to 4 weeks. Shake twice each day. If necessary, add more vodka as the herb swells and absorbs the liquid. At the end of three weeks strain and pour into a clean glass jar. Cork and keep in your herb cabinet or other dark, cool place. These are best stored in clean, dark glass jars.

The important thing to remember about making tinctures is that the strength of the herb increases with the alcohol, and you should be wary of taking too much. Usually, I take 1 or 2 teaspoons when needed. Also, remember that if you start with a poisonous herb you'll end up with a very poisonous tincture that can kill you. Make sure you know your herbs when you are working with them.

Sachets: Small cloth or leather bags that contain magickally charged herbs, crystals, and other natural ingredients such as sea shells or stones, sachets are easy to make. Take a piece of cloth, about four inches square, in a color relevant to the spell you want to do. Raise energy on the herbs as you crumble them in your hands. Raise energy on any crystals or other objects that you are adding to the sachet. Place everything in the center of the cloth and pull the corners together. Tie the ends firmly together with a ribbon in the color that matches the intent of your spell.

You can carry the sachet with you or leave it at home near your altar or your bed. Sachets are easy charms to make for other people.

Incense: Incenses have long been used to invoke states of altered consciousness. The smoke is used for smudging, cleansing, scrying, and purifying the air. While there are several ways to create self-burning incense, I buy most of mine since the process for making them is quite elaborate. If I want a very specific result, I burn pinches of powdered herbs on self-igniting charcoal.

Stick incenses, granular incenses, and resins like frankincense all work with equal success. Just match the type of incense to the spell you are doing.

Teas: Teas are used to promote changes both medicinally and psychologically. There is nothing better than a cup of orange spice or apple cinnamon tea on a cool autumn day to make you feel cozy and safe. Teas can be made from bulk herbs (chamomile, mugwort, lemon balm), or you can buy pre-mixed herbal teas like Celestial Seasonings. While I don't often use them in ritual, I do drink them before bed to promote healthy sleep and dream work and in the early morning while sitting with a favorite magazine to promote a calm, refreshed space from which to greet the rest of the day. If you like, buy a teapot that you will use solely for magickal brews and keep it with your ritual gear.

Washes: Herbal washes are used to effect physical changes on the body. For example, a comfrey wash is effective for easing bruises. One of the easiest ways is to make an infusion of the herb using hot (not boiling) water. Drop the herbs into the water, either loose or in a muslin or cheesecloth bag (I do not recommend using a metal tea ball for this), then strain the water and use a gauze pad to wash the affected area. Consult a good herbal encyclopedia for medicinal uses of herbs and remember—this is one area of magick where it is better not to experiment. Be sure that anything you rub onto or ingest into your body is something proven benign, or you could be setting yourself up for trouble.

Powders: Spell powders are usually made from ground and powdered herbs and roots. Use a mortar and pestle to grind the herbs separately then mix them together and charge them by raising energy.

Roots can be nearly impossible to grind this way unless you have hours and hours of spare time, so I recommend an electric coffee bean grinder. Use the grinder for herbal use only—you don't want to mix herbs and coffee together.

Use spell powders by sprinkling them on altars or on your body (keep in mind that this can be itchy), add them to sachets or put them in your shoes. You can roll your spell candles in them after anointing the candles with oil.

Woods: Sacred woods are used to make wands and staves. You can also carve runestaves on them, and make runes and talismans out of them. The process for gathering the piece of wood should follow the process of gathering herbs. Always ask the tree for permission to remove part of it first, and leave something behind as an offering. Never hack at a tree or twist the branch off. Use a knife or saw to cleanly cut the branch or limb so that you don't traumatize the tree any more than necessary.

HERBAL VOCABULARY

anaphrodisiac: a substance that cools the sexual drive

aphrodisiac: a substance that acts as a sexual stimulant

bane: that which destroys life or energy; poison

botanomancy: divination through the use of herbs

chaplet: wreath or crown of flowers and herbs, worn on the head to promote energy or healing

charm bag: sachet, medicine bag

hallucinogen: mind-altering substance

herb: a plant used in magickal, culinary, or medicinal arts

herbal: pertaining to herbs; written collection of information about herbs

herbal infusion: an admixture created by steeping or soaking herbs in hot, but not boiling, water; herbal tea

macerate: to make soft by soaking in a liquid

narcotic: a drug or herb that dulls the senses, induces sleep or stupor

sachet: a small packet filled with herbs and/or other objects.

simple: an infusion made from a single herb

steep: to soak herbs in hot liquid

tincture: herbal infusion made with alcohol instead of water (be aware that some herbs, roots especially, need alcohol to extract their essence)

wortcunning: herbal knowledge; the use of herbs

A Short Compendium of Herbs for Workings

Divination
anise

camphor

hibiscus

lemon

lilac

Banishing
basil

copal

dragon's blood

frankincense

myrrh

Healing
angelica

calamus

cedarwood

eucalyptus

lemon balm

Love
jasmine

lotus

orange

rose

vanilla

Lust
clove

ginger

grains of paradise

patchouli

tuberose

Luck
allspice

fern

heather

nutmeg

vetiver

Money
basil

chamomile

cinnamon

dill

vervain

Peace
gardenia

lavender

meadow sweetgum

rosemary

violet

Magick
carnation

ginger

mastic

tangerine

vanilla

Protection
bay

black pepper

heather

petitgrain

rose geranium

Purification
benzoin

fennel

lemon

pine

vervain

Spirituality
cassia

heliotrope

lotus

sage

wisteria

This list comprises only a small spectrum of the possibilities for using herbs in your magick. There are so many possible combinations that you will need a good magickal herbal to fully explore your work.

A NOTE ABOUT SYNTHETIC OILS

Natural oils are usually preferable, but can be extremely expensive or difficult to obtain. Because it is the essential scent that you are after, the synthetic oil will work if you can't afford or find the natural one. Use what you can afford, buy the best you can, and put more energy into it.

TOOLS USED IN HERBAL MAGICK

Magickal tools were discussed in chapter five, but there are some tools that are specifically needed for herbal work. The following is a list of the basic tools you will need, along with descriptions.

Censer: A heat-proof dish used to hold charcoal and incense. I recommend filling it with salt or sand.

Charcoal: Self-igniting (you just hold a match to it), they are usually round pieces of charcoal one or two inches in diameter. Do not use the charcoal briquettes intended for outdoor grilling, you can give yourself carbon monoxide poisoning.

Eyedropper: Used to measure oils, waters, dosages, and so on. You will want several of these.

Herbs: The backbone of herbal magick. Start with some of the basics and build up your supply as needed.

Incense: Buy a wide variety of powders, sticks, and resins. Incense can be avoided if you are allergic to it, but is really helpful in changing the atmosphere and mood of a ritual space.

Mortar and Pestle: A bowl—often of marble or wood—and grinding tool in which herbs are powdered.

Sewing supplies: You will need needles, thread, fabric, ribbons, and so on, for making sachets and poppets. Keep a variety on hand. You can find some wonderful fabrics by visiting the thrift stores and looking through the old clothes. If you use material from old clothing, at least be sure you wash them thoroughly before using them. It is a good idea to cleanse and raise energy over these discarded items to avoid using someone else's energy in your work.

Oils: Use them to anoint yourself, candles, ritual tools, and anything else. Essential oils are usually expensive, so you may have to choose some basic ones first and build up your supply as you can.

Oil Base: Olive oil, almond oil, and sunflower oil are all good bases to use for mixing your magickal oils. You will notice in my spell and oil recipes that I often include the type of base to use for a particular oil. While you can substitute vegetable oil if need be, try to remain close to the instructions for the best possible results.

Oil Bottles: Small bottles, often holding less than two drams, in which magickal oils are blended and stored. The darker the bottle, the longer your oil will retain its potency.

Salt: Used in ritual and for some sachets and charms. You can use table salt, but sea salt is more appropriate. Other special salts may also be appropriate. For my Pele rituals, I use Hawaiian Red Salt.

HOUSEHOLD MAGICK

Part of living a magickal life includes extending your spellwork to the space you occupy when you aren't in a circle or other sacred space. While there are a number of easy things you can make and do to create a more harmonious living space, you should start with a strong magickal foundation by thoroughly cleansing and purifying your home. See the "Moving In" and "Moving Out" rituals in this chapter, as well as chapter twelve for other protection and purification spells. Using these suggestions will not only secure your home, but provide a firm basis so that your other household spells and magick will work to their fullest extent.

MOVING IN

Anytime you move into a home, be it one room or a whole house, there are several traditional rituals that you should consider incorporating into the move. I have been using them for years now and wouldn't think of doing without them.

Performing certain rituals at this time can be very important for several reasons. As you prepare to leave your old home to move into a new one, you are leaving a space that you have imprinted with your energy. To be considerate of the new inhabitants of your old space, you should cleanse your essence out of that apartment or house.

On the same note, when you move into a new space, you can't be certain that the old tenants left with all of their astral baggage. You will want to cleanse your new space before you move in.

Once you have been given the keys to your new home, the first thing you should do is go there, taking with you a box of salt, as many bowls as there are rooms, your ritual dagger or wand, your magickal broom, a smudge stick or purification incense, and a charm for protection that you have already made in circle. (I like using Holly for protection, bound with red thread.)

Fill each of the bowls with water and add ½ cup salt to each bowl. Stir lightly, then place one bowl in the center of each room. The salt water will attract any leftover negativity and trap it.

Next, disconnect the smoke alarms and smudge the entire house. Fill the rooms with sage smoke and open windows to let it blow away any leftover negative vibrations that might be trapped in the corners and closets. You might want to set up a fan to help blow out the smoke. After the smoke dissipates, reconnect the smoke alarm.

Now, use the broom and sweep the air, widdershins, in each room, completing a full circle, chanting:

Sweep, sweep, sweep the air
Sweep old energies out of here!

After you have cleansed each room, close the windows (no sense giving vandals or burglars easy entrance) and leave, locking the door behind you.

If you can wait overnight to return, so much the better. If not, try to give it a couple of hours before you go back.

When you return it is helpful to take a sympathetic friend willing to spend an hour or so helping you. Pour the salt water down the drain, washing it away with plenty of cool water. IF YOU ARE ON A SEPTIC TANK, DO NOT DO THIS! You don't want water full of trapped negativity sitting underneath your house or in your back yard. Instead pour the water into a jar and put both the bowls and the jar outside while you complete the ritual. Then, take the water to a river, stream, or place where you can flush it into the sewer system. Wash the bowls thoroughly with soap and water. Light a protection incense.

With a clean bowl full of salt water, go through each room. At every window, door, outlet, water faucet, phone jack, ventilation grill, any exit to the outside that you can possibly reach, you will draw an invoking pentagram using your finger dipped in the salt water. (Obviously, don't let the water drip into the electrical outlets.) Draw the pentagram on the window, on the door, or other exit, and say:

> With the powers of Water and Earth,
> I do consecrate and protect this space.

Have your friend wave the incense over the opening and say:

> With the powers of Fire and Air,
> I do consecrate and protect this space.

If you are working alone, then this will take a little longer. This process does consume time—I have spent over an hour consecrating a new home, but it's worth it. Don't hurry the process if you can help it. The energy that you focus in protecting your new home will repay you many times over in peaceful sleep, cozy security, and magickal safety.

After you have finished going through the home, take your athame and cast a circle, walking from North to West through each room. I just walk along the outlines of the rooms of the apartment or house (a bumpy circle indeed!), and as I enter each room, circle it deosil, exit, and proceed to the next one.

As you cast the circle it helps to sing the Triple Goddess Chant on page 48. Continue to sing it over and over until you have circled through the entire house.

If possible, you might want to cast a circle outside, around the boundaries of your home and yard. It's too difficult to try this in an apartment or duplex but in a one-family dwelling, you should be able to manage it. If you're worried about people seeing you, then wait until dark and cast the circle in silence using your hand to direct the energy.

The last things you should do before moving your belongings into your new home are:

- Hang your protection charm near the front door. You might want to make one for each door leading outside.

- Buy a brand new utility broom and throw away your old one. Never bring a used utility broom into a new home. It carries on its bristles all the worries and troubles of the old environment.

- The first possessions you should bring into a new home are: a loaf of bread (for prosperity), a box of salt (for protection), and a bottle of wine or juice (so that you may never thirst).

You can then move in with the knowledge that you have thoroughly cleansed the space of negative energy. Sometimes you might find a strong spirit has latched on and doesn't want to leave. In this case, you may have to do a stronger banishing or exorcism spell (see chapter twelve).

MOVING OUT

Just as it is important to cleanse a space before you move in, it is equally vital to take your energies with you when you are ready to leave a house.

You will want to dismantle all protection charms, prosperity charms, and the like, and make new ones when you have moved into your new space.

Before you move your possessions into your new home, smudge the boxes to cleanse them of vibrations hanging on that you might not want to take with you.

Then after everything (but the old broom) is out of the house, and after you have finished cleaning up the space, you should cast a widdershins circle (using your hand) through the entire home, saying:

> *So now I go, my energy goes with me.*
> *I disengage myself and all of my belongings from this space.*
> *I release my hold on this space and leave it cleansed and renewed*
> *for those who will follow.*
> *Bléssed be.*

Next smudge every room and let the smoke dissipate through the windows. When you leave, place three pennies on a windowsill to leave hopes of prosperity for the new tenants, then once outside, break the broom and throw it away. I usually crumble the smudge stick, after making sure it is no longer smoldering, and toss it into the woods or a stream.

THE HEARTH

Remember that chimneys are magickal entrances to the house. With this in mind, you must guard and protect them as such. A simple way to keep negative energies from entering through this route is to cross the fire poker and tongs in front of the fireplace or wood stove.

The wood you burn can also affect the energy of your home. If you want to use your fireplace for magick, burn oak for strength, apple for love and beauty, pine for prosperity, ash for energy, and rowan for protection.

Cold ashes sprinkled over the roof of a house (make sure they are cold) are said to protect against lightning. I suggest a good lightning rod as well. Ashes from different woods are valuable, as well. They can be used to make magickal inks for spells. It gets a little messy, but it works.

PORTALS

I have cleaned up more than one dwelling where some nasty spirits were gaining entrance to the home through portals. It is important to not place mirrors directly facing doors, windows, or one another. These positions create powerful magickal portals that attract spirits and other entities. It isn't easy to dislodge entities once they've found a way in, so try to avoid opening these kinds of magickal doorways in the first place.

For further security from astral entities, draw runes of protection on the door. You can use tape to make them, you can make a rune stave and tack it up. If you own your home, you can simply carve the runes into the doors.

RUGS AND FURNISHINGS

Pay attention when you buy furniture and rugs. If they're used, you might want to smudge them so that they don't carry anyone else's energy into your home. We own a chair that belonged to our roommate who is now deceased. His father died in that chair. I had to cleanse it many times to rid it of both their energies.

Also take into consideration what the furniture is made of—a bed made out of oak, for example, will be very protective.

BEDROOM

Harmony in the bedroom is particularly important. There are a few simple precautions you can take to help ensure a good night's sleep. Don't point your headboard towards the south unless you want nightmares and strife in the bedroom. Sleeping with your head in the east invites awareness and intellect; towards the west invites psychic dreams. Sleep with your head in the north and you draw restful slumber.

Use dreaming pillows (herbal sachets made to slip inside your pillowcase) for deep sleep and to contradict nightmares. Dream Catchers, those beautiful webs made of leather and beads, are a Native American solution to nightmares and uneasy sleep.

BATH

Bathing is long connected to pagan rituals—in fact, during medieval days people seldom bathed because of this connection. Drenching yourself in water was also considered to be a prime cause of illness. I'm glad we've altered our views today!

The bath can be a sanctuary. Fill your vanity with bath salts, bubble bath, perfumes, and creams to feel pampered and luxurious. Bath salts and bubble bath can be charged by raising energy and aligning your focus to the scent of the potion. Focus on charging vanilla bath salts with the power of love; lavender can be charged for peace and tranquility, and so on.

Cosmetics have long been used in ritual. I treat my make-up with respect and joy. It's fun, and a ritual in itself.

Cast a circle in your bathroom, light a candle, put on some soft music and soak in charged bubble bath. See how quickly this changes a bad mood into a good one.

For ritual baths, I use clear water and a very lightly scented soap. If the ritual has a specific orientation toward love, or prosperity, or some other objective, I align the scent of the soap and color of the bath water with the specific focus of the ritual. While I sit in the bath, I focus on letting the mundane world slip away, out of my body, into the water. As the water drains out of the tub so does my connection with the day-to-day tribulations that heighten our stress levels. I often follow a ritual bath with a quick, cool shower to energize myself.

KITCHEN

For years the kitchen has been the cradle of more magick than all the circles put together. During the Burning Times it was safer to disguise magick and wortcunning as cookery. So the butcher knife became the athame and the wooden spoon, the wand.

Today, Pagans still have a romantic view of the kitchen Witch and all the glorious magick performed by these women.

The kitchen Witch! What a symbol.

An old woman is baking apple pies and brewing tinctures in the herb-laden kitchen of her house in the country. Her husband is long dead, of course, and the folk that live near her come to her for cures and spells, though they don't stay long because she's rather intimidating.

Once in a while a rare close friend drops by and they sit over tea and scones, cackling about times long forgotten by most.

At some point a young woman stumbles onto her doorstep needing help. She is alone in the world, an outcast, and the old woman takes her in and passes on her ways. When the old kitchen Witch dies, the young one carries on the tradition. She probably won't marry, but if she does it is a beautiful, star-crossed match. He has been warned against loving her and their marriage, passionate and vibrant, ends tragically.

Now, truthfully, doesn't this image conjure up a commonly held view about Witches?

I always wanted to end up like this, until I realized my computer and television don't fit with the image. I also like fashionable clothing and want my marriage to survive to a long and healthy old age.

The more I thought about it, the more I realized that the kitchen Witch is more likely to fit the image of several good friends of mine:

One woman is thirty-five, with three children clambering around her feet. Together with her husband (who works a full-time job away from home), they tend their fifteen-acre farm as well as their house in town. They grow the vegetables and fruit that they put up every harvest, feed and water the livestock that they send out to be butchered every year. She sews her own clothes and scrimps to make ends meet. Someday she wants to go back to school and get her Master's degree. When she gets the energy, she lights a candle and asks the Goddess to bless their family with prosperity and joy.

They celebrate the harvest festivals with a few friends who live in similar circumstances, they bake Yule treats and Samhain breads and her six-year old daughter is excited because she once made the rain stop.

They live in tune with the Earth but they don't always have time to stop and ponder what they are feeling—farming is hard work.

They accept their lives and enjoy them and every now and then during one of her reading spurts my friend says, "I wonder if I'm a Witch; hey, I cast my spells and I try to keep the kids out of the altar. It works." And it does.

Another is forty-six, still young, unmarried, and childfree. She calls herself Pagan but doesn't call herself a Witch. She walks at night and talks to the Moon. She lights a birthday candle every night and focuses on what she needs as the little wax candle burns into oblivion.

She celebrates the Sabbats with friends, plays her music, works in a day care and watches television. She silk-screens t-shirts with her own designs and makes cards every Imbolc. She's very laid back, calm beyond calm, and sees a bright side to every cloud.

She says, "I don't know what to call myself, but that's okay. I do what I do."

She does what she does. And it works.

There have been entire books written on magickal cookery and the magick of food. These are entertaining and contain some good information. But I find, for myself, the most magickal books about home and hearth are not books at all. I've read *Victoria Magazine* for years, encountering some incredible seasonal recipes (i.e., Pumpkin Chocolate Cheesecake, Roast Goose with Apple Stuffing) and the magazine seems to focus on the change of seasons in a graceful, delicate manner.

SIMPLE CHARMS FOR THE KITCHEN

There are some simple charms you can keep in your kitchen. A clove of garlic sitting on the sink board draws illness away from the family. Don't eat it, instead throw it away every month and replace it with a new one.

When you are cooking, especially something for a ritual or seasonal gathering, stir and blend in a deosil manner. Don't go widdershins unless you want to stir the energy out of the food!

Running out of salt supposedly foretells a loss of prosperity. Always keep an extra box that you never use on a high shelf to help ensure good fortune.

Wash all the dishes every night if you work with faerie magick. The faeries don't like dirt and clutter and they won't let you sleep until the kitchen is clean!

But truthfully, the most magickal energy of all comes from a clean, well-kept kitchen stocked with good, healthy food. Clear jars filled with pastas and beans are beautiful and functional. Home-made bread is sure to invite unexpected company. No time to bake? Buy a bread machine. It's not as romantic but it tastes great and the aroma still fills your kitchen.

Garlic braids ward off negativity as well as spice up your soups. A steaming teapot filled with raspberry tea, delicate old china cups and saucers found at a garage sale or a secondhand store, and a gleaming jar of honey with a wooden dipper combine to make a friend feel more welcome than all the other charms you could concoct.

When the morning sun pours through the window to wake you up, and the cats are sprawled on the table, when you look outside to see frost on the leaves, you'll be glad that your kitchen is clean and waiting for you to brew the coffee and fry up the eggs.

PETS AND ANIMALS

Pets are like children. We have four cats and they are our babies. They are also members of this game we call life and deserve our respect as well as our care.

While I am not a vegetarian, I try to do my best by the other species on this planet. That includes not wearing fur because I don't need it in the climate I live (though faux furs are fun); I do wear leather because I also eat the beef that comes from the cow. I use cosmetics that aren't tested on animals. I contribute to the Audubon Society and the Nature Conservancy (there are many good groups like this; these are two that I feel close to).

I hold mixed feelings on animal testing; on one level it infuriates me; on the other is the very real fact that through this research my husband, a Type I, insulin-dependent diabetic, will be able to live a relatively normal life. Don't ask me to debate the politics of it, I can't give you a straight answer.

I perform spells and rituals to send magickal aid to endangered species on this planet and most importantly, I vote. One voice isn't much. Thousands of voices joining together can change reality.

It is within this context that I try to coexist with my fellow creatures in relative comfort and peace.

There are many charms you can make to protect your pets. Call on the Gods and Goddesses who guard and protect them when you do so (Bast for cats, Artemis for dogs, Flidais and Mielikki for wild forest animals, Cernunnos and Herne for the stag, Odin and Tapio for wolves—there are many, many more choices).

Buy an image candle shaped like your pet (cat, dog, bird or whatever). Carve protection runes on it and anoint it with a protection oil, then burn it, asking that your pet be guarded and watched over.

Locate a statue that looks like your pet and paint protection runes on it. Keep it in a safe place and occasionally anoint it with protection oil, calling on the Gods to protect your friend.

Keep a charm in your car filled with rowan and cedar and a little bit of cat and dog hair. Charge it, asking that you always see the animals on the road, that your car never hit them, that you always be alert and able to see clearly.

Too many people are too lazy to get their animals spayed or neutered, and they refuse to vaccinate them against the deadly diseases that permeate the feline and canine worlds (feline leukemia is a virulent and painful disease). If you aren't willing to take care of your pet, don't get one in the first place. There are far too many unwanted puppies and kittens in this world and hundreds of thousands are killed in animal shelters every year. Be responsible and help stop the problem.

The easiest, safest way to protect your cats from being hit by cars is to keep them inside. They adjust. It may seem cruel to keep them inside but I've met many a contented indoor cat. If you can't stand that thought, then build an outdoor run where they can play in the grass but won't be able to run wild. Remember, the exploding cat population has decimated many species of birds.

Keep your dogs fenced in. When you're walking down the street keep them on a leash. A dog chasing a blowing leaf isn't necessarily going to listen when you shout for him to stop—and he just might run out in the road and get hit. It's also frightening to be harassed by a strange dog—will he bite? Will he get his muddy paws on my shirt? Rover may be a perfectly nice, well-behaved, gentle dog, but how am I going to know that? Have consideration for other people.

Remember, all the magick in the world won't stop an accident if you don't use your common sense. Practical solutions first, magick second.

The Troth of Nine: Living Righteously

Many years ago, I developed an oath (*troth*) that I decided was my credo in life. I try to live by this oath, and when my husband and I were married we adapted it and incorporated it into our wedding vows. You might want to think carefully, honestly, and come up with a set of truths that you live by. My oath isn't going to be right for everybody, and as you discover your own ethics, you can create a troth that fits your life.

Remember that when a Witch takes an oath it is binding. I seldom swear to anything because I take my vows so seriously. The term *warlock* actually means oath-breaker and refers to those who were sent to infiltrate the villages during the Inquisition to discover the heathens, Witches and heretics. That is why all male Witches are referred to as "Witch." Anyone calling himself a Warlock should think twice. You don't want to break oath with the Gods; it's neither safe nor wise.

Yasmine's Troth of Nine

Courage: the courage to stand for what I believe in, for what I know I must. The courage to take an unpopular stance if need be.

Truth: above all to be honest to myself, and to avoid hypocrisy.

Troth: to be faithful to my pledged Gods, to loved ones, and to those bound by oath—blood and soul.

Discipline: the patience to master my talents, the will to create and learn.

Self-reliance: the will to be unique, to care for myself. The knowledge and willingness to ask for help when truly needed.

Perseverance: the will to continue against all odds when I know I am on my true path.

Love: the will to love on a basis beyond superficialities, to commit myself to my beloved and my loved ones.

Passion: the passion to live life to the fullest, to not fear intensity and to celebrate the joys of the body without exploitation.

Wisdom: the will to learn, to gather knowledge on both intellectual and intuitional levels, and the common sense to apply said lessons.

This is the Troth of Nine. I do solemnly swear by all that is Holy to me, to hold it and follow it in my heart, my soul, my mind and my actions.

THE BOOK OF SHADOWS

The Book of Shadows, also known as BOS, is a journal of your magickal workings, rituals, and spells. I am haphazard about keeping records of my rituals but I always write down my oil and spell powder recipes and at least a brief notation of important events. I am, however, an avid diarist so sometimes my magickal entries get intermingled in my daily journals. It all evens out. In the end, a BOS is worth the trouble, although you may find, like I have, that it is almost impossible to capture some rituals and energy-workings in words. I mainly use the entries to jog my memory.

MORNING RITUAL

I developed this ritual when I felt a lull of magick in my life and decided that I needed to get back in touch with the elements. I performed this ritual every morning, shortly after I woke, over a period of a month. It worked. Soon I felt balanced and ready to greet each day, grounded in my magick, yet not feeling pressure to do more than I had time for.

Every now and then, I will drag it out and use it again for a period of time until I'm back in balance. It's like an old friend whom you don't necessarily see every day but that you occasionally need to spend some time with.

If you have only one altar, make sure that you have a representation for each element on it when you use this ritual. If you have different elemental altars then you can face each in turn. If you have no set altar, then you can stand in the center of the room—or better yet, go outside into your yard.

Face the North. Raise your hands to the sky and say:

Good morning, Spirits of the North
I am successful
I am the body of the Earth
the cornucopia showers blessing into my life.

Stand for a moment and let the energy of the Earth pour into your body and soul. Turn and face the east. Raise your hands to the sky and say:

Good morning, Spirits of the East
I am creative
I am the spirit of the wind
my mind soars to other realms and back again.

Stand for a moment and let the energy of the Air pour into your body and soul. Turn and face the south. Raise your hands to the sky and say:

Good morning, Spirits of the South
I am passionate
I am the glow of flame and lava
I magnetize and inflame the senses as I heal and burn.

Stand for a moment and let the energy of the Fire pour into your body and soul. Turn and face the west. Raise your hands to the sky and say:

Good morning, Spirits of the West
I am beautiful
My blood contains the tears of the Mother
I am joy and hidden depths transcended from the moon.

Stand for a moment and let the energy of the Water pour into your body and soul. Let your head fall back and face the sky. Raise your hands to the heavens and say:

Good morning Spirits of the Spirit
I am the balance
My body, mind and spirit are in harmony
I stand in the center of my web, weaving.
Good morning Lord and Lady
I am your daughter (son)
Guide me and guard me throughout this day
blesséd be.

Stand for a moment and feel yourself coming to a place of balance. When you are ready, salute the day and go about your usual routine.

You do not have to cast a circle for this ritual. It is very simple and takes only about ten minutes. It's a good alternative to that cup of coffee when you first get up.

8

LIFE TRANSFORMATIONS

There are all kinds of magick you can use to help affect change in your life. Most of what is used in this book is based in ritual, charms, and spellworkings. In this chapter, I present some opportunities to work with magickal energy in creative and interactive ways that can provide a new twist on your workings. Fairly informal, they offer a fun way to work magick with your friends and I hope that you enjoy them as much as I have. They can provide startling results.

CREATIVE COLLAGING

Creative collaging, called treasure mapping by some, is one of the easiest and most enjoyable ways to invoke objects or energies into your life. I learned this technique years ago and have used it for everything from prosperity to love to personal transformation.

One thing I have noticed through the years is that you will often start your collage with one theme in mind but find that as you go further and further into the spell, another theme crops up and won't go away. I always pay attention to these changes because our subconscious often knows more than our conscious mind does.

You will need:

Poster board
Glue sticks
Scissors
A stack of magazines that you are willing to cut up.

I use the 22" x 30" sheets of poster board. The color you select depends on what you are focusing on—see color charts in chapter two. I have found, however, that black works well for work I'm doing. Be open-minded when gathering magazines for this endeavor. Don't be fooled—I've found some of my most successful and unique words and images in the oddest places. Hunting magazines often have beautiful pictures of stags and bears, retirement magazines have pictures of money, women's magazines are host to a plethora of words like *magic, enchantment,* and *bewitching*—just look through the cosmetics advertisements.

You can do the work in circle if you like, though I find that the lengthy process of searching for images and phrases creates its own mystical space.

To begin, clear a large table or a wide space on the floor. This is a fun activity to do with friends. You can include your children in this, too, encouraging them to make their own collages.

Each person brings their own poster board, glue sticks, and scissors, and a pile of magazines to be shared by others. Each person gets first shot at their own magazines, then they're piled in the center for anybody to grab.

When you start looking through the pages, don't worry about how much space you have on your poster board. You will be layering images on top of one another, and when you actually go to assemble the collage, some pictures will naturally sort themselves out, while others you will discard or save for different maps.

When a word or image crops up that represents your theme, cut it out and set it aside. You can make up your own words and phrases too, out of ones that you collect.

For example, Jenny is working on a collage to bring out her natural beauty and self-confidence. She sees an image of a lipstick she likes, so she cuts that out. Then she sees a picture of a dress she would feel good wearing. She adds that to her pile. Next, she finds a picture of a meadow with wildflowers. She loves to be outdoors so that goes in her collection. A phrase catches her eye from a perfume advertisement—"To bring out the mysterious woman inside." By the time she goes through ten magazines Jenny has more than enough material to make her collage.

In another example, Brenda wants to encourage prosperity in her life. She cuts out pictures of cash, clothes she wants, furniture she could use, a fruit-laden peach tree to represent an abundance of food in her life, a house that looks like one she would like to own, a wicker basket overflowing with harvest produce.

Once you have assembled your pile of pictures and words, start playing with them on the poster board. Arrange and rearrange to find the most pleasing and complimentary arrangement. Don't be afraid to layer pictures. Overlap as necessary. I fill every inch of my poster board and over the years my collages have taken on an artistic and beautiful nature. I've even framed a few because I like them so much.

As a rule of thumb, try to let the images speak louder than the words; too many words and phrases can make a collage feel cluttered and clumsy.

Once you find the arrangement you like, start gluing the pictures down using the glue sticks (the sticks do work best—liquid glue will make a big mess). Begin in one corner and work your way across the board, always gluing the underlying images first. When you have finished, raise energy and charge the collage. Then hang it up in a place where you will see it every day. You'll be surprised at how fast things start to happen.

Over the years I have made collages for prosperity, beauty, and personal transformations. I've made magickally oriented collages; collages to inspire my writing career; collages to represent each element; for the God and Goddess; for Mielikki, Tapio and Pele; and for each season (Yule is fun—with so many sparkling images).

TRANSFORMATIONAL MAGICK

Transformational magick, or transformational drama, is best performed with a partner who is a willing and enthusiastic participant.

Remember when we were children? Remember the games of "let's pretend"? At its core, transformational drama is a return to that game, only we are consciously using magick to invoke the scenes we are portraying.

For this type of magick you really only need yourself, your partner, and a few candles. I find performing the magick in candlelight adds to its strength. You can also set up an altar if you like. I also find that performing the magick in your regular, daily clothes is a bonus because it ties the energy in with your everyday life.

Each person should pick a subject they want to work on. Rather than elusive, esoteric concepts, transformational drama should focus on concrete events that you wish to manifest.

Some examples include finding a romantic partner, finding a job in a particular field, taking a vacation or a trip to a specific place, buying a house or a car or some other major purchase.

Because it is easier to teach transformational drama through interaction rather than description, I present an abbreviated example on the following pages.

Susan and Tom are working together. Susan is an aspiring actress and wants to land a supporting role in a musical. Tom is lonely, he wants to attract a woman with whom he can settle down and start a family. They cast a circle, call the elements, and Susan invokes Apollo (God of music and the Sun) while Tom invokes Hestia (Goddess of hearth and home). Both Apollo and Hestia are from the Greek pantheon and don't seem to have any clashing energies.

They sit quietly for a few minutes, each focusing on their desires. They have agreed beforehand to focus on Tom's goal first.

When he is ready, Tom gets up and moves into the west quadrant of the circle (the west is the seat of emotions, love, and joy). He begins to whistle, pretending that he is setting the table.

Susan waits for a moment, then "knocks" on the "door."

Tom: Sus! Hi, come on in.

Susan: (entering the west quadrant) Hey, Tom, how's it going?

Tom: You'll never guess what happened last week!

Susan: What? You sound excited.

Tom: (grabs Susan's shoulders) I proposed and my girlfriend agreed to marry me! It was so romantic.

Susan: (showing enthusiasm) Really? How wonderful.

Tom: I would have told you sooner but I know you've been busy with the play (reinforcing the work that Susan will be doing later). I'm so thrilled. She's everything I hoped for. Intelligent, pretty, and I love her so much.

Susan: What's even better is how much she loves you. So, are you two planning to have kids?

Tom: We've agreed to wait a year or two, then we want to adopt. I had a vasectomy, you know. Lucky for me my fiancée doesn't care whether she gets pregnant or not. She just wants to be a mother. It's amazing how we agree on things. Of course, we want different furniture for the living room, she likes florals and I like solids (throwing in a touch of reality), and she hates Mexican food and I love it.

Susan: Am I invited to the wedding?

Tom: Actually, I was hoping you'd stand up with me. After all, you're my best friend.

Susan: Your girlfriend doesn't mind?

Tom: She knows I love her and she knows you and I have a strictly platonic relationship. She thinks it's a great idea. In fact, her maid of honor is going to be a man of honor, so it would balance out.

Susan: I accept your offer with pleasure. Oh, Tom, I know how long you've wanted to find someone like this.

Tom: And to think that it happened in such an unusual way...I
        never expected to meet her when I did. It goes to show,
        open yourself to the universe and the universe won't let
        you down.

The drama can go on for a lot longer than this; Tom could tell
Susan about his plans for the wedding, they could discuss where the
happy couple is going to live—the key to transformational drama is
to put as much realism and energy into it as you can.

Once Tom is satisfied, they take a moment to quiet themselves
and then Susan has her turn.

After both parties are finished, reflection and discussion about
the evening takes place. Then, devoke the elements and the circle.

When performing transformational drama, really live what you
are saying and always keep it in the present—as if what you want has
already happened (or is in the process of happening). At first you
may feel a little awkward, but you should find that after a few ses-
sions you can slip into the "role" you want to assume quite easily.

If after working on a specific issue several times, you find you still
can't get into the swing of things, you might want to reassess
whether this is a goal you truly believe in, that you really want or
honestly believe you can reach.

There is no harm in changing your goals from time to time—we
have to adapt our expectations as we go along. Don't cling to an
idea just because you think you should.

If you aren't meant to be a doctor, teacher, writer, or whatever,
you won't be able to muster the energy for it during transformational magick. You won't be able to bring up the enthusiasm and in
fact, you'll probably feel silly. That's because if we can't imagine
ourselves doing something, then we won't be able to do it.

ISN'T IT THE SAME THING AS FANTASY?

There is a big difference between fantasy and transformational
drama. Fantasy tends to focus on unrealistic dreams that may happen but are highly unlikely. We all fantasize about what we would
do if we won the lottery, but using transformational magick for this
wish wouldn't produce as much energy as using it for a more specific and achievable goal.

A note about lotteries and sweepstakes: It's fun to play them, it would be wonderful to win, but think about how many people are aiming towards that same goal and you get an idea about how hard it is to sway the energy. I think it's okay to play, to daydream, even to do a few spells for it, but don't make it your main goal—the magickal odds are being pulled in millions of directions by millions of people who all want the same thing.

Transformational drama is best used by those who can ad-lib and let themselves play. It is a fun way to raise energy, and it works with surprising accuracy and swiftness.

TIPS FOR TRANSFORMATIONAL DRAMA

- Keep the action in the present. What you want has already happened, or is happening.

- Work with people who truly believe you can accomplish your goals. Don't work with friends who are cynical and skeptical.

- Transformational drama is best used for very specific issues.

- You can use transformational magick more than once for the same issue; you can adapt each scene as you need. You might find, in playing out a scene, that something you thought you wanted doesn't feel right. Next time, leave it out or change it.

- There will be certain issues that bring up extreme emotional responses. If you break down, start to cry, get angry, or feel other powerful emotions, then call a time out and, with your friend or partner work through what has come up. It may be that you want something so bad that it hurts to even talk about getting it. You might want to discuss why you have such an extreme need for your goal. Is it really going to bring you everything you think it is? Do you have unrealistic expectations of what achieving your goal will produce?

- Each person needs to be assured that their goals and their work will get equal attention—unless you agree otherwise in advance. No one should feel slighted, and neither person should feel like they are being used to create solely for their partner and not for themselves.

- Each person needs to play out their partner's drama according to their partner's wishes—don't try to impose your own agenda or vision on your friend's goals or you run the risk of interfering with their magick.

TOASTING THE GODS: GRATITUDES, BLESSINGS, AND REQUESTS

Another creative way to incorporate magick into your life is to have a toasting ritual. While you can perform this alone, it is more conducive to have at least one other person there and, in fact, is one ritual for which "the more the merrier" is true. However, I would suggest that a maximum of seven or eight participants is a good rule.

You don't have to use alcohol, though if you do drink, this is a good time in which to do it. You can also use juice, though I recommend using sparkling cider or non-alcoholic wine instead of regular fruit drinks. Plan on having more wine or other libation than you think you need. This ritual can get pretty boisterous, and the longer it goes on the more creative people seem to become.

I also recommend having food present, especially if you are serving alcohol. If necessary, collect car keys at the door before beginning or have a supply of money for cabs. (Both are good ideas for any party at which you are serving alcohol.)

When everyone is present and has made themselves comfortable, cast your circle and invoke the elements.

Then give everyone a glass filled with wine, mead (really nice for toasting), or juice. You might want to have both; some people might choose to imbibe while others prefer to stick to the cider. Keep the bottles on hand for easy refilling when needed.

Now salute the Gods. If you have deities that rule over the group or the house, salute them first. Saluting a deity is different than invoking one. It is recognition without asking that they be present. For example, if the party were at my house, I would make the first toast something like this:

Mielikki, Queen of Fey, Lady of the Hunt, You who rule over this household, I salute You and toast Your presence in my life.

Everyone toasts Mielikki with a sip of wine. Then, I would continue:

Tapio, Wolf-father, Pack Master, Lord of the Forest, You who rule over this household, I salute You and toast Your presence in my life.

Everyone toasts Tapio with a sip of wine. After this, working deosil, each member of the group salutes—not invokes—their God, Goddess or both. Each salutation is honored with a drink.

When the Gods have been toasted, the host begins the next round. I call this phase of the ritual Gratitudes.

Again, I would begin the round with something like this:

I thank the Universe for giving me the chance to publish my books and fulfill myself in my choice of careers. Salute!

Everyone drinks. Then, again working deosil, the next person gives thanks for something for which they are grateful. Gratitudes can last a number of rounds, but when people start to wind down then we begin the Blessings.

I would start this round with:

I invoke a blessing on my niece and her children that they might prosper and be healthy, strong, and happy. I ask a blessing for my sister, that she might find a better job that matches her talents.

Each person toasts, then one by one the group invokes blessings for those in need.

The next and final rounds are the Request rounds.

Once more I would start, perhaps with:

I ask the Gods to bless the work that I am doing, and that They strengthen my health and help me find a way to buy a new computer so my writing won't suffer. I also ask that They bless my efforts in getting signatures on my petition to protect the bears from bear-baiting.

Again, a toast, and move on to the next person.

One thing I have noticed time after time is the tendency for requests to become more universal, calling for help for the planet, endangered species and the forests. Each person has personal requests and these are quite valid, but I also notice that just about everyone begins to express planetary concerns. Sometimes after the last round a chant will spontaneously spring up (you can start one if it doesn't) and the energy raised during the ritual will infuse the singing and build a cone of power on its own.

Usually everyone ends up holding hands and more than once I've seen tears mingled with the laughter as we build the chant and let it go.

Perhaps a little lugubrious from the alcohol? I suppose, but I think it rises more from the sense that while we each have personal desires and real needs, as a group we recognize the overwhelming problems facing our planet. At the same time, by just focusing our energy in their direction, we start to solve some of the world's ills.

I do not believe our civilization will ever be completely at peace. Human nature thrives on competition, on the struggle to go beyond our limitations, but there are moments when we can catch a glimpse of a better path, one that is both practical and environmental.

During toasting rituals, as people settle into the energy of giving thanks, of sensing what we truly have, we begin to explore beyond our own lives as we ask blessings for those in need.

9

PROSPERITY AND ABUNDANCE

I have always found it curious that some spiritual disciplines place such an emphasis on the need for material deprivation. On one hand, I understand that they believe material comfort might divert their focus from spiritual matters. On another front, it has been a good way for some disciplines and governments to keep the poor from feeling too upset about their current situations. By promising the poor rewards after their life on Earth, anarchy and revolution have often been avoided.

My personal belief is that if you are hungry, if you don't know where the money to pay your rent is coming from, if your teeth hurt and you need dental care but can't afford it, then you aren't going to have a whole lot of energy to expend on more esoteric thoughts.

It took me a long time to rid myself of concepts ingrained during my upbringing. In my family I always got the impression that rich people weren't trustworthy and they must have done something underhanded to get their money.

Then, through studying the Eastern religions for a while, I absorbed some of the "poverty equals spiritual righteousness" mentality. Along the way I also managed to develop the attitude that all technology is evil and everyone needs to get back to the land.

Thank Goddess I've gotten rid of those beliefs.

The amount of riches and wealth—not necessarily financial—to be had in this world is phenomenal. We don't have to destroy the Earth to be prosperous.

A new fuel-efficient car is easier on the environment than an old hippie van that guzzles gas and spews exhaust into the air.

A well-insulated house reduces the amount of electricity, gas, or wood that we consume to heat ourselves during winter.

Hair dye is better for our hair than henna. Just talk to your hairdresser and you'll find out if you don't believe me. The metal oxides in henna will eventually make your hair brittle and coarse.

Using a computer saves a tremendous amount of time that can be spent on other pursuits—especially for writers.

If we lived like our ancestors you wouldn't be reading this book. You probably couldn't read at all. Education was a privilege for the rich, powerful males in most societies. Forty was considered old; women died because they had too many babies or because their husbands could legally beat them to death (which is still the case in some countries); men worked themselves to exhaustion to eke out a living, most of which went to the landowners for taxes. Life as a peasant wasn't very pleasant!

Remember, just one hundred years ago if you developed diabetes, pneumonia, cancer, polio, measles, small pox, or any number of diseases, it signified a death sentence.

Yes, modern technology has the potential to be fatal, lethal, and horrendous (Hiroshima and Nagasaki prove this). But it can also be life-saving, time-efficient, and can give us the luxury to explore other realms and other realities.

When I was struggling for money, when I was scrambling to find enough change to feed the cats, let alone myself, I didn't have the energy to write. I couldn't do what I loved best because I was too worried.

There are many definitions of prosperity.

For one person it means having enough good food to eat, a nice apartment, and a job they like.

For another it means owning a five-acre parcel of land with a lovely home, an orchard, and the time to do what they want most.

For still another it means having enough money to walk into a store and buy anything without asking its price—to wear designer clothes and drive a BMW.

Only you can decide what is right for you, and you need to stick by your truths. Some time ago I was talking to some friends and we were discussing my book *Trancing the Witch's Wheel*. I mentioned that I didn't expect it to be a bestseller, but that I hoped it would do well. It is, after all, geared to a very specific audience.

I added that, like many authors, I would love to have a bestselling novel out on the stands. I want to own a house, I want better health care, I want to know that my husband's health care is fully covered and I want to see my work widely received. In essence, Sam and I want to be prosperous with a lifestyle where we're comfortable and happy. We are willing to work hard toward that end.

A loud silence followed my statement. I might as well have said that I wanted to single-handedly destroy the Earth. There was an awkward pause in the room then everyone started talking at once. Some of the statements I heard that afternoon included:

"No you don't—all you really need is enough to get by," said a friend who already owns her own home and acreage.

"Yeah, just enough to live on and eat."

"Money is so evil."

"Don't sell out your art, man. Don't go commercial."

Inexplicably another woman added, "Computers are a complete waste of time and money."

I gathered my courage to face the animosity that I felt was aimed not toward me, but my desire. I refused to defend myself, just firmly reiterated my position.

"Listen," I said. "I've put up with pain for years because I couldn't afford dental care. There have been times I've been hungry with no food or money. I want a better life. We aren't bad off now, but this isn't where we want to be. I want to own my own home, I want to continue writing and I want Sam's career to continue to blossom out in the directions he hopes to take it. There's nothing wrong with that."

I don't think they bought it, but that doesn't matter. What matters is that I didn't let them shake my beliefs.

You have to be strong and you must also be careful not to step on other people's dreams. You don't know what their lives are really like. You can give an opinion, but always tender it as such. Remember that some aspirations may sound stupid, they may seem like pipe dreams, but you have no right to tell your friends they don't know what they want.

The only exception that I can think of is when someone's goals involve harm to innocent bystanders or if they're headed down a path leading to self-destruction. In the latter case, be aware that they probably won't listen.

A friend recently told me she had the brief fantasy that the house next door to her, which was unoccupied at the time, would burn down so that she and her husband could buy the land at a low price. My first thought was that the people who own the land would get less for it than they would if the house was still standing, and that it was a very selfish wish.

I do realize that fantasies are fantasies but still I told her to be careful. If the house next door catches fire there's a chance it will spread to hers.

PROSPERITY SPELLS AND RECIPES

In this section, a variety of spells, charms, and oils are presented that can help you attain those things that you want, both materially and emotionally. Use them with positive intent for yourself and for others.

CORNUCOPIA RAINING

This spell can easily be done on a daily basis. If you have real need, it will work very quickly. It is a simple spell—you need nothing more than a block of time to yourself and a quiet place where you will not be disturbed to sit and visualize.

Sit quietly and think about what you want or need. Focus, not on lack, but rather on those items you desire.

Now close your eyes and visualize a large cornucopia over your head, filled with an unending supply of treasures. See a trap door underneath the horn of plenty, and reach out with your mind and open the door. The treasures from the cornucopia will rain out, showering through the open portal, to pour blessings upon your head and shoulders.

See gold coins, money, jewels—whatever it is that you desire showering around you, piling up around your chair.

Say:

May the blessings of the universe shower from the cornucopia of the Goddess, an unending supply that eliminates all need from my life and the lives of my loved ones and friends. There is plenty in the universe to share and I accept my portion of good fortune. My life is filled with abundance and prosperity. Serendipity rules in my life.

GOLD MONEY BAGS

You can use this charm to help bring financial prosperity into your life. It is an easy talisman to make and the ritual to charge the Gold Money Bags is short and simple. For the best effect, keep the bag with your checkbook or where you keep your bills and invoices.

Take two pieces of gold cloth and, using green thread, sew them together into a pouch.

Fill with equal parts of:

Rosemary	Ginseng
Sage	Mandrake
Lavender	Fern

Add one piece each:

Jade
Peridot

Add:

A folded dollar bill
a penny, a nickel, a dime, and a quarter

Sew the bag shut.

Set the bag in sunlight and sprinkle lightly with a few drops of Sun Water. Let the sun warm the material.

Raise energy and charge the charm bag, saying:

I call on the Spirits of prosperity and the Spirit of the Sun to infuse this charm with the power to attract abundance and prosperity into my life. Let my wallet fill with money, let my checking account overflow with money, let my old debts be paid easily and without strain, let my health be robust, let my cupboards be filled with good food. Let my life be rich like the golden sunlight. So mote it be.

MAPLE MONEY CHARM

I keep several of these charms in different parts of the house and make new ones every few months when it feels right. Keep the charms around the house, tucking them into nooks and crannies where they can work their subtle magick. Among the ingredients are a special oil and powder that you will have to make yourself, the recipes for which are included below. Instructions for making oil blends are on page 115. If you would prefer, substitute similar oils of your own choosing.

You will need:

1 large maple leaf
   a feather quill or felt pen
   dragon's blood ink
   Money Draw Oil (page 153)
   Prosperity Powder (page 153)
1 long fern frond
   green or gold embroidery thread

Figure out what type of prosperity you want to invoke into your life.

Consult the rune charts for runes you will need and write out any phrases you might want to add. Spread out the leaf, making sure that it is dry and clean. Using the feather quill or felt pen (a felt pen that has dried out is ideal for dipping in magickal ink; it absorbs the ink readily) dipped in dragon's blood ink, write the runes on the maple leaf. Anoint it with oil, then sprinkle with Prosperity Powder. Fold the leaf, runes inward, into a small packet. Wrap with fern frond, then tie with embroidery thread and say:

Spirits of the Earth, Spirits of the Wood, let my prosperity grow as do your roots, branches and leaves. Let abundance flow through my life.

Prosperity Powder
See page 118 for instructions for making powders.

¼ ounce dill	1 tablespoon ground cloves
¼ ounce parsley	1 tablespoon ground nutmeg
¼ ounce basil	21 drops Money and Luck Oil
¼ ounce chamomile	or Calling Abundance Oil

Money and Luck Oil

¼ ounce olive oil	13 drops oakmoss oil
8 drops dill oil	9 drops tonka oil
13 drops bergamot oil	6 drops clove oil
21 drops nutmeg oil	flower: dill
9 drops earth oil	gem: peridot

Calling Abundance Oil

¼ ounce olive oil	13 drops clove oil
20 drops chamomile oil	flower: basil
20 drops cedar oil	gem: lodestone
20 drops patchouli oil	

Money Draw Oil

¼ ounce olive oil	7 drops cedar oil
21 drops patchouli oil	flower: chamomile
14 drops chamomile oil	gem: peridot
7 drops cinnamon oil	

LUCKY NUTMEGS

These little charms are among my favorites—they work very well. When you're feeling the need for a little extra luck, keep one of these safe in your purse or in a charm bag next to your heart. Keep in mind that nutmeg is poisonous in large doses. If you have children or animals, keep your whole nutmegs safely out of their reach. Consult page 115 for oil-making instructions.

Assemble your ingredients and cast a circle. Invoke the elements and the God or Goddess you have chosen to work with.

You will need:

1 whole nutmeg
long needle
Prosperity Powder (page 153)
3 drops Money and Luck Oil (page 153) or
    similar magickal oil
green candle
black or green netting or lace
green embroidery thread

Hollow out the top end of the nutmeg with a long, thick needle. Pack the hole with Prosperity Powder. Add three drops of oil. Light a green candle and when enough wax has melted, drop three drops of green wax on nutmeg hole to seal. Wrap the nutmeg in lace and tie with embroidery thread, either 3, 9, or 21 knots (these are widely accepted magickal numbers with healthy, strong vibrations).

While tying knots, say:

> *O Spirit of the Nutmeg, I call on you. Infuse this charm with good fortune and prosperity. Let it draw into my life the abundance of the universe. Spirit of the Nutmeg, I call on your powers. Hear me and answer.*

Raise energy and charge the charm.

Seven Day Prosperity Spell

This is a seven-day spell to focus your will over a period of time and bring a long-term abundance into your life. Sometimes I even do a fourteen-day spell, beginning a day after the New Moon until right before the Full Moon.

You will need:

1 seven-inch green taper candle or seven-knobbed candle
   a ruler
   a push-pin thumbtack
   a piece of paper
   dragon's blood ink (you may substitute green ink)
   quill pen or felt pen
   Money or Prosperity Oil (page 153)
   Prosperity Powder (page 153)

The day after the New Moon, lay the taper candle on its side. Mark off each inch using the point of the tack. (If you are using a seven-knobbed candle, you don't have to do this). There will probably be a slight discrepancy (candles are hard to make in exact proportions). Don't worry about whether one area is a bit larger than the others.

Next, using the tack, carefully draw a circle around the candle at each point, to divide it into seven sections.

Now sit down with the piece of paper and, using the dragon's blood ink, write the following information: the date you are starting your spell (anytime between the New Moon and the Waxing Moon—but you must start it in time to be finished by the Full Moon), your name, and the following words—Prosperity, Health, Happy Home, Successful Career, Abundance of Material Goods, Freedom From Debt, Joy.

Draw these runes (consult chapter six) on the paper in a decorative manner: Money, Caduceus, House, Gort (Ivy), Fehu, Ruis (Elder), Wunjo.

Set the paper aside to dry.

Using the tack, in section one of the candle, carve the word *Prosperity* and the rune for "Money." In section two, carve the word

Health and the rune for "Caduceus." In section three, the words *Happy Home* and the rune for "House."

In section four, carve the name of the career in which you want to succeed, and then carve the rune for "Gort." In section five, carve the word *Abundance* and the rune for "Fehu." Section six should bear the words *Freedom from Debt* and the rune for "Ruis." In section seven, write the word *Joy* and the rune for "Wunjo."

Now, dress the candle, using a prosperity oil to anoint it, then, if you like (and if the spell is for you), add a drop or two of your blood.

Raise energy and charge the candle.

Fill the candle holder (brass works best for this) with Prosperity Powder and fix the candle snugly into the holder, on top of the powder.

Set aside until you are ready to begin your spell.

Each day that you cast the spell sit in a quiet, clean room and focus on the piece of paper. Think about what that day's workings will mean in your life. Visualize them as if they've already happened.

Light the candle and burn one section until the flame reaches the line signaling the next day's work.

Carefully extinguish the candle and set it aside on your altar until the next day, when you will burn the next section.

Do not skip days with this spell. When you have finished burning the entire candle, take the paper outside and bury it under a tree. You can also burn the paper in a heat-proof bowl if you like.

You should see some results, however small, before this spell is over, but I usually find the major results come within two or three months of casting it. The Seven-Day Prosperity Spell is more useful as a long-term investment rather than a short-term "I need cash now" working.

DOMESTIC LIFE

This is a complex oil that can help to increase happiness in your existing home or help you to find a new one. This oil has a lot of ingredients, but it really works—and it smells wonderful. After all, if you're going to anoint your home's doors and windows, it should have a pleasing aroma. See page 115 for mixing directions.

HAPPY HOME AND HOMEFINDING OIL

¼ ounce olive oil base
16 drops tonka oil
7 drops new mown
　hay oil
7 drops oakmoss oil
4 drops earth oil
8 drops bergamot oil
4 drops dill oil
4 drops lilac oil

4 drops jasmine oil
7 drops thyme oil
16 drops dragon's blood oil
6 drops high john oil
14 drops violet oil
18 drops rose geranium oil
　gems: peridot, tiger's eye
　flowers: oak, cedar

FINDING A JOB

This has to be one of the most trying activities in the history of the human race. Finding a job actually isn't that difficult, but finding a job you like is another matter.

I have found that using Transformational Drama (see chapter eight) is a good way to attract a job but there are some other things you can do to increase your chances of landing a position.

- Herbal charms kept in your purse or pocket are good ways to carry magick with you during interviews. Sprinkle a little sage, lavender, dill, basil, and parsley into a green cloth and add a tiger's eye chip. Tie with a golden ribbon. Carry this to magnetize prosperity while you radiate wisdom and knowledge.

- Take applications home with you if possible. After you have filled them out, raise energy and charge them with the intent of drawing the right position to you.

- Draw or paint the runes Ansuz, Tir, and Mannaz over your heart (with a non-toxic marker) before you get dressed to go to an interview. Allow to dry before you put on your shirt or your dress and I recommend an undershirt or a slip between your skin and your outer clothing. These runes enable clear communications and will encourage others to come to your aid. These same runes, drawn on the phone, will invite good news to come over the wire.

- Don't forget—sometimes your best ally is your mouth. Let people know you are looking for a job, tell everyone you see, and check back where at places where you applied.

Again, all the magick in the world won't help you if you don't put forth some sort of effort!

10

LOVE AND LUST

Love and lust magick are two of the most misunderstood and abused forms of magick in the world. It is human nature to crave love, to want to be desirable. Unfortunately, our heads often have little to say about what our hearts are feeling.

THE IMPORTANCE OF LOVING YOURSELF

As a professional Tarot reader, I have clients who return over and over again hoping I will tell them that their abusive partner will change, that the married man they're involved with will suddenly decide in their favor—that love is just around the corner and everything in their life will magickally blossom once they've found Mr. or Ms. Right.

Time and again I tell them that if you are in an abusive relationship, leave, go to a shelter, no amount of wishing and magick in the world will do any good until you get out of the situation. I tactfully suggest that the married paramour has it pretty good—a home life and a mistress on the side—he's not likely to give up that situation.

Most importantly, I find myself continually reminding people that until they love themselves and treat themselves with the respect and care they want from someone else, a successful love life isn't going to magickally appear.

Only in loving yourself, only in accepting your own company, can you attract a person who will add to your life instead of drain you. People treat you the way you treat yourself.

It wasn't until I left a nine-year, emotionally abusive relationship and learned to live with myself and for myself that I was able to see what I truly had to offer. Once I had re-established my self-esteem and decided that sometimes being alone was better than being with just anybody, only then did I meet my current husband and form a relationship based on truth, self-integrity, mutual love, and admiration.

I met my husband in a truly magickal way. We had a whirlwind courtship and long engagement, and even though we're content and happy, we realize that marriage takes continuing hard work.

I always remind those who come to me seeking a love spell, a potion, a prediction of love, that it took me two years of self-discovery to be ready to enter a successful relationship, two years of serious work, scrupulous honesty with myself, and getting my fingers burned in a couple minor affairs along the way.

Love isn't a cure. It's an enhancement. If you are unhappy in your job, if you hate your looks, and you aren't doing meaningful work, then getting involved with a lover won't make everything okay. It may take the edge off your unhappiness at first, but the irritation and the anger will creep back in and can easily spoil your relationship. You need to be happy with yourself, you need to find worth in yourself if you expect a romantic partnership to work.

I WANT HIM TO LOVE ME!

"Can you cast a spell for me?" It was ten o'clock at night and the voice on the phone sounded vaguely familiar. "Who is this?" I asked.

"Joanie," she said. (Not her real name, of course.)

I remembered now, she was a new client. I had read her cards the week before.

"What do you want done?" Sometimes if a person has a real need I will help them out. More often I advise them to buy a book or two and work it out for themselves. Magick is usually most effective when done by the person who needs it.

She sounded a little embarrassed, then said, "My boyfriend. Can you cast a love spell on him for me?"

"No," I said. "I told you last week that I'm not going to help you."

"But I really want him to love me!"

I spent a few more minutes reiterating what I had explained to her the week before. You can't make someone love you if they don't already have the inclination. Her boyfriend, a married man, wasn't likely to give up his house and children just to marry her and take care of her kids.

I explained—again—that when you try to manipulate someone's heart, you're the one likely to get hurt. When I finished, she was quiet, but only for a moment.

"So you won't cast a spell on him for me?" she said, plaintively.

I hung up.

Joanie's problem wasn't that she couldn't find a boyfriend, it was that she wasn't ready to find a stable relationship. She had been hurt in the past and expected to get hurt in the future. She set herself up for failure by getting involved with unavailable men, with men who refused to commit. Joanie wasn't going to let anyone get near her heart. She wasn't going to expose her vulnerability.

The problem was that Joanie didn't understand that her attitude was attracting only those men who wanted superficial connections.

Joanie came back to me a couple of times after that. Each time I would tell her that she needed to work on loving herself; that she needed to spend some time finding out what she had to offer and to break off the unproductive affairs. But she didn't want to do the work. It wasn't quick enough, it wasn't easy.

She left me as a client but I am pretty sure she still makes the rounds of the psychics and readers hoping someone will tell her that her boyfriend will leave his wife if she just waits long enough, or that a new love will drop into her life and sweep her off her feet.

CONTROL IS FOR REMOTES

The problem Joanie faced, and the same problem facing many people, is the concept that we can make someone love us. All the magazines tell us—especially women—that if we look a certain way, if we use this make-up or that perfume, any man we want is ours. All we have to do is walk by in a pair of sheer nylons and a miniskirt and we'll control him.

Along the same vein, men believe that money and power will make a woman's head turn.

What we don't fully realize is the fact that lust and love are not the same, that not everyone is going to like us, let alone love us, and that we simply don't have the control over others that we'd like.

So we turn to outside remedies—a new shade of lipstick, a new dress, a fat wallet, two hours a day in the gym. All of these things can be fun and healthy but not when used to try to manipulate another person's emotions.

The same goes for magick.

There are love spells and potions and powders and they can help draw the right person to us, but we have to give up the idea of who that person is going to be and let the Gods decide.

It is, however, perfectly acceptable to decide what *type* of person you want. My list included these traits among others: must be intelligent, humorous, fun, loyal, faithful, and mature; must accept my size without negativity; must find me sexy; must encourage and support my writing; must love cats . . . there were about twenty-five or thirty traits that I decided I couldn't compromise on.

At first I worried that I was being too specific but then decided that I couldn't be happy with someone who didn't have those traits in one form or another.

So I cast my spells (more about that later on) and within two weeks met my current husband. He fit almost every trait on the list and the three he didn't, he developed later on.

But if I had set my sights on one particular person, thinking that that person was right for me, then I would have been disappointed. The man I suspected was going to be drawn in by the spell turned out to be someone I wouldn't have wanted, once I got to see what was inside his heart.

If I had focused on him, instead of leaving it up to the Universe, we might have actually started a relationship, but it wouldn't have gone anywhere and it wouldn't have afforded me the chance to be married to the man I'm now with.

That would have truly been a tragedy.

Shouldn't the whole concept of love and lust be to attract someone who finds you irresistible even at six in the morning when you've got sleep gunk in your eyes? Whom you find adorable even when they're sick with the flu?

If attraction is one-sided then you're never going to know the joys of reciprocal love.

HEART ALTAR

Pick a spot in your house where you can leave the altar set up. Find a beautiful rose-covered wall paper or sturdy wrapping paper and use it to cover a strip of wall behind your altar from floor to ceiling. Tack it smoothly to the wall.

Center your chosen table in front of the strip of rose paper and cover it with a pink, red, or rose-covered tablecloth. In the center of the altar, place a heart-shaped rock or stone (naturally or artificially created). Add a red or pink candle in a beautiful candle holder to one side and a vase of flowers to the other. Other things you might want to add to the heart altar may include:

- Pretty beads, silk flowers, ribbons

- Pictures of you when you've been happy

- Pictures of beloved friends, family, lover, and pets

- Chocolates

- A carafe of wine or brandy

- Pieces of amethyst or rose quartz

- Figurines of deer, otters, tigers

- Perfumes, magickal love and lust oils

- Incense holder and incense

Spend some time each morning or evening in front of the altar, thinking of what love and friendship mean in your life. This is a good place to cast your love spells.

FULL MOON TRIPLE CANDLE SPELL

This spell takes some advance planning. I used it with wonderful results about two weeks before I met my husband. I had come to the point where I was comfortable with the idea of being by myself, I didn't need anyone to "complete" me, and was at a stage where I felt, "This is who I am, either accept me this way or find someone else."

I asked Mielikki (my Goddess) for help in drawing the right person to me and She gave me the directions for this spell in a dream.

The spell begins on the night of the New Moon. Sit down with a pencil and three sheets of paper. On the first sheet of paper list the attributes you are looking for in a mate. Don't be afraid to get specific. If you have a gender preference, you should list it.

Think carefully as you make your list. The qualities you list should be compatible with your own attributes—I may entertain the thought of tromping thirty miles up a steep mountain road—it's rugged and wild and I want to see the pictures, but I'm not going to be doing that anytime in the foreseeable future. If my mate's hobby turns out to be mountain-climbing and he wants me to participate then we're going to have problems.

On the second sheet of paper, list all the qualities you have to offer someone else. Don't write an idealized version of yourself, but be honest and give yourself the credit you deserve. List your hobbies and interests and what you won't compromise on in life.

On the third sheet of paper, list all the qualities you would like your relationship to have. Do you want a cozy, quiet relationship? Do you need someone who prefers excitement and parties? Do you want to get married or are you happy with separate lives? Do you want children? Again, be very honest with yourself and don't leave out anything important.

Over the next two weeks refer to the three lists. Change them if necessary. Spend a little time each day reviewing the lists and make sure they resonate as truth.

For the actual spell you will need:

- your three lists

- one red image candle of the gender you want your mate to be. If it doesn't matter, use the gender you lean toward most.

- two candles about one inch in diameter, one pink and one green

- Passion Powder (see page 174)

- Love oil (Any will do. If you don't have access to a magickal blend, rose essential oil will work. See my recipe on page 173.)

- rose or vanilla incense

- red embroidery thread

- a push pin thumbtack

- a large metal bowl filled with salt

- a metal stand to hold the bowl off the counter or bathtub

Two nights before the Full Moon, cast a circle and call the elements. Light a stick of incense. Refer to your list of desired qualities in a mate and carve each one onto the image candle using a thumbtack. Don't leave anything out. Focus on each quality, visualizing how it will enhance your relationship.

Next, carve each quality you have to offer a potential mate onto the round pink candle, again focusing on the positive and visualizing how your attributes can enhance a relationship.

Third, refer to your list and carve each desired quality of a relationship onto the green candle, once more envisioning how it would feel to be in this type of relationship.

Take the Love Oil and anoint each candle thoroughly. After you have done this, spread several drops of your blood onto each candle.

Roll each candle in Passion Powder, arrange on a cloth and set outside under the moon. Cover with a clear piece of plastic if there's a chance of rain. Bring inside the next morning and set them on your altar.

The night before the Full Moon, again place your candles outside under the moonlight and bring in the next morning.

On the day of the Full Moon, cast a circle and call the elements. Invoke whichever Gods or Goddesses you are working with.

Light a stick of rose or vanilla incense.

Bind the candles together in a triangle with the image candle in the center. Join them with the embroidery thread.

᷍d charge the candles.

᷍ candles in the bowl of salt and set the bowl on ᷍ivet or holder so that the bottom does not touch the ᷍᷍o or the counter where you are casting the spell. Be very sure ᷍nat nothing flammable is near the candles. Sometimes the flames from this spell can grow very tall and wild.

Light the candles. While they are burning, read each list aloud and explain to the God or Goddess why each quality is important to you. When you have finished, let the candles burn until they're gone.

Take the remaining wax and, together with the three lists, bury it right outside your front door. If you live in an apartment building bury the remains in a plant pot and set it right inside your front door. You should see results within three months.

Extra Plate for Love Spell

This is a simple addition to other charms and spells you might be doing to attract love. It is easy to perform when you don't have much time to devote towards love magick. If others at your table give you odd looks, just smile. You know what you're doing.

Each night when you eat dinner set an extra plate at the table. Put a small portion of food on it and say:

> This place I set at my dinner table,
> Come my love, when you are able,
> Knock at my door and enter in
> In my life you are welcome.

Give this spell time. It's a quiet spell and will eventually work its magick and someone will enter your life to claim their place at your table.

Braided Love Spell

You will need three nine-foot sections of cord for this spell—one pink, one red, and one white.

Cast a circle and invoke the elements. Invoke the God or Goddess you are working with.

Pick up the red cord. This represents passion. Run it through your hands and think of the passion you would like to have in a relationship.

Now pick up the pink cord. This cord represents companionship. Run it through your hands and think of the companionship you would like in a relationship.

Pick up the white cord. This cord represents trust, fidelity, and spirituality. Run it through your hands and think of these qualities and how they relate to the relationship you would like to have.

Tie the tops of the three cords together and firmly secure the knot to a broom handle or chair. Braid the three cords, visualizing that you are braiding passion, companionship, and values together. While you braid the cords, chant:

> *I lust, I love, I trust, I weave*
> *Around the Loom, Around the Loom*
> *I braid, I knot, gifts I receive*
> *From the Loom, From the Loom.*

When you have finished the braid, knot the end with a triple knot and hang it in your bedroom next to your bed or next to your front door.

DANCING LUST SPELL

I often find dancing to be one of the best ways to raise energy. For this spell, compile a tape of passionate songs with good rhythm.

On a night during the Waxing to Full Moon, preferably a Friday, take a bath using Fire Lust Bath Salts (see the recipe on page 168). Dress in a dancing outfit that feels sensuous and sexy yet allows you to move.

Light three red candles on your altar and other candles around the room (make sure they are secure so your clothes won't brush against them and so you won't knock them over).

Cast a circle, invoke the elements and whichever God or Goddess you are working with.

Turn on the music and begin to dance, keeping in mind the passion and love you would like to share with another.

Dance to build power, and as you dance, raise energy by fluffing up your aura with your hand movements. Get primal here, then send the energy out into the universe, asking that it be directed towards the appropriate partner for you.

Once you have expended yourself, eat something wonderful and sensuous while still in circle, like strawberries and cream, or chocolate, or grapes and cheese. Drink a glass of sparkling cider or wine and relax.

FIRE LUST BATH SALTS

1 cup epsom salts	10 drops rosemary oil
⅔ cup table salt	8 drops cinnamon oil
⅓ cup baking soda	(any more may irritate
14 drops orange oil	your skin)
14 drops lime oil	orange food color

When making bath salts, mix the salts and soda together first, then add the oils, drop by drop. Blend together with your hands until thoroughly mixed. Store in air tight container. They may get hard, but all you have to do is add them (about ½ cup) to hot water and they will dissolve.

WOODLAND LOVE SPELL

This spell is designed for those practitioners of the Craft who are very focused on the natural world around them. This ritual provides a way to use the earth-focused forest energy and woodland spirits to draw love to you.

On a bright and sunny day, go into the woods to a favorite spot. Take with you some fruit and cheese, bread, and a knife. Also take a felt pen, a small piece of rose quartz, and some green cord.

Make yourself comfortable and relax, let go of the mundane world. When you feel yourself beginning to tune in to the woods around you, cut a small cube of cheese, a slice of bread, and a piece of fruit into small pieces. Dig a hole at the base of an oak, maple, or apple tree, and put the food in the hole.

Then on a large, broad leaf—maple works well—use the felt pen to carefully write this:

> Lord (Lady) of the forest, Lord (Lady) of the Vine,
> Bring to me the love that is mine.
> Blesséd Be.

Wrap the leaf around the rose quartz, taking care not to tear it, and tie it with the green cord.

Raise energy and charge the leaf charm. Place the charm on top of the food and, if you are trying to attract a man, say:

> O Ancient Hunter, I come seeking you
> Come to me, Cernunnos, Pan, The Master of the Hunt,
> Tapio, Osiris, Green Man, Lover, Horned One.
> Bring to me a man suited to be my partner.
> I will accept and love the one you choose to
> Embody Yourself within.
> Let us bind together, play together, love together,
> Lust together, learn together,
> Entwining our souls and minds
> Entwining our hearts and bodies
> Entwining our paths and lives.
> So mote it be.

If you are calling for a woman, say this:

> O Ancient Huntress, I come seeking you
> Come to me, Artemis, Flidhais, Mistress of the Hunt
> Mielikki, Earth Daughter, Green Mother, Lover, Creatrix.
> Bring me a woman suited to be my partner.
> I will accept and love the one you choose to
> Embody Yourself within.
> Let us bind together, play together, love together,
> Lust together, learn together
> Entwining our souls and minds
> Entwining our hearts and bodies
> Entwining our paths and lives.
> So mote it be.

Now fill the hole with dirt and draw an invoking pentagram on top of the mound, then cover with leaves. Eat your lunch, secure in the knowledge that the Woodland God and Goddess have heard your need. When you leave the area, don't look back.

LOVE, LUST, AND ATTRACTION RECIPES

The following recipes for bathsalts and oils are time-proven to draw passionate results into your life. Along with each recipe is a brief notation of the kind of energy you can expect to attract—ranging from the wildly sexy to the gently companionable. Remember, for instructions on making a bath salt, see the recipe included on page 168. For oil creation, consult page 115.

APHRODITE'S BATH SALTS

Perfect for a bath before an evening of passion, this blend is named for the foam-born Goddess of love and lust.

1 cup epsom salts	15 drops rose petal oil
⅔ cup table salt	7 drops ylang-ylang oil
⅛ cup baking soda	5 drops orange oil
2 drops lavender oil	7 drops jasmine oil
7 drops violet oil	violet food color

ATTRACTION OIL FOR MEN

This blend creates a sexy, masculine scent. Designed for men to use, it's musky and reminiscent of the satyr.

¼ ounce apricot oil	6 drops sandalwood oil
3 drops rosemary oil	flowers: patchouli or
4 drops patchouli oil	cinnamon shavings
4 drops dark musk oil	gem: amber
1 drop cinnamon oil	

COME AND SEE ME OIL

There are many similar versions of this oil, which is based on a Voudoun recipe. Use it with care; it is seductively intoxicating.

¼ ounce olive oil
5 drops patchouli oil
1 drop cinnamon oil
3 drops rose oil

6 drops sandalwood oil
flower: patchouli
gems: carnelian or garnet

NYMPH AND SATYR OIL

This is a very powerful oil. I've had many women tell me how well it works for them, so be sure you really want to attract men before you wear it.

½ ounce olive oil
25 drops rose oil
11 drops anise oil
13 drops violet oil
15 drops jasmine oil
15 drops ylang-ylang oil

12 drops narcissus oil or
   4 drops lotus oil and
   8 drops lilac oil
flowers: rose or jasmine
gem: peridot

PAN'S DELIGHT OIL

This was developed for a friend on her birthday who wanted a playful, sexy scent to attract a partner to have a good time with, not necessarily to settle down with for the long haul.

½ ounce olive oil
15 drops rose oil
11 drops jasmine oil
4 drops violet oil
2 drops carnation oil
1 drop dark musk oil

2 drops orange oil
5 drops rose geranium oil
3 drops lilac oil
15 drops ylang-ylang oil
flowers: rose or lilac
gem: garnet

SHEHEREZADE OIL

Just like the name suggests, this oil conjures images of Arabian nights and opulent surroundings. It is a seductive, feminine scent.

¼ ounce apricot oil
11 drops hibiscus oil
10 drops poppy oil
20 drops rose oil
15 drops carnation oil

25 drops honeysuckle oil
15 drops ylang-ylang oil
    flowers: poppy or rose
    gem: garnet

FIRE LUST OIL

One of my most highly requested oils, this spicy selection is sure to stoke passionate flames.

¼ ounce olive oil
35 drops orange oil
15 drops citronella oil
20 drops carnation oil

10 drops rose geranium oil
    flower: orange blossoms
    gem: garnet

LOVE OIL

The opposite of Pan's Delight Oil, this oil will help to draw companionship and a partner who is interested in a long-term relationship.

½ ounce olive oil
10 drops rose oil
5 drops jasmine oil
7 drops musk oil

10 drops ylang-ylang oil
2 drops lavender oil
    flowers: rose, jasmine
    gems: garnet, rose quartz

LOVE POWDER

Similar to Love Oil, the powder attracts love and a long-term partner.

¼ ounce lemon balm
¼ ounce peppermint
13 drops love oil
    (page 172)

1 tablespoon ground cinnamon
1 tablespoon ground ginger

PASSION POWDER

Not only can this powder be useful in drawing lustful attentions, it can also be used to empower yourself—a little extra verve when you need it.

¼ ounce patchouli
¼ ounce jasmine
    flowers
¼ ounce rose petals
¼ ounce peppermint
¼ ounce orange
    blossoms

3 tablespoon cardamom seeds
1 tablespoon ground cinnamon
1 tablespoon ground ginger
1 tablespoon grains of paradise
13 drops Fire Lust Oil (page 172)
    or Nymph and Satyr Oil
    (page 171)

CREATING A ROMANTIC, PASSIONATE ATMOSPHERE

Creating a romantic atmosphere doesn't take a lot of money, but it can require creativity. Remember, just because something is romantic to you doesn't mean that it's going to be romantic to your partner. I love black lace and satin; my husband would just as soon have me bare breasted.

But, you can come to some compromises. Talk to your partner, discuss what turns both of you on and find an acceptable balance. She doesn't want black sheets and bedspreads? Maybe she'd like black roses on a Victorian comforter.

He wants the television in the bedroom? (Tough one, that.) Well, maybe you can cover it with a beautiful scarf when it's not in use.

Some ideas on creating a romantic atmosphere:

- Fresh flowers are always nice.

- Incense (providing no one is allergic to it).

- Pictures that you both find erotic or romantic.

- In the morning, spray the bed with a very light coating of your favorite perfume. By nighttime it will just barely linger in the sheets.

- Set up your Heart Altar in the bedroom.

- Keep the condoms in a lovely candy dish next to the bed.

- Drape beautiful scarves around the headboard of your bed.

- Giant urns with huge stalks of dried grass and plumes (pampas grass, for example) always bring to mind the harems of the Far East.

- Use your own imagination.

Sex Magick

Let me just say this up-front: never use someone else's energy for sex magick without their permission. It's wrong, wrong, WRONG!

Sex magick should be performed between two partners who are sexually active with one another in the everyday world. Even the symbolic Great Rite can bind two people together if they don't realize what's going on. If you are in a relationship with one person and you perform sex magick with another, there will be fallout, both magickal and emotional.

Having said that, I now add that sex magick can be a very potent way of achieving results. In the first place, sexual power is tightly connected to psychic energy; both run up the central spine (the kundalini force) and it is easy to mistake one for another when you are in circle.

A lot of grief would be spared if people just took a few minutes for a reality check, asking, "Am I really attracted to my coven-mate, or is it just her magickal energy that I find seductive?"

Sex magick utilizes the process of building energy through sexual excitation, then orgasm releases it. There are books written on the subject, some I agree with, some I don't, but really, all you need to do during sex magick is agree with your partner on a common focus, keep that focus in mind as you go about your sexual play, and try to delay orgasm until the energy is super-charged.

Then, much like releasing the cone of power, you release the spell through orgasm.

Enough said. Try it if you like. You don't have to, there are plenty of other forms of magick to work with if you don't want to mix your magick with your sexual life or if you have an uncooperative partner.

THE GREAT RITE

The Great Rite, or the Hieros Gamos, is a term used to refer to the sacred marriage between the Goddess and the God. It is reenacted between mortals either physically or symbolically as a recognition that without both Feminine and Masculine principles the world would not flourish and life would not procreate.

The Great Rite is a sacred charge; if you decide to enact it, it must be with utmost respect.

There are several ways (some traditions have very specific wording and processes they go through) to approach the Great Rite, or Divine Marriage.

THE SYMBOLIC GREAT RITE

The symbolic Great Rite is perhaps the easiest and least volatile form of the Hieros Gamos to perform. You can do this alone or with another person during ritual. I recommend casting a Circle, invoking the elements, and calling the Lord and Lady.

Then, one person (usually male) holds the chalice filled with red wine (representing the blood of the Goddess' womb). He blesses the chalice in Her name.

His partner (usually female) holds the athame high (representing the phallus of the God). She blesses the athame in His name.

Slowly, she lowers the athame into the chalice, saying:

> As the athame is to the God's phallus, so He descends into the Goddess' loins.

Her partner says:

> As the chalice is to the Goddess' womb, so She accepts Her Lord's seed and is made fertile.

Together, they say:

> The Divine Marriage is complete. As They couple in joy, the Earth is renewed and Their passion brings life to the world.
> Blesséd be.

THE SACRED MARRIAGE

The Sacred Marriage is comprised, not only of a symbolic act representing the union of the Goddess and God, but also a physical act between two consenting adults. The culmination of this rite is sexual intercourse. If a couple decides to perform the Sacred Marriage, I provide a few guidelines:

- The woman represents the Goddess; she should be treated with the respect and honor any Witch would pay to the Gods.

- The man represents the God, he comes to the Goddess and asks permission to enter Her womb.

- If you are doing this with others present, it is a good idea to screen off the area of actual intercourse for privacy.

- Remember, you entangle your energy with another's when you have sex with them. Ask yourself if you truly want your magickal life intermixed with this other person's energy.

- Safe sex, please!

- If a coven insists that you must undergo ritual sex with the Priest or Priestess as an initiation, or that you can't be a real Witch without this step, then turn around and run the other way. In the past some traditions worked this way but I find the concept manipulative and destructive.

- The Hieros Gamos shouldn't be used as an excuse for an orgy. If you are looking for an orgy, that's fine, just don't use your religion as an excuse for it. Have the guts to admit that this is what you want and don't lead anyone else to believe otherwise. It isn't fair to pretend that you want a highly sacred experience when you're just out for an easy lay.

SWEETS FOR THE SWEET

Chocolate and romance go together like the birds and the bees. Chocolate and sweets, candy and little heart-shaped cakes, delicately scented teas and scones with jelly, all add to the experience of romance, whether or not you're involved with anyone.

Too much sugar isn't good for the body but, unless you are diabetic, a taste for sweets probably isn't going to hurt you as long as you get a balanced diet.

With that in mind, I present a few recipes.

ROSE MIST TEA

1 part rosebuds
2 parts chamomile
1 part lavender

2 parts lemon balm
2 parts lemon grass

SOFT MEAD

1 quart water	¼ teaspoon ground cloves
1 cup honey	¼ teaspoon ground cinnamon
¼ cup lemon juice	pinch of salt
½ cup lemon juice	

Boil water, honey and ½ cup lemon juice in enamel or glass pot until reduced to 3 cups. Add ¼ cup lemon juice, spices and salt. Chill. Shake before serving.

ROSE PETAL JELLY

4 cups rose petals (organic, washed)	3½ cups boiling water
2 teaspoons chamomile	1 package pectin
	4 cups granulated white sugar

In large stainless steel, glass, or enamel bowl, cover rose petals and chamomile with boiling water. Cover and steep for one hour. Strain liquid into a large stainless steel or enamel kettle and discard the herbs.

Add pectin to the liquid. Bring to a boil, then add sugar all at once. Bring to a rolling boil (which you cannot stir down), stirring constantly. Boil exactly one minute.

Remove from heat. Skim foam from surface of jelly. Pour into sterilized, hot jars and seal.

Makes about 5 cups.

BLACK FOREST CAKE

2 cups flour, pre-sifted	6 squares unsweetened baking chocolate
2 teaspoons baking powder	1¼ tablespoon vanilla
½ teaspoon salt	1¼ cups milk
½ cup butter	1 can vanilla icing, pre-mixed
1¼ cups white sugar	3 cups cherry pie filling
2 large eggs	

Preheat the oven to 350 degrees F.

In small bowl, stir flour, baking powder and salt.

In large bowl, cream butter and sugar until fluffy. Add eggs, one at a time, beating after each addition.

Melt chocolate in microwave or in small pan over water bath, stirring so it doesn't burn. Let cool five minutes while you grease and flour a 13" x 9" pan.

Add chocolate to butter mixture, beating until thoroughly mixed. Add vanilla.

Add the flour mixture, ½ cup at a time, alternating with the milk until both are blended in.

After last addition, beat for two minutes at medium speed. Spread in prepared cake pan and gently tap on counter to remove air bubbles.

Bake for 22-26 minutes, until toothpick inserted in center comes out clean.

When the cake has completely cooled, spread a thin layer of vanilla icing on the top. Spoon the cherry pie filling over the icing and serve.

Keep the following tips in mind when making this or other magickal cakes:

- Stir batter deosil, never widdershins. If you use an electric mixer, move the mixer in a clockwise motion. There's not much you can do about the beaters.

- Allow the cake to cool thoroughly before icing.

- Remember, if you have love and friendship in your heart, then it will seep into the foods you prepare and will make a difference in how they taste.

- If you like, before adding the pie filling, cut the cake in heart shaped pieces and put on individual serving dishes. Then pour the filling over the cake.

11

Beauty and Glamour

Beauty begins on the inside. Beauty is a state of mind. Beauty is as beauty does. True beauty assumes no particular size, shape, color, or ability except to the beholder.

Everything that could possibly be in style, be considered seductive, has at one time or another been popular.

Greased hair, long hair, short hair, no hair . . . .

Beards, mustaches, clean shaven . . . .

Thin, fat, robust, Rubenesque . . . .

Tall, short, somewhere in between . . . .

Black, white, red, yellow, brown . . . .

White teeth, black teeth, no teeth . . . .

You name it, and sometime, somewhere it's been considered sensuous, beautiful, desirable.

The desire to look attractive drives some people to extremes—the woman who chooses to have plastic surgery in order to look like a Barbie doll, the man who has gastric bypass surgery to lose weight, the bodybuilder who spends hours and hours lifting thousands of pounds of weight, the make-up junkie who slaps down two hundred dollars for a jar of wrinkle cream that may or may not work.

But the essential truth is that attitude makes the difference.

The most perfectly manicured, spotlessly dressed, stylishly thin woman in the room may have personality so horrid that her mere presence makes your skin crawl, and it will show. Sure someone might want to sleep with her, but put up with her on a long-term basis? No way.

That handsome hunk who spends two hours getting his hair slicked back and who freaks out if he drops a spot of ketchup on his leather jacket could be hiding an obsessive-compulsive disorder that would drive you nuts if you lived with him.

Think twice about basing your opinion of others on superficialities. But, it is also true that our feelings about our looks—our own sense of being in the physical realm—make a difference in how we act. If we feel sexy we're apt to project an aura of sexiness. By boosting our self-esteem and by increasing self-confidence we free our inner beauty to be seen by the outer world.

BLESSING THE VANITY

Like most women in this country, I love make-up. I buy more than most of my friends because I think it's fun, I love to dress up, and enjoy the way I look when I "do my face." My vanity is filled with jars and bottles and tubes and my cosmetics case weighs more than my purse.

I just don't expect miracles from it.

Occasionally I like to perform a quick blessing over my "stuff." I take a ritual bath, then light a few candles near the vanity and quietly reflect on myself in the mirror.

When I'm in a calm, peaceful state I cast a circle and invoke the elements. Then I invoke a Goddess of beauty (Hathor, Egyptian Goddess of Women and Beauty or Rauni, the Finnish Goddess of Lightning) and say:

> Oh Great Lady, let Your beauty and Your wisdom shine down on this vanity.
> Infuse these potions and creams with Your energy.
> When I use them, let my natural beauty shine forth and let me see in myself
> the beauty that is the face of the Goddess.

After I have blessed my vanity I wait a few moments then put on my make-up in circle and dress for either a night out on the town or for a romantic, passionate evening with my husband.

You can repeat this spell once a month with good effect, if you like.

Please, when you buy your cosmetics, buy from companies that don't test on animals. Also, try to invest in quality perfumes. There is a profound difference, both in scent and energy, between the low-grade varieties and the more expensive names. This is one area where you truly get what you pay for. I wear Opium and Casmir, and I wouldn't think of wearing an imitation version. Period. I buy the eau de toilette which is less expensive than the concentrated parfum. It's worth it.

THE GARNET DRESS

Have you ever had a vision of yourself that took your breath away?

A number of years ago, I had a sudden flash. I saw myself standing there, dressed in a long gown made of sparkling garnets. I immediately coveted that dress and how it made me look.

Well, besides the fact that there's no feasible way that I can make a dress out of garnets, I knew that what I craved was to possess the energy of that vision.

Garnet is the stone of passion and sexuality and that's what I wanted to project.

This prompted me to develop a spell to invoke the power of that vision into my daily life and it worked. I remember one night I was at a meeting and all the men were congregated in my corner! It was fun, although I was careful not to abuse it. Unfortunately, the women in the room didn't find it so charming. Beauty and glamour do have their downsides.

I don't use it often but once in a while I'll feel the need for a little extra sparkle, a walk that says "I'm here, notice me." On those occasions, I use this spell.

Sit in front of a full-length mirror. You should either be in your undergarments (preferably pretty ones) or dressed for an important, glamorous event like a party, dinner, or dance.

Light two red candles, one on either side of the mirror, so that they are positioned at just below eye level.

Turn off any other light sources in the room and play some sensuous music.

Stare at yourself, just above eye level (never stare directly at your own eyes in a mirror, it will give you a headache).

Envision yourself in a garnet dress. A long gown that flows to your ankles, that sparkles every time you turn.

You are exotic, the tiger prowling outside the window, the snake slithering through the treetops.

Throw your head back, laugh and feel your voice ripple with passion. Look into your eyes, see the smoldering gaze that stares back.

Quicken your breath, feel your heart and pulse jump, know, inside, how very sexy and sensuous and incredible you really are.

When you have captured that feeling, when you can hold it and know it's part of you, then snuff the candles and go to your party and sparkle as much as you want.

AN HERBAL BEAUTY CHARM

You can use this charm to "fluff up" the glamour in your aura. This combination of herbs works to give you not only radiance, but also increased attractiveness and self-confidence. Keep the sachet on your altar (if you have a Heart Altar, that's a good place for it) or near your bed where you can see it daily. To make it, you will need:

1 six-inch square golden cloth
1 seven-inch square green lace
1 teaspoon witch hazel bark
1 teaspoon cardamom seeds
1 teaspoon grains of paradise
1 teaspoon basil
1 teaspoon caraway
1 inch piece of dried sugar ginger
1 inch piece of cinnamon stick
13 apple seeds
1 piece of rose quartz

    1 garnet
     red ribbon
     tiny red ribbon roses

Lay out the gold cloth squarely on top of the lace. In the center, sprinkle the witch hazel, cardamom, grains of paradise, basil, and caraway.

Hold the sugar ginger in your hands and focus on your inner beauty; see it as a ray of light making its way into your aura. Place the sugar ginger on top of the herbs.

Add the cinnamon stick, the apple seeds, the rose quartz, and the garnet.

Bring the corners of the cloth and the lace up to bundle; wrap three times with the ribbon. Tie three knots.

Put the ribbon rose stems directly over the ribbon and wrap the ribbon ends three more times, tying three more knots to secure the ribbon roses to the sachet.

Trim any ragged ends.

Raise energy and charge the sachet, saying:

> *Treasures without, treasures within*
> *the glamour comes from my heart,*
> *Beauty without, beauty within,*
> *Never from me to part.*

OTHER BEAUTY HINTS

Dancing is a good way to exercise your body, to give you a sense of grace and fluidity. Even a few minutes a day can make a big difference. Also, stretching loosens the body and calms the mind. A little every night can bring inner peace and the good, restful sleep that makes you a pleasure to be around the next day.

Your choice of clothes can alter your perceptions of yourself. Even if you can't afford to go buy a new wardrobe, try to make sure all your clothes are neat, clean and mended. Fixing a rip in a dress can mean the difference between feeling pulled together and feeling unkempt. Wearing clothes that are too tight will only make you uncomfortable. You'll project the aura of someone who is unwilling to accept their physical size. I am a short, large woman and I love satin and lace and leather, but now I make sure that everything fits, that I can breathe in my clothes, and I generally buy a half a size larger than I need for comfort's sake. Imagine my surprise when I realized how much better I look that way.

Walk tall. Good posture gives you a sense of stature and dignity. Hold yourself like you're proud to be you and people will notice.

Clean up your language. You want someone to listen to you? Make sure your speech is clear and your words coherent.

SOME HERBS TO INCREASE BEAUTY AND HEALTH

All of these can be ingested, but note the following:

Valerian is mildly addictive. Do not use it for longer than two weeks at a time. It is also very pungent and bitter so you might want to take as a tincture or mix with more fragrant herbs.

Mugwort tea tastes pretty ugly. My suggestion is to stuff a dreaming pillow with it and tuck it into your pillowcase so the fragrance drifts through.

Pau d'Arco is easiest obtained and taken in tincture form.

If you are pregnant, some of these herbs can cause complications. Consult a good herbal or herbalist before taking any herb when you are pregnant.

Beauty	Health	Mental Clarity
apple	orange spice	peppermint
rose	spearmint	sage
yarrow	slippery elm	black Tea
cucumber	blackberry	lemon

Sleep	Menstrual Cycles
chamomile	wild yam
valerian	red raspberry
lemon balm	shepherd's purse
mugwort	pau d'arco

12

PROTECTION, PURIFICATION, AND HEALING

One of the most common questions I am asked is how to magick-ally protect the self. Another is how to know when one is being psy-chically attacked.

First, allow me to address the latter. It is my belief that active, malignant psychic attack is exaggerated. I don't think many people waste their time and energy by using the astral realm as a conduit to battle. Most often, those who think they're being attacked are having a run of bad luck and have usually brought on most of it themselves.

We are capricious creatures. We don't like to admit when some-thing is our fault, especially when it affects us. We'd rather look for someone else to blame. For many of our parents it was the Rus-sians—the Cold War gave us the perfect scapegoat. In the New Age community, it's often the space aliens who are causing havoc. In the Pagan community it's usually a psychic attack that gets the blame.

Please understand, I'm not making fun of these people; psychic attack can and does happen. But we must not jump to conclusions. When several things go sour at once, try to figure out if you've slipped a few lemons in the works.

So you didn't get the job you wanted. How many people applied? 350? 1,000? Well, 998 of those people are in the same boat as you—they don't have the job either. Do you truly think everyone was under psychic attack? Maybe your résumé just wasn't up to snuff, maybe the person who got the job knew the personnel director. Sometimes bad luck is just bad luck.

Your boyfriend left you for another woman? Could it be he's not worth the trouble? That he's just a jerk? Could they be better off together? Or is it possible that you really didn't want to be in the relationship and you subtly pushed him away? It happens.

When things start going haywire try to keep a clear perspective on the issue. Sometimes things seem to go the worst just before a turn of good luck.

"I Still Think I'm Being Attacked"

Okay, there are several things you can do.

You can directly confront the person you think is attacking you.

You can protect yourself both physically and magickally.

You can stop the attacker with a binding spell.

You can fight back.

In the case of magickal attack, direct confrontation usually doesn't work. You probably have no real proof that they're doing anything to you. It can, however, alert your attacker that you know what they're up to and they may stop. It can also make you look like a paranoid fool if they aren't perpetrating the attack.

Protecting yourself on both physical and magickal levels is always a good idea—it keeps stray spirits out of your path as well as those energies headed directly towards you.

A binding spell may work, though I've found it more appropriate for someone doing actual physical distress—whether it be slander, theft, or abuse.

Fighting back is best left as a last resort. You've confronted the person, you've cast your protection spells, you've tried to bind them and it didn't work. A mirror spell can help at this point, but it can produce some startling and sometimes disturbing results. Be certain you really need to cast this spell before you begin.

MAGICKAL PROTECTION

There are a number of spells and charms you can make for protection but I want to say this:

Before you cast any protection spell ask yourself if you have done everything you can on a physical level to protect yourself. Do you lock your doors? Do you drive defensively? Do you stay away from the bad areas of town where people are known to get hurt?

My point is that magick is used for enhancement. You can't enhance what isn't there. If you don't take precautions on the physical level, magick may help you for a little while, but the spell is going to break down if not backed up by action and you'll eventually get hurt through your own carelessness.

You must exercise common sense. Don't blame a spell for not protecting you from burglars if you leave the windows open at night when you're gone.

I would also like to stress that if you are in an abusive situation, magick isn't the answer. Go to a shelter. Go to a friend. Forget the television and the Waterford crystal. Those are replaceable. You are not. Take yourself and your kids and get out while you still can. Too many women are murdered by men who are supposed to love them; too many children are abused. You need a lawyer and a cop, not a Witch to protect you.

HOLLY PROTECTION CHARM

This is a simple protection charm you can use even if you are not concerned about a psychic attack. Hang each sprig of holly near one of your doors. Renew the charm every six months.

You will need:

1 sprig of holly for each door
   Protection Oil (page 192)
   red ribbon

Rub the holly leaf with the oil. Wrap the ribbon around the stem while saying:

Holly, holly, berries bright
Protect our home day and night
Thieves and rogues all be caught
So pass this house, tarry not.

WITCH'S BOTTLES

There are a number of different Witch's Bottles you can make for protection. A Witch's Bottle is a glass bottle with a narrow, long neck, into which magickally charged objects are placed. Generally used to trap negative energy, they act as active discouragement of attacks. These are two of my favorites.

Thread Bottle

You will need:

1 long-necked clear bottle
   thread leavings, none longer than two inches

Over the course of time fill the bottle with thread snippets. These should be left over from sewing projects, they shouldn't be cut to order. When full, raise energy and charge the bottle, then place it in a window. The tangle will confuse burglars and thieves so they won't be able to get into your house.

Sand Trap Bottle

You will need:

1 long-necked bottle
   clean dry sand
   splinters of rowan or oak

Raise energy and charge the sand with the intent to protect, to suck down negative energy. Carefully fill the jar ⅛ full of the sand.

Raise energy and charge the splinters with the intent that they defend against intruders. Carefully fill the jar ⅛ full of splinters.

Now, fill the jar to the neck with more charged sand. Cork tightly.

Say:

> *Into the sand, may it suck you down*
> *If ever you should intrude on my house*
> *Defend against foes, splinters of wood*
> *But to my friends bring only good.*

Set the jar in a corner near the door. This Witch's Bottle will work to keep negative people from coming into your home.

CANDLE OF PROTECTION

This a a general spell for your home and family. It does not necessarily guard against psychic attack, but it is effective against negativity. For instructions on mixing the oils, consult page 115.

You will need:

    1   three or four inch white pillar candle
        Guardian or Protection Oil (page 192)
        gold metallic paint
        a paint brush
        saucer at least four inches larger than candle
        aluminum foil
        gold shiny origami paper
        scissors
        glue

Anoint the candle with the oil. Let it dry.

Using the paint brush and the gold paint, carefully paint the rune of Algiz on all four sides of the candle. Again, allow it to dry.

Cover the saucer with foil, keeping it as smooth as possible.

Use the scissors to cut Algiz runes out of the origami paper (you can draw them on the white side of the paper so you have a guide to follow). Arrange the runes around the edge of the foil-covered saucer and glue on. Let dry.

Put the candle in the center of the saucer. Raise energy and focus an intent of protection into the candle.

Use the following chant to build power around the candle and when it peaks, release it:

Light to light, sparkling bright
Protect us through the long, cold night.

Burn this candle a little every night, especially when you feel the need for extra protection. When the candle is almost gone you can either make a new one or, if it has burned down in the middle but not the sides, you can charge a small white or gold votive for protection and put it in the center of the pillar candle to make a perpetual candle.

Protection Oil

This is a good oil to select for your candle of protection when you are concerned with physical, as opposed to psychic attack. It can also be used to anoint yourself before you leave on a journey or undertake a potentially hazardous situation.

½ ounce olive oil
15 drops lemon oil
8 drops lavender oil
   drops cajupet oil

6 drops rose geranium oil
4 drops citronella oil
   flower: lavender
   gem: clear quartz

Guardian Oil

If psychic attack is your fear, then Guardian Oil is a good choice for anointing a candle of protection or yourself.

½ ounce olive oil
15 drops lemon oil
10 drops clove oil
15 drops patchouli oil

5 drops pennyroyal oil
10 drops rosewood oil
   flower: rose
   gems: carnelian, citrine

HERBAL PROTECTION CHARM

This herbal protection charm is perfect to keep with you in your car. It provides protection for you while you are on the road—not just from physical damage to your automobile, but also protection against any of those mishaps that occur on the highway.

You will need:

1 six-inch square of white or gold cloth
   red embroidery thread
   needle
1 teaspoon basil
1 teaspoon burdock
1 teaspoon clover
1 teaspoon frankincense
1 piece of dragon's blood resin
1 tiger's eye chip
1 sprig of rowan or ash

Embroider the Algiz rune on the outside of the cloth. If you can't embroider, you can use red fabric paint. When done (or when it's dry), lay the cloth out with the Algiz rune touching the table.

Raise energy and charge the herbs for protection. Place them in the center of the cloth. Add the dragon's blood and the tiger's eye.

Catch the corners of the cloth together and bind with red thread. Bind the sprig of rowan to the charm and keep with you in your car for protection on the road.

SINGLE HERB CHARM

Like the Holly Protection Charm, this single herb charm is good for a general protection of your home. Hang it from the ceiling. If you use garlic, you will need to renew this charm monthly. If you choose one of the other herbs, you can wait about three months before renewing it.

You will need one of the following:

   a sprig of Rowan
   a sprig of Holly
5 acorns
1 bud garlic
   a sprig of Ash

You will also need:
    Protection or Guardian Oil (page 192)
    Red netting
    Red embroidery thread

Anoint your chosen herb with the oil. Wrap in the red netting and tie with the thread, knotting it five times. Raise energy, charge the charm and say:

Magickal herb, heed my charm
Protect this home from all that harms
By Stone and Flame, Wind and Sea
Protect my loved ones, protect me.

OTHER PROTECTION TIPS

- Bells hung from the doors guard against intruders and stagnant energy. Hang them where the air currents can ring them. They will set up movement in the air and clear the psychic energy of your home.

- An onion on your kitchen window will absorb ill will. When it starts to decay, replace it and throw it away (under no circumstances should you eat it).

- Salt water left out in the center of a room all night will absorb negativity. Wash it away with flowing water the next morning. If you are on a septic tank, either pour the water into the woods or into a body of running water.

- Healthy house plants, especially ferns and ivies, will create an aura of protective, positive energy. Just make sure your children or pets can't get into any poisonous plants.

- Totem animal statues can be blessed and used to protect your home (see chapter fourteen).

- Hang a mirror over the top of your bed to repel nightmares and other astral entities from your dreams.

- Native American dreamcatchers are also used to catch and tangle up nightmares before they have a chance to enter your dreams.

MAGICKAL PURIFICATION

Purification clears away doubts, worries, and concerns, and cleanses the aura of negative vibrations that muddy up the psychic sense. You can also purify an object (also known as cleansing) or place.

It is safe to do a purification ritual anytime you feel the need, but I will say that I see some people focusing more on cleansing their auras than living their lives. So use your common sense. Sometimes a quick smudging is all you need to get rid of the daily "gunk" that accumulates in your energy field. Sometimes, you will need something more elaborate.

SELF-PURIFICATION RITUAL

Use this ritual when you need to let go of something. A wonderful working for alleviating sorrow, I recommend it when you are feeling melancholy.

You will need:
    salt
    a bowl of New Moon Water (bottled spring water will do)
    yourself

Cast a circle, then invoke the elements and the Lord and Lady. Sit quietly and think about what you want to clear out of your aura.

When you are ready, add three good-sized pinches of salt to the water and stir widdershins.

Breathe deep into the bowl and as you do, let your fears and doubts pour into the water. Breathe them into the salt water where they will dissolve away. Do this until you feel that the negative energy has passed out of your body.

Next, hold the bowl in the air and visualize a gold or white light flowing into the water, transforming the negative vibrations and cleansing them. Carry the bowl to the sink and flush the water down the sink with cold, running water. Again, if you are on a septic system, do not put this water down your drain. Instead, take it somewhere it can be flushed into the sewer system or poured into a body of running water.

Smudge yourself with either lavender or jasmine incense (or another scent that promotes peace) and open the circle.

SUNLIGHT PURIFICATION SPELL

As opposed to the Self-Purification Ritual, this spell focuses on re-energizing yourself. It helps to clean out the "gunk" and help you get ready to take on challenges. It is also effective to restore energy after getting over a cold. Oil-blending instructions are on page 115.

You will need:

> a sunny day
> sunscreen
> Sun Oil or Solar Rites Oil (page 197)

Put on your sunscreen thirty minutes before performing this spell. You don't want to get skin cancer from your magickal workings.

Go outside and find a spot where you won't be bothered by interruptions. Sit in the grass and let the sunlight begin to relax you.

Anoint your forehead with the oil. Now lie down on your back and put your hands flat on the ground. Close your eyes.

Feel the warm earth against your back. Let all the muck in your aura sink to the bottom; let it flow out of your body into the Earth.

Visualize the Earth acting as a sponge, soaking up the negative vibrations as the sunlight pushes warm, healing, purifying energy into you from above.

The sunlight pushes all the negativity into the Earth where it will be absorbed and transformed.

When you feel clear, sit up and let the sunlight play on you a little longer, renewing your energy. Then, thank the Earth and the Sun for helping you.

Sun Oil

¼ ounce almond oil
30 drops orange oil
40 drops lime oil
5 drops ginger oil

10 drops vetiver oil
3 drops cinnamon oil
flower: orange blossoms
gems: clear quartz, carnelian

Solar Rites Oil

¼ ounce almond oil
18 drops orange oil
5 drops patchouli oil
14 drops ginger oil

9 drops pennyroyal oil
20 drops citronella oil
flower: orange blossoms
gems: clear quartz, citrine

THE BURNING COFFIN SPELL

The Burning Coffin Spell is especially good when you are coming to the end of a major event in your life and need to let go of the emotional baggage that the cycle or trauma has left with you. While this spell can provide you with closure, it will not work if you aren't absolutely certain that you are ready to let go of the negative "stuff" you are carrying. Instructions for blending oils are on page 115.

You will need:

1 large sheet of white paper
a ruler
a black marker
a red pen
a heat-proof container, stainless steel or ceramic
Excalibur Oil (page 198)
scratch paper
matches

Using the ruler, draw the shape of a coffin onto the large sheet of white paper. Set it aside.

Now, on the scratch paper, list those things in your life that you want to get rid of—those traits or qualities you don't like in yourself; those energies that aren't any good for you anymore; relationships you're ready to let go of. Think carefully as you decide what energies to dismiss, you don't want to let go of something before its time.

Once you have completed your list, use the red pen to write each thing to be released in the middle of the outline of the coffin.

When you've finished, take the black marker and color in the coffin, so you can't see your words. Visualize closing the lid on these things in your life.

Now, anoint the coffin with the oil and let dry. Destroy your scratch paper list—you can tear it up and throw it away.

When the coffin is dry, place it in the heat-proof bowl (which should be large enough to contain the flames of the burning paper).

Say:

> *You have been part of my life.*
> *I now release you back into the Universe*
> *To be changed and transformed,*
> *Forever separated from me.*
> *I bid you go, leave my life and don't*
> *Come back.*
> *You are dead to me.*
> *So Mote It Be.*

Now, light the paper on fire and watch the coffin containing all of the unwanted energies burn away into ashes. Either flush the ashes away using running water or take them, once they are cold, away from your home and bury them deep in the ground. You can also sprinkle them in the ocean when the tide is going out. If you are on a septic system, do not flush these ashes into it. It will be difficult to remove the negativity if it is still lingering in your water system.

Excalibur Oil

¼ ounce almond oil	5 drops rose geranium oil
15 drops lemon oil	1 drop cinnamon oil
9 drops orange oil	14 drops lavender oil
4 drops thyme oil	flower: thyme
2 drops ginger oil	gem: clear quartz

NOTES ON PURIFICATION

- You can throw bundles of herbs in a bonfire to purify the area for an outdoor ritual.

- Ritual baths are a good way to cleanse your aura. Use lavender bath salts and then rinse off with a shower after you've finished your bath to wash away the last remnants of negative energy.

- Magickal rattles are good for clearing the aura's energy; you can also use your magickal broom to "sweep" the negative vibrations out of your aura.

BINDING SPELLS

A binding spell is used to stop someone from harassing you. If you can't do anything on the practical level to make them stop (for example, they might be spreading rumors about you that are untrue), a binding spell can be an effective deterrent. The best binding spell I've created follows.

You will need:

1 black taper or image candle (gender depends on who
   you are trying to bind)
push-pin thumbtack
black cloth
a large piece of black felt
red ribbon
cotton or cotton balls
needle and thread
Banishing Oil (page 201)
loose tobacco
small mirror that can stand by itself

If you can obtain hair or nail clippings from the person you intend to bind, or their picture, you can also use these in this spell.

Fold the felt in half and cut out a rough shape of the person you want to bind. Make the figure large enough so that you will be able to stuff it after you have sewn it together.

Sew the pieces of the poppet (the figure) together, leaving a hole through which you can stuff the poppet. Fill it with cotton and tobacco, and if you have hair or nail clippings of the person, add those to it. Once it is filled, sew the opening closed.

If you have a picture of the person, staple it to the front of the poppet.

Next, carve the name of the person onto the black candle with the thumbtack and add these runes: Thurisaz, Isa, Eihwaz, Dark Moon, Bars, and Widdershins.

Anoint the candle and the poppet with the oil.

Cast a circle, invoke the elements and the God or Goddess you are working with. Light the altar candles.

Light the black candle and adjust the mirror so the flame is reflected in the glass.

Hold the poppet out in front of you and say:

> *Creature of cloth thou art,*
> *Now creature of flesh and blood you be.*
> *I name you* (name of the person you are binding).
> *No more shall you do me harm,*
> *No more shall you spread false tales.*
> *No more shall you interfere in my life, nor in*
> *the lives of my loved ones.*
> *By the power of the Gods and by my will,*
> *So Mote It Be!*

Draw an invoking pentagram over the poppet.

Now take up the ribbon and begin to wrap the poppet like a mummy, leaving no space unwrapped. Say:

> *I bind your feet from bringing you to harm me.*
> *I bind your hands from reaching out to harm me.*
> *I bind your mouth from spreading tales to harm me.*
> *I bind your mind from sending energy to harm me.*
> *If you do so continue, let all negative energy*
> *be cast and reflected directly back at you!*

Tie off the ribbon and hold the poppet in front of the mirror while you visualize all negative energy this person has sent to you being reflected back to them.

Wrap the poppet in the black cloth and tie with another length of ribbon. Say:

Great Mother, I have bound this person
from harming me and my loved ones.
By the powers of three times three
By Earth and Fire, Air and Sea
I fix this spell, then set it free
'Twill give no harm to return on me
As I will, so mote it be!

Let the candle burn out while the poppet sits at its base, then take the poppet and the remains of the candle far from your home and bury it deep in the ground or toss it in the ocean and walk away without looking back.

This spell is very powerful and works quite well. I've never had the need for a different binding spell. Sometimes binding spells work in unexpected ways. The person you are binding may suddenly decide to move away, they may have a change of heart and turn into a decent person after all, they may go through a horrible streak of bad luck and learn their lessons the hard way.

There is an outside chance that if they are projecting enough negative energy, they might end up hurt. Be assured, they were only caught in the backwash of their own negativity.

BANISHING OIL

½ ounce olive oil	10 drops peppermint oil
15 drops pine oil	flower: crushed black
12 drops rue oil	peppercorns
7 drops pepper oil	gem: obsidian or black onyx

Some of these oils are rather volatile. Do not anoint yourself with Banishing Oil. You could burn yourself with it if you aren't careful. Wash your hands after using. Consult page 115 for instructions on mixing oils.

MIRROR SPELL

There are some people who might consider this hexing, but I believe that at times this is a necessary and appropriate spell to perform.

You should cast this spell only when direct confrontation, physical and magickal protection, and binding spells have not done any good. It is meant to be used against those who are invading your space, or the space of another, and who are an active threat whether emotional or physical.

You will need:

> 1 black taper candle
> Banishing Oil (page 201)
> a free-standing mirror that can reflect the entire candle
> push-pin thumbtack

The wording of this spell is very important. It must be exact in order to avoid backlash and hurting anyone you shouldn't (we all do make mistakes at times). Cast a circle. Invoke the elements and one of these Goddesses: Cerridwen, Hecate, Persephone, or Kali-Ma (only invoke Kali-Ma in cases of extreme need).

While in circle, carve these words on the candle:

> *You who attack me, you are cruel and unjust to me, this spell I bind to you. May all the negativity and pain you have caused me be returned to you threefold now. I reflect back the anger you project, the envy and hatred you show. May it manifest in your life and prevent you from harming me again.*
>
> *By the powers of* (Goddess), *so mote it be!*

Do not carve a specific person's name on the candle. You may be mistaken about who is attacking you. If you list the wrong name, the spell could affect the wrong person. Instead, by saying "you who attack me," you can be certain that the spell will find its appropriate target. I cast my mirror spells in this manner to avoid making mistakes and involving innocent people.

Next, raise energy on the candle, focusing on everything you think this person has done to you. Be honest about the wrongs, don't try to throw in something you know was your own fault. Anoint the candle with a good dose of Banishing Oil and fix it in a candle holder. Set it up in front of the mirror and light. As the candle burns, build power through this chant:

> *Let harm return to sender,*
> *Let pain return to source,*
> *Know that you have done me wrong,*
> *Be filled now with remorse.*

Peak the energy, let it go, and leave the candle to burn out in front of the mirror. To make this spell effective, you should have as little to do with the suspected offender as possible after the spell has been cast. If something happens to them, know that all you have done is reflected in the energy they've been sending your way.

EXORCISMS

There are times when it is necessary to exorcise a spirit from a house or piece of land. This is really best left to an experienced Witch—I've seen eager teenagers stir up trouble when they got in over their heads—but sometimes you may not have anyone there to help you.

Be aware that there are many different types of spirits and they have different reasons for being tied to this plane.

My friends Tony and Daniela, who are both experienced Witches, joined me to help a mutual acquaintance a few years ago. She had a nasty spirit running around her land. She operated a daycare at that time and several of the children had seen the ghost. They said it was an old man.

We found a plethora of entities there.

The old man was definitely a threat. His energy was mean—downright vicious. We started up the steps to where he felt centralized and were hit with a wave of panic. We ended up running back downstairs to regroup and formulate a plan. It was easy to see that the spirit was holding on to this plane out of spite and malice.

The house also held the spirit of an old woman who wandered through the daycare. If our information was correct, she had stepped in to try to protect the children from the spirit of the old man. She made it clear she would leave once he was gone.

The spirit of a little boy who had been murdered had also found his way onto the land. A number of children in the daycare had seen this ghost, who was apparently drawn to their youthful, playful energy. We needed to help him through the gateway so he could go on.

The fourth entity I can only call a "Land Deva," the soul of a very powerful Earth Spirit. It ran right through the house and was attracting other entities. Neither malignant nor benign, we knew we couldn't get rid of it. The best we could do was appease it so that the energy wouldn't be so tumultuous.

After we sorted out the entities we were dealing with, we inspected her house. She had mirrors facing doors (remember what I said in chapter seven about that?) and she never warded or protected her home, yet she worked with psychic energy. Her home life wasn't the happiest, and that added to the chaos as well.

We had her move all the portable mirrors and cover those that were fixed in place. We then began to tackle the spirits.

First we decided to help the little boy. We found him in one of the bedrooms, and together we used visualization to form a magickal pathway. We could feel him moving toward it, but he was still scared to go. We projected the image of a cute, fuzzy animal on the other side of the doorway (the gate that would lead him out of the physical realm). He ran toward the animal and slipped over to the other side. We felt him leave and knew that he would be okay.

Our next step was to tackle the land deva. I have the gift of being able to connect with plants and land spirits, and we discerned that the deva wanted a way to channel its energy. There had once been a large tree where the house stood, and when it was cut down, the deva's energy no longer had a focal point. So we constructed an altar of crystals and branches through which the deva could channel its energy and instructed our friend to leave it in place.

The third step was to exorcise the old man. This proved the most difficult task. He didn't want to go and he tried a lot of cheap tricks on us. At one point, Daniela and I turned our attention to a door with a window in it and we saw the image of a skull floating there, glaring at us.

As we continued, Tony and I were in a storeroom where a child's plastic toy lay. The eyes, which were painted on, began to move around. Then, tangible waves of hatred and anger boiled through the room. It was actually like a low-budget horror movie now that we look back on it, but being in the midst of that energy was truly terrifying.

Using a combination of incense, rattles, chants, and our combined, focused wills we drove him out and over to the other side. It is difficult to describe the process, but it's like being a psychic bully, saying, "You're going whether you like it or not."

He couldn't stand up against the three of us.

Once he was gone the old woman's spirit quietly left.

After that, we thoroughly smudged the place, asperged it, and warded it against other entities. It is my belief, however, that because of the combination of the land deva's energy and the chaotic nature of our friend's life, it won't be too long before other spirits are attracted to the place.

In another case, Tony and I went out to investigate a pond where the spirit of a murdered girl had become trapped. A group of local teenagers had tried to exorcise her on their own and had stirred up a lot of negative energy.

We went into trance to seek information and discovered that the girl's spirit had attached itself to the land and was slowly becoming part of the area, mingling with the energy of the pond. She had also managed to attach herself to the man who killed her (now in prison) and was feeding off his energy as a way of vengeance.

We told the kids who had attempted an exorcism earlier to leave well enough alone. The spirit wasn't bothering anyone and she was too entangled with the pond and the land to be separated from it. She had worked out her own form of karmic retribution and we weren't about to interfere.

So, you see, there are times when exorcism isn't the answer.

There are also times when you might want to allow a spirit to co-exist in your space if they aren't bothering you or causing problems. They have their own reasons for being here.

Each exorcism will require a different method of approach; you might find that a simple acknowledgment of the spirit's presence takes care of their need to be recognized.

Do not automatically assume that a spirit is unwilling to leave; they may simply not know how to leave this plane. That commonly happens with victims of violent crime who were suddenly cut from life. To help these spirits find their way out, raise energy and visualize a line of light leading to the gateway that divides physical reality from the spirit world. Tell them to go along that light, to use it as a guide.

If the spirit is unwilling, you might find that a thorough smudging works. Sometimes just cleansing the house (as in chapter seven) and warding it can clear out unwanted visitors.

You might have to resort to more drastic methods—using rattles, oils, chants, and the force of your will to drive out a spirit. This is difficult, and is usually more effective with a group of people focused on the exorcism rather than just one.

Last but not least, if you simply can't budge an entity and it's causing real problems, then you have several options.

- You can move to another place.

- The entity might have been such a strong Christian that only a Christian clergy member can convince it to leave. Or perhaps they were Native American or Buddhist, and will only respond to that specific type of energy.

- You can research the house's history to see if anything violent happened on the premises. I've heard about houses where slaves were killed and their deaths left unacknowledged. In the process of researching the house, the owners came across hidden rooms where the slaves had been chained, and bones that needed to be put to rest. Also, remember that something might have happened on the land prior to the building of the house (are you on an old graveyard? Was there a fire that burned down a house and all its occupants?). You never know until you look into it.

- You can live with the entity and hope for the best. Ghosts are usually benign, though there have been a few cases where people have been physically hurt by astral entities. Most frequently, they can wreck your sleep.

- Remember, sometimes a creaky house is just old, sometimes that whistle you hear is the wind, and sometimes the chill on your back is telling you to turn up the heat.

HEALTH AND HEALING

If you break your leg, if you are having chest pains, if your teeth hurt, go to the doctor. Healing magick is best used after medical treatment, to help speed along recovery. It can also benefit emotional trauma, although again, go to a counselor first if you need one before seeking your answers from magick.

GENERAL WELL-BEING SPELL

When you have been sick, but are beginning to feel better, this is a good spell to cast. It is energizing and will leave you feeling healthier than when you began. For periodic maintenance, you may want to use the spell twice a year. See page 115 for oil-making guidelines.

You will need:

1 white or pink image candle
   powdered rose petals
   push-pin thumbtack
   Star Oil (page 208)

Carve your name, or that of the person for whom you are casting the spell, onto the candle. Carve the runes Sigel, Flame, and Caduceus in the wax.

Anoint the candle with the oil and sprinkle with powdered rose petals.

Raise energy and focus on general well-being as you charge the candle.

Burn under the Waxing Moon, chanting:

Earth, Air, Fire, Water
Peace, Health, Joy, Laughter.

Peak the energy and let it fly out to the universe. Let the candle burn completely.

Star Oil

¼ ounce almond oil
10 drops lemon oil
7 drops jasmine oil
7 drops rosemary oil

17 drops chamomile oil
5 drops sandalwood oil
flower: jasmine
gem: clear quartz

EMOTIONAL PEACE SPELL

When you are feeling overwhelmed emotionally, this is a good spell to help pick you up. It is particularly effective following emotional upheavals.

You will need:

Clear Thought Oil (see page 115 for mixing instructions).

Clear Thought Oil

¼ ounce almond oil
10 drops cajupet oil
10 drops lemon oil
12 drops lavender oil

15 drops siberian fir oil
flower: cedar
gem: clear quartz

Sometime between the Waning Moon and New Moon anoint yourself with the oil and go outside. Sit where you can see the moonlight—near a small stream or pond would be ideal. You should also be in a place where you can scream without causing a fuss. If you have to sit in your car, that's okay.

Let all the thoughts and worries that have been haunting you bubble up to the surface. Let them churn and roll until they feel like they're drowning you.

Raise your arms to the sky and open your mouth. Begin to let out the sound of the worry, the sound of the troubles. It can be a scream or a moan or a low groan, but let it fully pour out of your body.

When it feels like you've let go of the stress, anoint yourself again with the oil and take a short walk, focusing on the stillness of the night around you.

STRENGTH OF BEING OIL

This oil not only smells wonderful, but it helps strengthen the will to be oneself (see page 115 for mixing instructions). Wear it when you need to stand up for yourself, or when you feel like you are losing sight of your own goals and ethics.

¼ ounce almond oil
4 drops cedar oil
5 drops cypress oil
9 drops ginger oil
1 drop lemon oil
9 drops lotus oil
6 drops camphor oil

4 drops frankincense oil
9 drops siberian fir oil
4 drops lavender oil
1 drop carnation oil
5 drops jasmine oil
   flower: lavender
   gem: amethyst

Part Three

Shadow Work

13

FAERIE MAGICK AND RITUAL

The Sidhe . . . the Dark Folk . . . Sirens . . . Dryads . . . Gnomes . . . Brownies . . . Elves . . . Undines . . . Kelpie . . . Kobolds . . . Metsanhaltija . . . Menahunes . . . Naiads . . . Jenny Greenteeth . . . Black Annis . . . Faeries, all of them.

What are faeries? Some research maintains they're an offshoot of the human race that evolved in a different direction. Still others believe they are plant and nature spirits who happen, at times, to take human form. I agree with the latter.

Legends of the Little People permeate almost every culture from Native American to Celtic to Hawaiian to European to African. If these beings are nature spirits, it would account for the multitude of forms since the ecosystems of the different cultures vary so widely.

Also, when in human form, the Faeries seem to resemble the race of people with whom they share the environment. Therefore, I see them as taking human shape only when necessary. When those times occur, they would naturally mimic the humans around them.

I have seen and interacted with Faeries on several occasions (I count my unicorn sighting as one of these). Each time, I come away from the encounter feeling like I've stepped out of a dreamworld. The otherworldly nature of the creature or being shrouds the experience with a cloak of starlight and mystery. It is difficult to describe the process of how I talk to the Faerie. I speak and then listen and a message will form in my thoughts. Channeling, I suppose, though I am loath to use that word because of all the negative connotations it has acquired.

During all of my Faerie interactions I find that I haven't been fed a line of "this is how it is" but only "this is what I can tell you." None of the Faerie have ever told me they hold all the answers to the mysteries of the Faerie Kingdom. They don't claim to be omniscient. Over the years I've accumulated what at first seems like a lot of information. Yet when I lay it out, the pieces seem fractured and mysterious, like the fossils of a dinosaur.

There is an unseen, unexplored world out there. In some ways I hope it remains a mystery. Humans have dissected too many creatures and cultures that never recover from the shock.

If we continue to have brushes with the world of Faerie, fleeting glimpses of their realm, we will be richer for the experience—kissed by enchantment, so to speak. It is when we attempt to analyze every contact, to catalog every case in order to create a linear framework, that we destroy the very magick that we seek.

So how do we really know what the Faerie Kingdom is all about?

We don't. We ask for answers, and sometimes we get them. But those answers run the gamut of experience and they will differ based on who you ask.

It seems impossible to get a full view of the Faerie Kingdom from where we stand. We find a bit here and a piece there and try to fill in the blanks as best we can. Toss all the information in the ring, stir, and hope something coherent comes out.

This chapter presents my own experience with the Faeries. I am pledged to a Goddess who rules over "the thousand daughters of creation" (wood spirits known as the Metsanhaltija) so I work extensively with what I call Faerie Magick. In my studies I've done my best to integrate what I experience with what I've learned through research.

DEFINITIONS OF FAERIE MAGICK

In my work with Faerie Magick I have developed several terms and definitions. You might find that you've experienced these energies or events but have given them different names—perhaps you've experienced them but didn't know what to call them.

Faerie Magick: Magick specifically connected to the Faerie Realm, whether through invoking the Faeries, working in a Wild Place, or working with energy that feels specifically connected to the realm of Faerie.

Faerie Fire: A green light or energy that glows but does not burn, often seen in enchanted places at night during summer. When raising energy, focus on Faerie Fire and you will find the energy tingles and crackles more than usual.

Mists and Shadows: The veiled space between the physical realm and the world of Faerie. It's possible to enter this realm in a physical state, and often you will 'lose time' in this space. Shape-shifting is easier here, and when we subconsciously slide into this realm we often catch glimpses of the Faerie Folk.

Green Man: The masculine aspect of the Forest, often seen in entwined ivy, the bark on trees, or in the twisted limbs of a bush.

Crystal Grove: This is what I call the magickal space of the Faerie. I visualize this space as a grotto with lush vegetation, sparkling lights from the phosphorescence that floats in on the tides, huge dark trees with moss hanging down and overlooking it all, a Full Moon. The energy of this space can be re-created through the use of candles, crystals, finding a lovely spot in the woods or by a stream (I found two such places—one on Big Island of Hawai'i and one here in Washington State. I know there must be more.).

Wild Place: A spot in nature that has wild, untamed energies. Unkempt lots where the brambles and briars have overtaken the land tend to be where Faeries congregate. I was pixie led in one such area. I had been through it dozens of times in the daylight, and knew the path blindfolded but one night got lost and ended up in the middle of a patch of scotch-broom three times—each time returning to the beginning of the path and starting over again. I finally took the long way home. The next day I checked—nothing out of the ordinary, the trail hadn't been altered in any way by human hands. After that I avoided it at night because the energy wasn't very welcoming.

Deva: A plant, land, or faerie "oversoul" who has more knowledge and insight than the others—kind of like an elder. One who has guardianship over a territory or group of plants or faeries.

Tips on Working with the Faerie

- Faeries don't like iron. I thought this was a silly belief, until I started working with Faerie Magick. I found that I was beginning to get rid of everything I had that was cast iron—pots, pans, candle holders and the like. Then I realized that I had pledged myself to a Goddess who rules over wood sprites, and I had to laugh. What I had put down to superstition played itself out to be true in my life.

- Faeries aren't all light and fluffy. There are numerous instances in both history, legend and experience that show Faeries as chaotic. They can be mischievous or downright nasty if they feel like it.

People tend to forget that the Faerie, don't play by human rules and they don't ascribe to human ethics. The modern "cute" version of the Faerie became popular during the romantic Victorian era, just like the cherubic view of angels. Neither is grounded in fact and legend but rather in the desire to see Nature as a loving, forgiving entity.

- You might find that certain gems or stones seem to attract Faerie energy more than others. This may differ based on your own interaction with the stone. For me, peridot and moonstone are two of the strongest Faerie stones.

- Certain scents and flowers seem to attract Faeries more than others—but this could be based on which Faeries are near you. Violet, thyme, lemongrass and ylang-ylang are traditionally strong Faerie scents.

- If you work with Faerie Magick long enough, expect to occasionally find jewelry and other small objects missing. I stand in the middle of the room and yell, "Give me back my ring (keys, or whatever seems to be missing)!" The object in question usually shows up again in a couple of days, though a few years ago, one of my favorite rings disappeared for good. My ruby ring vanished one August and showed up in the Ostara altar box when I took it down the next Spring to iron the altar cloth. How my ring got from the coffee table into the box on the closet shelf I don't know—but I got the distinct feeling that it showed up again thanks to Mielikki. The Faeries also brought back an earring I had lost years before, so I suppose that makes their pilfering square in their eyes.

GREEN MAN RITUAL

This ritual works well when you have an evenly mixed group of men and women. Lively and fun, it is a good ritual to perform during the Spring.

Discuss the ritual a few days beforehand with all of the participants so everyone knows what to expect. The day before ritual each man should spend some time focusing on the Green Man aspect of nature (see chapter sixteen and the bibliography for more information).

For this ritual you will need:

> as many different colored strings of embroidery thread as there are men involved
> a basket

a space big enough to dance in
an ivy wreath
as many roses as there are people in the ritual
cakes and wine

In addition, each person should bring a small gift that can be hung around the neck of the Chosen One (a crystal, a charm bag, a tiny penny whistle, a cute key chain on a ribbon—use your imagination).

Ritualists should dress in nature colors—green, brown, yellow, black, gold, rust, tan. Altar decorations can include sprigs of ivy, green candles, a green or gold altar cloth, and herbal charms.

Four people are selected to invoke the elements during Circle.

Set up the altar and light the candles. The roses are placed by the altar. The gifts are kept by each member.

When everyone has congregated, the Priestess for the evening ties a thread around each man's wrist. Each thread should be of a different color. A matching piece of thread is put into the basket.

Everyone files into the ritual space and takes their place in circle (holding this ritual outdoors would be ideal, if possible).

The Priestess casts the circle using the Triple Goddess Chant (see page 48). The elements are invoked. Then the Priestess says:

We are here tonight to celebrate the Green Man of Spring. We call on His essence, that lush, verdant masculinity that entwines the fruit of the Goddess.

Green Man, Jack O' The Green, Lord of the Greenwood, we call upon you, Great One, Vibrant One, to come into our midst and empower our ritual with joy and life.

The Priestess holds up the basket of strings.

One man will be chosen to represent the Green Man in our ritual tonight.

Another woman, chosen before the ritual, steps up and closes her eyes. The Priestess guides her hand to the basket and says:

Lord of the Green, use the hand of this woman to choose Your representative.

The assistant reaches into the basket and lets her intuition guide her to one thread. She pulls it out and opens her eyes.

The Priestess takes the thread and, with her assistant, walks the circle, stopping at each man in turn to compare the thread with the one tied around his wrist.

When the chosen man is discovered, the Priestess holds his arm up, saying:

We have the Lord of the Green!

Everyone crowds around him. He is escorted (picked up and carried, if possible) deosil around the circle while everyone begins chanting and clapping over and over:

Green Man! Green Man! Green Man!

The Green Man should let himself drift into a trance.

After carrying him around the circle, deposit him in the center, and everyone should take their places again. The Priestess stands near the Green Man. While the Green Man lowers himself deeper into trance, the person with the strongest voice should begin this chant while clapping in rhythm. The others should then join in when signaled by the Priestess:

Green Man of Spring, welcome to our circle,
Green Man of Spring, welcome to our rites.
Green Man of Spring, welcome to our circle,
Green Man of Spring, dance with us tonight.

As the chant continues, the Green Man should grab the hands of one of the ritualists and pull them into the circle, beginning in the north. As the spirit moves him, he dances, chases, or teases them around the inside of the circle back to their place.

Continue chanting as the Green Man, working deosil, gives everyone a turn. He should take as much time as he pleases.

When everyone, including—lastly—the Priestess, has been danced around the circle, then the Priestess fades out the chant.

The Green Man picks up the vase of roses and goes back to the first person he danced with. If he is deeply in trance he might find he has messages to convey. Otherwise he should simply give each person a rose, then kiss their head and say,

Blessings from the Lord of the Greenwood.

Each should then thank him and give him their present, tucking it around his neck.

Once this is done the Priestess joins him in the center and says:

Lord of the Green, thank You for joining us this night. Be with us in our hearts, be with us in the forests that stand guard around us. Help us protect those endangered woods and the creatures that make their homes there. Go if You must, stay if You will, but please leave this man's body for now. Thank you, and Blesséd Be.

The Green Man should take a few moments to come out of trance. During this time, cakes and wine can be passed (see chapter two) and quiet conversation about experiences during the ritual is appropriate. Then devoke the elements and open the circle.

The Green Man's representative gets to keep his presents—he might want to leave an offering to the Green Man out in the woods in the next few days.

If you really want to add to the energy of the ritual, a week or two in advance get everyone together to build a giant Green Man. Bring grape vines and sticks for the framework, cedar and fir boughs to cover the body, and daffodils make fantastic eyes. The one we built stood well over seven feet tall. Later on, at Summer Solstice or Lughnasadh, you can burn him in a bonfire.

When I led this ritual with a group of friends several years ago the man chosen as Green Man was obviously possessed. His energy, usually mild and passive, became wild, fool-like and wonderful. When he danced me around the circle he grabbed my hands and we spun around and around as we circled the space—over the years since then I've had dreams of dancing like that out in the fields, only in my dreams I was dancing with the true Lord of the Forest.

He grabbed me by the shoulders when we reached my space in circle again and as I stared into his eyes, I could see that my friend wasn't there. A wild, feral spirit gazed back at me. He whispered, "Who are you?"

I wish I had not been so startled, so surprised. I could only answer, "I'm me."

He asked again and I was speechless. I think, if I could replay that night, I would be able to find out just what he was trying to ask—because he didn't want my name; there was some other link there that he wanted me to acknowledge. Alas, sometimes we are unprepared and we lose what could be incredible opportunities.

CRYSTAL GROVE RITUAL

This is another good ritual for a larger group. You will need four participants to lead the ritual: one to represent the Forest Lord, one to represent the Lady of the Shore, one to represent the Ocean Mother, and the fourth to lead the other members of the ritual into the circle and give them instructions (this person is referred to here as the Priestess).

You will need:

3 tables
3 altar cloths (one forest green, one white or gold, one blue)
    tokens (i.e., dimes or blue hearts) for each participant

Forest decorations for the forest altar should include a dish of pine cones (enough so each member of the ritual can have one). A long, crystal dish filled with clean sand into which you have poured gold glitter works for the beach altar. Seashells and a bowl of Full Moon Water should be used on the ocean altar.

Place the tables in a triangular pattern in the middle of the circle. Those representing the three Elementals should set up their altars and take a few minutes to attune themselves to the energy. Forest Lord, Lady Shore, and Ocean Mother should be in position behind each table, dressed and made up to represent the element they are guarding.

The Priestess leads the other members of the ritual into circle. They take their places and the circle is cast.

Only three elements are invoked: Forest (Earth), Shore (Wind and Sun), and Ocean (Water). The Forest Lord, Lady Shore, and Ocean Mother should invoke their own elements.

The Priestess stands in the center and says:

We gather tonight to experience the Crystal Grove. We will travel through the Forest where we whisper our desires, down to the Shore where we set our wishes free, then into the Ocean where we are cleansed and renewed.

The members of the circle are instructed to think about one of their deepest desires. One by one they are to go to the forest altar and whisper their desire to the Forest Lord. There he offers them a pine cone to represent their wish embodied.

Then, paying respects to the forest, they travel to the shore altar where they are greeted by the Lady of the Sands. She bids them to plant their desire (i.e., the pinecone) deep in the sand where it will be safe and nurtured. They do, then leave, traveling to the ocean altar where Ocean Mother greets them.

Ocean Mother bids them to cleanse their hands in the water of life (the bowl of water). After this, she blesses them and offers them a token of their journey.

When finished, each person resumes their place in circle and silently meditates on their experience. When everyone has made the rounds, clasp hands as the Priestess leads all participants in this chant:

May you weave by Starlight
May you glow in the golden Sun
Flow with the waters, Grow in the Forest,
Ancient Ever-Young.

The Priestess guides the Cone of Power and releases it as it peaks. Everyone ground and center. Follow with cakes and wine, then devoke the circle to end the ritual. The sand and pine cones should be scattered in the forest.

MAGICK OILS

Consult page 115 for instructions for mixing these oil blends.

Faerie Magick Oil
This oil is very useful for working with Faerie Magick. Wear it on Midsummer's Eve to increase chances of Faerie encounters.

¼ ounce almond oil
7 drops lemon oil
10 drops gardenia oil
7 drops jasmine oil
11 drops violet oil
5 drops lavender oil
7 drops lemongrass oil
7 drops rose geranium oil
7 drops ylang-ylang oil
flowers: jasmine, violet
gems: peridot, moonstone

Gnome's Cap Oil
Useful for contacting the Faeries connected with the Earth Element (Gnomes, Dwarfs, etc.).

¼ ounce almond oil
10 drops cypress oil
5 drops lilac oil
2 drops narcissus oil
25 drops siberian fir oil
10 drops dark musk oil
flowers: cedar, fir
gem: tiger's eye

Gossamer Wings Oil
Useful for contacting the Faeries connected with the Air Element (sylphs, elves, etc.).

¼ ounce almond oil
12 drops violet oil
10 drops lemon oil
5 drops cajupet oil
20 drops lavender oil
flower: lavender
gem: clear quartz

Faerie Fire Oil

Useful for contacting the Faeries connected with the Fire Element (Will o' the Wisps, Flame Dancers, etc.).

¼ ounce almond oil
12 drops peach oil
4 drops dark Musk oil
2 drops chamomile oil
2 drops poppy oil

5 drops ylang-ylang oil
4 drops new mown hay oil
2 drops dragon's blood oil
flowers: chamomile and oat straw
gems: peridot, garnet

Siren Song Oil

Useful for contacting the Faeries connected with the Water Element (Undines, Naiads, Sirens, etc.).

¼ ounce almond oil
3 drops lemon oil
4 drops lavender oil
3 drops primrose oil

3 drops rose geranium oil
15 drops camphor oil
flowers: geraniums, roses
gems: iolite, amethyst

Crystal Grove Oil

This is a wonderful oil with which to anoint your magickal tools.

¼ ounce olive oil
10 drops anise oil
20 drops violet oil
15 drops jasmine oil

3 drops ylang-ylang oil
10 drops honeysuckle oil
flower: oat straw
gem: peridot

Mists and Shadows Oil

I use this oil when I want to work in the space between the Faerie Kingdom and our realm.

¼ ounce olive oil
4 drops heather oil
3 drops lemon oil
4 drops lilac oil
5 drops rose oil
10 drops Faerie
Magick oil (page 223)

10 drops green forest oil
5 drops siberian fir oil
5 drops honeysuckle oil
2 drops dark musk oil
flowers: oat straw, oakmoss
gems: peridot, amethyst

14

ANIMAL MAGICK AND SHAPE-SHIFTING

The concept of being linked to a totem animal spirit has evolved in most aboriginal cultures inhabiting our planet. A totem animal is an animal form or spirit you feel connected to. Your totem is not necessarily going to be your favorite animal, nor is it necessarily going to be one living in your area.

My three totems are the black panther (occasionally it grows spots and becomes a leopard), the green boa and the peacock. While I have seen peacocks I have never actually encountered a black panther or green boa running through my back yard, nor is it likely to happen.

DISCOVERING YOUR TOTEM ANIMAL

To discover your totem animals, you should start paying attention to your dreams, signs and pictures, your daydreams, visions, or other sources. Before I discovered that the black panther was one of my totems, it cropped up in pictures and nature shows everywhere I looked for a three or four-month period.

Don't rely on other people to tell you what your totems are—I believe that only the seeker can find the answer. Psychic friends and acquaintances may see glimpses of your totems in your aura. If they do, they should tell you without insisting that the animal is your totem.

WHAT DOES MY TOTEM ANIMAL MEAN?

There are several fine books that focus solely on this subject. I direct you to one of those for your answers, as it is a topic too wide to cover within this book (see Bibliography). I would also like to suggest that one of the best ways to interpret the animal is to observe it. Watch nature shows, visit zoos and animal farms, spend quiet time just watching. You will learn what nature wants you to know.

DO MY TOTEM ANIMALS EVER CHANGE?

For some people, yes. For some, no. It depends on whether you need to learn something from the animal, in which case, after the lesson is learned the animal spirit might leave, or whether you have a soul connection with the animal, in which case the animal spirit will probably stay.

WHAT CAN I DO TO STRENGTHEN MY TOTEM?

There are several ways to strengthen the connection between you and your totem animal. A friend gave me a beautiful wax candle of a black panther that sits on my altar and I cut the wick off so it can't be burned. You can buy a statue and focus your energy on it, asking the totem animal to use it as a reference point.

You can make a collage (see chapter eight) using pictures of your totem and its habitat, or you can paint pictures of your totem. There are even services that will morph two photographs together—you could morph a picture of your totem with a picture of your face and create an otherworldly photo. I plan to do this using my black panther totem.

You can also talk to your totem, asking it to remain at your side and to make itself known.

Totem Animal Protection Spell

A good spell for protection lies in summoning the spirit of your totem animal and 'fixing' it to an object in the room so that it can protect you. This can also work with animal spirits that aren't your totems.

When I left my first marriage I was frightened of being alone—it had been a long time since I had lived by myself. Even though I was glad to be out of the relationship, I admit I was scared.

I slept with a big, white teddy bear named Frosty. One night I noticed some psychic activity going on in the living room, near the sliding glass doors. I dropped into trance and "peeked."

There was a polar bear in my living room!

It paced back and forth from the front door to the sliding glass doors and radiated protective energy. I realized that Frosty had become so important to me (I couldn't sleep without him on the bed) that I had attracted a wandering animal spirit to the apartment and it had become "fixed" to the stuffed bear. I had a guardian. As I grew used to being alone and less frightened the polar bear vanished, leaving Frosty, once again, just Frosty.

You can summon up an animal spirit to guard you in this way:

- Choose what form you would like your guardian to take. For this spell, you can even choose a dragon if you like. The spirit will assume the animal form.

- Buy a statue, stuffed animal, or large poster of your chosen animal.

- Choose a place in your home where you can leave the statue without disturbing it.

- Leave gifts for it. Dragons like jewelry and money (and never take the jewelry or money away. If you give something to a dragon, it's gone!); big cats would probably like milk or steak (after a day or so, place outside in an area reserved for offerings); my polar bear liked it when I gave Frosty a good tummy scratch.

- Speak to it often. Talk to it—guardians get lonely. Thank it for guarding your space.

- If you decide you don't want the guardian anymore, formally release it and show your gratitude for what it has done for you.

INVOKING THE GUARDIAN SPIRIT

To invoke the guardian spirit, you will need:

> your athame
> the statue, poster, or other object
> a gift for the spirit
> a clear mind
> frankincense incense
> Guardian Oil (page 192 for recipe, 115 for method)

Light the incense and sit quietly, focusing on what you are intending to do. Cast a circle and invoke the elements. Invoke a deity aligned with the animal you've chosen. Examples include Artemis for dogs and bears, Bast for cats, Mielikki for stags and bears, Merlin or Morgana for dragons, Mab or Titania for unicorns, or Epona for horses.

Anoint the statue with the oil. Raise energy on the statue and say:

> *I invoke thee, O Spirit of the* (your chosen animal). *Send one of your representatives here, to my home, to be my guardian, to watch over and protect this space.*

> *I will feed and nurture you, I will respect and love you. I will not hold you should you choose to leave.*

> *Please, come to this space, Guardian, and keep it safe against all unwelcome intruders.*

Draw an invoking pentagram over the statue. Then set the statue in place and give it the first gift. Repeat this spell, leaving the statue in place, for two more days.

Talk to the statue daily, as a friend. Ask it how things are going, and so forth. Anoint the statue with Guardian Oil on a regular basis.

Soon you should begin to notice little things that tell you the Guardian Spirit has manifested. My friends Tony and Daniela have a dragon who guards their Witchcraft shop. It ruffles papers, occasionally sets off the alarm, and when I began hanging out with them, the dragon came up and bumped my arm. I didn't know it was a dragon at the time, but I sure knew something was there!

I occasionally watch the shop for them and I can tell when he's lonely. We have some interesting discussions.

PET PROTECTION SPELL

While it is important to work carefully with your totem animals, it is also important to remember your pets. This spell will help protect your animal friends on the physical plane.

For each animal you will need:

  1 six-inch square piece of black felt
     fabric paints and brush
     a clipping of hair or stray feathers from your pet
  2 teaspoons dried cedar
  1 bay leaf
  2 teaspoons catnip (even if you have a dog)
  1 teaspoon comfrey
  ¼ teaspoon dried garlic
  1 teaspoon heather
     Protection or Guardian Oil (see page 192)
     cotton
     needle and thread

On what will be the outside of the charm bag paint your pet's name and these runes: Algiz, Koad; the Forest Rune; the Pentacle and the Goddess Rune. Let dry.

Fold the felt in half (painted side in) and sew two sides of it, leaving one open. Reverse the bag so the painted side is facing out.

Raise energy on the herbs then powder and pour into the pouch. Add the clipping of pet hair, then stuff the rest with cotton to which you have added a few drops of the oil. Finish sewing the pouch. Cast a circle, invoke the elements and the Lord and Lady.

Say:

> *O Gracious Lord and Lady, Protector of all creatures who walk upon this Earth. Guard my* (pet's species and name) *against harm and illness. Watch over him* (her) *with every step he* (she) *takes. Help me protect him* (her) *and strengthen the connection of love between us. Let this charm be blessed, to hold the energy of protection. blesséd be.*

Keep the charm bags in a safe place, perhaps on your altar, where the animal can't get to it. Renew this charm every six months.

Remember, as I said in chapter seven, the best protection for your animals is to keep them inside, to keep their vaccinations current, and to give them plenty of love, food, and clean water.

SHAPE-SHIFTING

In some shamanistic cultures the "witch" doctors, shamans, medicine men and women could shape-shift. There are two ways of doing this. One is by projecting your essence into the body of an animal while you see through their eyes—this is perhaps the easiest method.

The other method for shape-shifting is to physically change into that animal. Highly spiritual cultures still exist in which the shamans claim this is possible. I believe them. I also believe that in our culture, surrounded by the influences of a Judeo-Christian religion, many of us have been brought up believing that we are separate from nature and that we have dominion over it. This, I think, makes this kind of transformation nearly impossible for most people.

I say "nearly" because of an experience some years ago.

A friend and I were going through a period of intense spiritual experimentation. We spent almost all of our spare time in trance, sneaking into the state parks at night and running through the woods in the dark. We would jump in the car right after work, buy bread, cheese, and fruit along the way, and drive wherever Spirit led us. We would spend the night exploring, prowling the woods. We crept home between two and six A.M., just in time to get an hour or two of sleep, get up and go to work, and start the whole cycle over again.

Keep this up for any amount of time and the sleep deprivation alone is going to mess with reality. We were sliding in and out of trance, working magick with yet another group and our consumption of the "ritual" wine and "herbs" had risen to match our ecstatic attitudes.

One night we were just too exhausted to go out. We had seen the movie *The Doors* that night and were sitting at home, drained from the intensity of the film.

All of a sudden I could see a mist rising around me in the room. I was a little concerned but felt oddly distant, as if I was drifting in the mist.

My friend then mentioned that she could see a fog around me. Instead of getting worried because she could see it too, I was actually excited.

As I sat there, I could feel my face start to change. The only way I can describe it is that it felt like time was marching through my body. I underwent so many emotional swings within a few minutes that I wondered if the past months had finally caught up with me. Then it passed and the mist vanished.

My friend told me what she had seen. My face had changed, physically changed shape, sex, color—she said it was like watching the ruffling pages of a picture book.

For my part, when I looked at her through the mist, all I could see was a glowing, golden figure. No face, no hair, just the golden silhouette of a person.

For the next few days we existed in that space. We had somehow managed to tap into an energy that allowed us to experience shape-shifting, if only through the face.

When I called out my panther, the energy had me creeping around the floor, growling. No, my body didn't follow suit—I didn't have black fur on my hands and feet—but my friend could see panther there in my eyes, my mouth.

And I could see the fox, one of her totems at the time, lurking behind her snarling teeth and cunning eyes.

Then we crashed. The Dionysian period was over and we couldn't keep the intensity up. Since then I've done little work with shape-shifting, not for lack of interest, but for lack of reason.

I had a great deal to learn then about the boundaries of magick—mainly that they aren't as limiting as we would sometimes be comforted to believe.

Reality isn't solid—quantum mechanics tells us that. From the experiments of that time period, I can still look at a wall and put myself into trance deep enough where I can see the atoms dance around and the wall starts to dissolve. I've never tried to put my hand through. I think I'm afraid it might work and that I might get stuck.

TIPS FOR SHAPE-SHIFTING

So you want to try this? First you have to accept that you won't be shifting into just anything that you desire. I believe that all of those faces my friend saw were past lives of mine. My connection with them allowed the residue of those spirits, of which I am a part, to manifest on my face.

Second, panther is my totem. If turtle was my totem, that probably would have shown up. If you've got a mouse for a totem don't expect to feel the energy of a hawk flowing through you. Why did panther and not boa or peacock come through? I'm not sure, but I suspect that I'm connected on a deeper level to panther than either of the other two.

- Start slow, with something familiar, which is why one of your totems is the perfect choice. Observe your totem, get to know it thoroughly.

- You must practice going in and out of trance at will, and you must work on deepening your trance. You can achieve this through practice, through use of music, through spending an entire day in trance. This is potentially dangerous so don't trance and drive, please.

- A little alcohol—not a whole bottle—can help, especially wine blessed in Dionysus' name.

- When you are ready to try shape-shifting, sit quietly and focus on your totem. Feel its power inside of you. Will it to come forth, to manifest its nature in yourself. Be content at first if you just find yourself acting like the totem—crawling instead of walking, growling, baying to the Moon—magick is sometimes learned in baby steps.

- My meditation for Samhain in *Trancing the Witch's Wheel* is designed to lead you into your totem's energy; it might be of help.

- Remember, fear can be healthy, but if you want to experiment with shape-shifting you are going to have to suspend that fear. Feeling panther come up, snarling and hungry, claws readied, was terrifying but I had to let go of the fear to allow panther to really manifest herself.

- Dancing your totems to music can help. Each member of the group goes into trance and calls up their totem, then spends the evening 'dancing' the energy. However—remember with whom you are working. I was dancing my boa one night while a friend was dancing her eagle and she was swooping toward me—eagles eat snakes. I happened to be dancing with my dagger (to represent fangs) and almost sliced her because I reacted in self-defense. This went on through the evening. After that, I've been careful to dance totems with people whose totems aren't contradictory to mine.

- If you do manage to get some shape-shifting done, I congratulate you. It is difficult and sometimes, I think, too dangerous for us to do. We are not raised in a shamanistic culture and we don't necessarily have the wisdom to handle this power. Then again, if we don't experiment, we will never know our own limitations.

SHAPE-SHIFTING OILS

This pair of oils are particularly effective in shape-shifting, trance-work and other meditative work. For instructions for mixing oils, consult page 115.

DREAMCHASER OIL

This oil is conducive to work done between realms—trance work, dream work, journey work, shape-shifting and totem animal work. It is also good to use before you go to sleep.

¼ ounce olive oil
7 drops lemon oil
13 drops violet oil
13 drops lavender
    or lilac oil

7 drops lemongrass oil
10 drops sandalwood oil
    or rosewood oil
    flowers: mugwort, valerian
    gem: clear quartz

BAST DANCE OIL

This oil is conducive to all dance work, to working with felines in any way, shape or form, and for Egyptian Magick.

¼ ounce almond oil
16 drops orange oil
10 drops earth oil
4 drops violet oil
2 drops jasmine oil

4 drops new mown hay oil
2 drops ylang-ylang oil
3 drops ginger oil
    flower: jasmine
    gems: garnet, ruby

15

Drawing Down the Moon: Goddess Rituals

The concept of magick is as old as the human race itself. Our ancestors were closely connected to the physical environment around them—they had to be or they died. Life depended on the ability to read the weather, to find water, food, and shelter. To this end, our ancestors developed a deep connection with nature, learning over eons to interact with the elemental forces that shaped their world and, ultimately, their lives.

The wind, rain, sun, and moon, while not understood in scientific terms, were viewed on a primal level and the energies behind these forces were revered. They could spell the growth and the decline of human life. Earth was worshiped as a Goddess, the feminine force from which sprang forth the trees, the ground, food and animals—just as life emerged from women's wombs. The Earth became the Mother, to be appeased in order for humans to prosper.

Our ancestors also began to understand that they could use the power behind these forces to affect everyday life. They could harness the power of the winds, they could summon the power of the fire into themselves and use that energy for other things.

Over the millennia as human culture grew and flourished, names were designated for these forces. Entities connected to the elements were discovered or made themselves known. It is impossible to say how magick developed during prehistory, but develop it did.

As basic survival became less of a priority, humankind began to look inward, and began to develop spirituality. Gods were discovered and named. Religion and magick entwined.

MAGICK AND THE
EARTH AND MOON GODDESSES

These primitive societies began to watch the cycles of the moon, the seasons of the year, and the cycles of women. They noticed a connection. At first men existed outside of this cycle. They weren't connected with fertility for there was no obvious link between the sex act and birth nine months later.

Women gave birth, however. They were fertile. The land gave birth. It was fertile. The moon affected the tides every month; it also affected women's menstrual cycles each month.

The Earth Goddess represented fertility; the Earth Mother maintained the eternal rhythmic balance of the food chain and was seen as both beneficent, when She provided for Her children, and merciless, when the land lay barren, when the harsh winter snows swept down on the people.

Original images of the Earth Goddess portray her as huge, rotund, with round belly and breasts and strong, thick thighs. At that time and for many centuries to come, being fat meant you were well-fed and would not starve. It was a sign of wealth and health and fertility. Thinness was often equated with a barren womb. And of course, the bulging belly of a pregnant woman meant new life was coming.

Worship of the Earth Goddess continued. Later as man's role in procreation was established, the Hunter God also became a fertility symbol, though as Progenitor rather than Creatrix as the Goddess was seen. Still later, after the patriarchy established itself, the king of the land underwent a ritual marriage to the Earth Mother via the hieros gamos.

The ritual of the sacred marriage varied depending on the culture but the essence remained the same: the King, to be officially proclaimed of royal lineage and acceptable to the land, underwent ritual sex with a Priestess of the Goddess, often after an exhaustive set of physical tests and trials. Coronation rites today hearken back to that connection with the Goddess, in this form known as the Goddess of Sovereignty. According to Proinsias MacCana, in *Celtic Mythology* (p. 95),

> The criterion of a rightful King is that the land should be prosperous and inviolate under his rule—and this can be achieved only if he is accepted as her legitimate spouse by the goddess who personifies his kingdom.

So the Goddess promised fertility. Women prayed to her when they wanted to get pregnant, men prayed to her for luck with their hunting (until the Hunter God became more deeply established); rituals and charms were created to call Her attention . . . magick connected to the Gods was born.

The Goddess was also associated with the moon. Since the night is ruled by the moon, it made sense to our ancestors that anything associated with the night also was connected to the Goddess: dreams, intuition, visions, passion, and to some extent the wild, feral side of nature (if you've ever been in the forest at night, you know what I'm talking about).

The New Moon was also seen as a powerful time: the time of the blood-flow (rather than the Full Moon which was associated with ovulation).

The word *sabbatu* is derived from ancient Assyrian rites observing the New Moon, the seventh, fourteenth, and twenty-first days of the cycle, corresponding to the Goddess' menstrual cycle. Both the Christian and Jewish terms *Sabbath* and the pagan *sabbat* find their origins in sabbatu.

Magick connected with the moon, then, was directed towards the Goddess, and many cultures viewed menstruation as a magickal, powerful (and for men—fearful) time when vision-quests were possible.

MAGICK AND THE DARK MOTHER

If She rules over life, She also rules over death. In Judeo-Christian philosophy and patriarchal thinking, the concept of polarity has degenerated into a state of conflicts rather than a state of complements. The internal polarity of the Goddess is intrinsic to the cycles of nature. These polarities are vast, yet each are an important link in Her make-up.

We can condense these polarities to two concepts: life and death.

In the pagan philosophy, death is not evil. Only when you get into more modern religions do death and evil become synonymous. Most Pagans and Witches accept that human existence is a great chain of life and everything must be sacrificed to make way for new growth when the time comes. From the void comes life into the womb. From destruction comes creation.

The Dark Goddess has been feared by patriarchal institutions for many thousands of years. She represents the female power of destruction and women's anger. She is the caring cloak of death, the rest-stop for the weary. She is the revenge of the ravished, the destroyer of rapist and abuser. She is the void from where we all began and the void where we return. She will destroy those who abuse Her (the land itself) and She protects women and children. To my thinking, she protects men too—men who are at risk, men who try to do right by their children, their loved ones, and the Earth.

The Dark Goddess is Nature's cleansing process. While this can seem ruthless from a human point of view, it is necessary and vital in terms of planetary survival.

Magick directed towards the Dark Goddess is the magick of binding, the magick of cleansing and purification, the magick of cutting away old growth without mercy. It is also the magick of protecting the abused by exposing the abusers.

THE TRIPLE GODDESS

The Triple Goddess phenomenon is a worldwide archetype, associated with three phases of women's lives. She is Maiden, Mother, and Crone. It is speculated that from this triplicity, the trinity of Christianity (Father, Son, and Holy Ghost) developed.

The Maiden is youthful energy, unbridled curiosity. She is the Seeker, the young woman who still plays with dolls but is beginning to notice boys (or other young women, as the case may be). The Maiden is footloose and fancy-free. She is adventure personified; she runs through the woods without fear and can easily defend herself if need be.

The Maiden is that part of our lives symbolizing new beginnings, springtime, laughter, and learning lessons—sometimes the hard way. The Maiden is virginal. That is, she owns herself and owes responsibility to no one else. If she takes a lover she does not wed him, she does not commit to him. She exists for herself and for the experience of life. Traditionally, the color for the Maiden is white.

The Mother has come into her own. She may or may not have children, but either way she is a Creatrix. She is whole and ripe, sensuous and full-bodied. She has dedicated herself to a path, be it child-rearing or artistry or corporate ladder-climbing, and she gives her all to this work. At this point she may be ready to take a mate— to commit to a relationship and therefore there will always be some compromise in the Mother's life. Even if she remains single and unattached, in her work she must find some grounds of cooperation with her other coworkers.

The Mother embodies passion and devotion, she is protective of her offspring and creative endeavors, she has earned the right to her position and defends it from all attackers. The traditional color of the Mother is red.

The Crone is wisdom and power. She embodies compassion but seldom mercy; she is still passionate but able to detach herself from situations in order to look at them more critically. The Crone is still sexual, but she need not fear pregnancy so her sexuality is purely for her pleasure. She has fully established her position in life and now can exist without fear of being dethroned, for though others may sit near her, none may have her place.

The Crone embodies the face of the Dark Mother for she is closer to death and through her merciless compassion, may judge and send others into the void. She is Spider Woman, weaving the threads of life . . . she is also the one who cuts the thread binding us to life. The Crone's traditional color is black.

The Triple Goddess is a mirror of every woman's life; she is the Goddess as a whole, yet each part exists independently. Magick worked under the Triple Goddess usually is focused towards one of the three aspects.

GODDESS RITUAL AND DRAWING DOWN THE MOON

In the Craft every woman is considered the face of the Goddess. The ritual of Drawing Down the Moon invokes the Goddess to enter the body of a Priestess during ritual. In many traditions, the Priestess is expected to memorize a passage known as *The Charge of the Goddess*. During the Drawing Down ritual she recites this charge.

Frankly, I don't understand this line of thinking. If you are truly possessed by the Goddess surely She's going to have Her own agenda and Her own thoughts. I've never bothered to memorize *The Charge* (though it is a beautiful work) and neither have my friends.

The times we've performed Drawing Downs, no matter which Goddess we have invoked, She's come through quite clear and has spoken Her piece.

There are several ways to Draw Down the Goddess. The one we have found to be most effective goes thus:

The Priestess selected to be the vessel should, if she can, fast for a day or so before the ritual is held. If she cannot fast she should eat light, protein-sparing meals centered on fruits and bread.

The day of the ritual, she should take a ritual bath.

The night of the ritual the Priest who will do the invoking should sit with the Priestess for a while, both meditating in silence.

When all members of the ritual are present, cast the circle and invoke the elements.

Then the Priestess stands in the center of the circle, raising her arms out, palms towards the ceiling. The Priest kneels in front of her. He kisses her feet and says:

Blessed are thy feet, which walk the paths of the Goddess.

He kisses her knees and says:

Blessed are thy knees, which kneel at the altar.

He kisses her womb and says:

Blessed is thy womb, from which springs life.

He kisses her heart and says:

Blessed is thy heart, in which beats the rhythm of the Goddess.

He kisses her lips and says:

Blessed are thy lips, which speak the words of the Goddess.

Then he will stand back and begin the invocation to whichever Goddess they are invoking that night.

As the energy of the Goddess descends into the Priestess she should not fight it but give over and let the Goddess settle into her body. She might totally blank out, leaving a shell through which the Goddess will work. Or she may be conscious of what's going on but from a distance, as if she were watching everything through a filtered lens.

Words will come if the Goddess truly decides to enter her body. If no words come, then perhaps it is not the right moment for the Goddess to speak. The Priestess should give these messages as she is directed.

The Priest should monitor the Priestess, watching for signs of fatigue. It is exhausting to go through a Drawing Down and the body cannot handle the energy of the Gods for too long. If the Goddess shows no sign of leaving, but the Priestess looks like she needs to let go, the Priest should respectfully remind the Goddess that mortals strain easily and he should ask Her to release the Priestess.

When it is time to bid farewell to the Goddess the Priest should, as he invoked the Goddess, devoke Her with a beautiful, respectful devocation.

As the Goddess slips out of the Priestess, one or two members of the circle should stand near in case the Priestess faints or needs help to sit down.

A woman who has had the Goddess drawn into her will be permanently changed. She will always, somewhere inside, remember the feeling of having the Goddess enter her.

Visible changes are often noticed during a Drawing Down. The Priestess may appear taller, her eyes may change color or her voice may change. Remember, after the formal ritual the Priestess should be treated gently for the rest of the night; she has just undergone both a great honor and a great strain. Bring her food and a blanket—after a Drawing Down the room can seem very cold, and respect her space if she doesn't feel like talking.

In turn, the Priestess should never abuse this power; she should remember that while not all women are good channels for the Gods, all women do mirror the face of the Goddess. Just because the Goddess has spoken through her, it doesn't set her above the rest of the human race.

INVOCATIONS TO THE GODDESSES

On the following pages, several invocations you can use during Goddess rituals are presented, along with tips on when to perform them. With each invocation I include an appropriate devocation (farewell) and an oil specifically made to enhance the energy of the ritual. Anoint your forehead, wrists and heart with it. Recipes for the oils follow each devocation, instructions for making oil blends appear on page 115.

MOON MOTHER

Use this invocation during rituals for which you choose to invoke the power of the Full Moon.

Invocation

Moon Mother, hear me. You are at your zenith, full in power tonight. We call you to shine down on us, bring your radiance into our lives, into this ritual and lend it strength and the force of your will. Beautiful silver orb, Moon Mother, guard the ebb and flow of our days and cast your light to guide our journeys in the velvet night. So mote it be.

Devocation

Moon Mother, you have joined us in ritual, we now invoke your spirit into our feast, that as we eat, we eat of your will. Enter our souls as we drum out your heartbeat, fill our bodies as we dance the spirals of creation. Life and Love await us. Lead us to their joy. So mote it be.

Moon Mother Oil

¼ ounce almond oil
15 drops lemon oil
7 drops citronella oil
6 drops jasmine oil

7 drops lavender oil
flower: jasmine
gem: moonstone

PELE

Use this invocation when working with the Hawaiian Goddess Pele. Her sacred berries are the o'helo berries. If you cannot obtain these (they grow in Hawai'i), cranberries make an acceptable substitute. Always offer them to Her first, then eat some yourself.

Invocation

Aloha Pele! I call You from across the miles! Hear me, E Pele! Madame Pele, Mistress of Volcanoes and Fire. Pele-honua-mea! Woman of the Sacred Earth! Come to me from across the mighty ocean. I have Your sacred (o'helo) berries. First I offer some to You, then some I also eat. Pele, be with us. Aloha.

Devocation

Pele, You have been with us in circle. We are grateful for Your presence and bid you Mahalo. You have shared Your mana with us and we will remember. Return to Kilauea if You must and think of us. Again, Mahalo and Aloha.

Tropical Fire Oil

This is a complex oil to make, but the result will sweep you away into the tropics.

¼ ounce almond oil
1 drop lavender oil
5 drops nutmeg oil
4 drops oakmoss oil
3 drops thyme oil
3 drops violet oil
4 drops narcissus oil
7 drops jasmine oil

9 drops dragon's blood oil
10 drops new mown hay oil
5 drops lemongrass oil
16 drops ylang-ylang oil
4 drops primrose oil
   flower: jasmine
   gems: garnet, olivine or
      carnelian

Isis

Isis is the loving, eternal Mother, the Egyptian Great Goddess. She is the comforter and nurturer. Turn to Her when you need a shoulder to cry on, when you need help and you don't know where else to look.

Mighty Isis, Mother of Civilization, I call out to you. Come to me this night, Queen of the Desert, enthroned among the palms and the date trees. Hear my sorrows and let me lean on Your shoulder. Share my burdens for I am weary and need to rest. Help me Great Mother, for You are the champion of the weak and the young. Be with me in ritual and wash away my tears with Your glorious light.

Devocation

Great Isis, Queen of the Night, I thank You for Your aid. You are comfort and joy, and I ask that, as You leave my circle, You still watch over me and protect me throughout the coming days. Blesséd be, Great Mother.

Isis Oil

¼ ounce olive oil
21 drops lotus oil
14 drops cypress oil
14 drops frankincense oil

21 drops rose geranium oil
flower: roses
gem: amethyst

ARTEMIS

Artemis is the Grecian Huntress, Mistress of the Bear and the Dog. The word 'bitch' comes from Her, and was originally a positive term ("son of a bitch" literally meant "son of the Goddess"). Artemis rituals are useful when you need the inner strength to enter new realms.

Invocation

Artemis, Queen of the Night, Lady of the Hunt, I call upon You to come with Your bear and stag and lead me into new directions. Give me the strength and courage to forge ahead. Help me run the path lightly, that I may pass without a trace, known only to those I choose. Be with me, Moon Lady, and teach me to rely on myself. Blessèd be.

Devocation

Huntress, I have raced the skies with you. Now I bid You farewell. May You traipse the woods forever more, protecting child and animal, guarding against assault. I ask that Your strength remain in my heart. Blessèd be.

Artemis Oil

¼ ounce olive oil
10 drops lemon oil
10 drops rose oil
6 drops violet oil
3 drops narcissus oil

10 drops ylang-ylang oil
3 drops carnation oil
flower: carnation
gem: moonstone

DARK MOTHER

Over the years, a number of women have found their way to my doorstep. They had either been raped themselves or their children had been victims of sexual abuse. Some were having trouble with the court system—there was either no physical evidence of the assault, or the abuser had a better lawyer than they did—the list of reasons people get away with these grotesque crimes goes on and on.

I developed a ritual to help the situations. I think of it as "karmic facilitation"—someone has to be a catalyst for karma, and I'm willing to take that role when need be.

I have also used this invocation and ritual to speed my own recovery from rape and assault and again when the women in Bosnia were being systematically raped. It was the only way I could help them.

Be aware that this is a very powerful ritual and if I had children I might not perform it—unless they themselves had been victimized. Those who are weak, frightened or hesitant should not work with the Dark Goddess—She is a terrible, awesome force and can exact a price.

I always cast a circle for these rituals—I don't want the energy or power leaking out to the rest of the house. Then, light one or more black candles and anoint yourself with Dark Huntress Oil.

Invocation

I call on you, the Dark Mothers of the Night!

Hear me and come to my side. You who are Hecate, Crone of Magick; you who are Persephone, raped and despoiled; you who are Kali-Ma, the Mother of Destruction . . . hear me. Mielikki, Dark Huntress who prowls through the treetops with poisoned arrows, come to me. Cerridwen, Sow-Mother and Reaper of the Dead, I call to thee.

There has been an act of violation that cries out for your attention. (Name of Victim) *has been* (raped, etc.) *by one who escapes justice. Dark Mothers, I ask that You turn Your eyes to this abuser and bring him* (her) *to justice. Let him* (her) *not hide from your eyes, let him* (her) *be exposed for all to see. Let the perpetrator of this atrocity be known to all.*

Then I ask, Dark Mothers, that You take him (her) *into Your realm and show no mercy, as no mercy was shown to the victim. Persephone, you have undergone this pain. I ask that you sweep* (Name of Victim) *into your arms and help her* (him) *live through it, give them strength to go on and the inner will to overcome the pain and memories.*

Dark Mothers, should you find this case worthy, I ask that You act, according to Your own wills. So Mote It Be!

The times I have used this have included these results: the courts reversed their decision in one case and refused the abusive father unsupervised visits with his daughter; in another, there was no physical evidence of the abuse during the first medical exam but during a second one, physical evidence was found to give proof to the allegations.

In still another, during the ritual I was hit with the certain knowledge that the woman who had asked for my help was lying—trying to get back at her husband. The Dark Mothers let me know that they weren't needed to protect the child, she was okay.

As I said, this is a powerful ritual and can be draining to do. I only perform this when absolutely necessary, but I am so glad that I'm able to help when I can.

Dark Huntress Oil

¼ ounce olive oil
7 drops jasmine oil
2 drops lemon oil
7 drops sandalwood oil
7 drops rosewood oil

10 drops dark musk oil
7 drops ylang-ylang oil
7 drops honeysuckle oil
   flower: wormwood
   gem: garnet

BRIGHID

Brighid (pronounced *breed*) is the Celtic Goddess of fire, poetry, smithery and healing. She is one of the many Goddesses the Christians demoted; some became demons, others, like Brighid, were given the status of Saint (St. Brigit).

Brighid's festival is commonly celebrated on February 2, also known as Imbolc.

Invocation

Brighid of the golden hair, Lady of Healing we call upon you to join our rites this night. We seek the wells of healing, that we might renew and strengthen life. We kindle the sacred fires of creation, forging our tools with your guidance. Let us tell the tales of the Gods, loosen our tongues as we sing out praises in lyric verse. Great Brighid, hear us this night and join us as we celebrate Your day.

Devocation

Sacred Lady of Flame, You have been in our hearts this night and we bid you now farewell. Remain in our lives, kindling our fires, healing our pain, inspiring our tongues. We thank You for Your attendance and wish You a joyous day. Blesséd be.

Imbolc Oil

¼ ounce almond oil
5 drops lavender oil
5 drops ginger oil
10 drops orange oil
4 drops nutmeg oil
5 drops primrose oil

5 drops frankincense oil
9 drops siberian fir oil
5 drops carnation oil
   flower: orange blossoms
   gems: garnet, ruby

MORGANA

Morgan Le Fey, or Morgana, may have been a character out of Arthurian Tradition, but She is a very real essence indeed, just as Titania cropped up in Shakespeare by name but was around in essence long before that.

Morgana is a Goddess of Faerie and magick. She is cloaked in shadows and mist and works with dragons and wondrous beasts that have, for the most part, left our dimension for other realms. In some legends Morgana is portrayed as evil, or willful—but this is primarily due to the patriarchal view that women should hold no powers beyond those of home and hearth. Morgana is a true feminist, standing up for her rights to work magick.

She is a Goddess of Witches and of wonder, a reminder of the powers of the night.

Invocation

Hail, Morgana, Queen of Fey! You who ride the winds of night and weave the magick of crystal and sword, we call Thee. Join us in our rites this night, strengthen our magick and teach us the hidden secrets of nature that wait just below the surface. Weaver, Cunning Woman, You whose lilting voice calls the Dragon, be with us and lead us through the night safely.

Devocation

Morgana, 'tis almost morning and we depart for our daily lives as You depart for Your shadowed realm. We thank You for the secrets You have shown to us, for the workings You've strengthened. We bid You farewell for now, Lady of Magick and Enchantment. Until we meet again, blesséd be.

Lady of the Lake Oil

¼ ounce almond oil
25 drops lavender oil
5 drops lilac oil
5 drops earth oil
1 drop jasmine oil

5 drops rose geranium oil
4 drops carnation oil
1 drop rosemary oil
flower: lavender
gem: amethyst

Priestess Oil

This is a good general Priestess oil for use in ritual and magick

¼ ounce olive oil
4 drops violet oil
6 drops lemon oil
1 drop lilac oil

5 drops honeysuckle oil
16 drops lavender oil
flower: lavender
gem: clear quartz

16

Drawing Down the Sun: God Rituals

Today there seems to be a similar reaction among some pagan groups towards the God as Christianity had, and still has, toward the Goddess. Though not as widespread, it does exist. Some people totally ignore the existence of the God, others prefer to refute the variety of attributes and aspects He encompasses. Still others accept His presence but won't include Him in their rituals. Then there are those of us who accept Him fully.

There are several reasons for this lack of acceptance, the most prominent being a reaction against patriarchal religion—against the monopolist view of the Christian, Jewish, and Arabic Gods, all claiming to be the only true God, and all of whom are tyrannical when They feel crossed.

Another reason finds its roots in the feminist reaction against worshiping a male deity. While I understand this to a degree I also realize that most separatists either won't or can't see that the God of Paganism refutes the male-having-power-over-female image.

Yes, some of the finite Gods are this way to be sure, but the concept of the Goddess' Consort is not. He emerges from Her, They complement rather than conflict. They are yin and yang, both necessary for the continuation of the other.

THE GREEN MAN

The image of the Green Man is found all over Europe and the United Kingdom. Known also as Jack-in-the-Green, Robin Hood, the King of May, and the Garland, he represents the irrepressible masculine life-force of nature, the masculine aspect of the Earth. He is the Vegetation God, and the Fool of the Tarot deck.

The Green Man is linked with the Earth Goddess, he is one of the oldest forms of Her consort. He is not the Hunter of nature, not the Horned God. The Horned God is more humanoid, more connected to the mortal condition. The Green Man is an intrinsic facet of nature. He is a cyclic God, for as nature burgeons and grows, so does He. As the plants wither and die, dormant for the winter, so the Green Man fades.

Images of the Green Man can be found anywhere from modern Morris dancing during which Jack-in-the-Green will emerge as an eight-foot tower of vegetation crowned with a wreath of flowers, to images found on cathedrals all over Europe. These sculptures envision a man's face made up of leaves, sprouting vines from his mouth.

THE OAK KING AND THE HOLLY KING

Another aspect of the Vegetation, or Nature, God is that of the Oak and Holly King pair. The Oak King represents the waxing year, from Yule until Litha. The Holly King rules over the waning year, from Litha until Yule. They are a duality much like the Dark Mother and Bright Mother essence of the Goddess—but again, a duality in which neither aspect can stand alone. Both are necessary phases in the natural cycle.

The Oak King represents growth, fertility, vigor, and strength. He is the erect phallus that fertilizes the Mother, he is the passion and wild joy of positive masculinity.

The Holly King represents the wisdom of age, death, and the reaping in of the harvest. He is the grandfather, the sage, the wise elder. Indeed, the image of Santa Claus originated from the Holly King.

At the two changeover points They meet in mortal combat. On Litha the Oak (or Sun) King gives way and dies, His light fading as the year wanes into the darkness ruled by the Holly King. And on Yule the new Oak (Sun) Lord is born, and His light pierces the Holly King's breast, killing Him as the Oak King once more comes into His reign.

THE HORNED GOD

The Horned God is probably the best-known aspect of the pagan God. He is Lord of the Animals, virile consort of the Goddess. He is known as the Challenger, the Hunter, the Horned One, and He is also Master of the Wild Hunt.

He stands in the forest, waiting with glowing ruby eyes and erect phallus. He is the howling of the wild wind and He dies with the corn harvest, making His way into the Underworld where He takes His place as Lord of the Dead.

He leads His Hunt across the land at night, the hounds racing forward, catching any who stand in their path. In Norse tradition, the Wild Hunt is a spectral phenomenon in which Woden (Odin) leads a band of the dead across the night sky. In Celtic tradition it is Herne, or Cernunnos, who masters the Hunt.

The Horned God is traditionally antlered, whether it be stag or goat horn. He is seen as playful and wry. One does well not to enter His forests without permission and certainly, you won't do anything to harm His woodlands.

No discussion of the Horned God's aspects would be complete without discussing the Piper. Pan is the God of shepherds, flocks, the woods and of hunting. He is also a God of fertility and music. The goat-God inspires ecstasy and passion. The fact that He is half-goat and half-man indicates the dual nature of humanity: both cerebral and carnal. Both aspects are complimentary, we do not rid ourselves of one in order to attain the other.

Pan is also a God of fear and awe—we derive the word *panic* from His name. He does not just skip around the fields all day, piping happy music. He takes what he wants and has ravished the nymphs who share the forests with him. He is the Rut Incarnate.

The horns of the God represent energy, vigor, life-force, and the phallus. Christianity co-opted the Horned God and renamed him Satan. In this way they controlled Pagans by convincing them that the God they worshiped was evil, a fallen angel, and so was born the concept of the Devil.

While I believe in demons, I simply view them as nasty astral entities who have never been human. No Pagan or Witch will believe in the Christian Devil, it simply isn't part of our religion and makes a mockery of the wonderful masculine force in nature.

THE SKY GOD

Many of the Gods in Paganism seem to be connected with the sky—with the clouds, thunder, lightning, rain, and wind.

They are usually creative and artful Gods, mastering the more intricate skills given to humanity.

Ptah is a builder of gateways and inventions; Ukko rules the wind; Zeus leads the Gods of Olympus after the overthrow of the Titans and uses His lightning bolts to drive home his displeasure; Thoth is the God of medicine and truth . . . the list goes on.

These Gods are more humanized, They concern Themselves with the actions of mortals and are often called on by the more cerebral Pagans or by those who need help in the physical and intellectual world. While They might not be connected to the forests around us, They play an important part in our daily lives and we should not disdain the Sky Gods for riding the winds instead of walking the Earth.

GOD RITUAL AND DRAWING DOWN THE SUN

Just as every woman is considered the face of the Goddess, every man in the Craft is considered to be a face of the God. The ritual of Drawing Down the Sun invokes the God to enter the body of a Priest during ritual.

I suggest that you review the procedure and comments in chapter fifteen relating to Drawing Down the Moon for guidance. Everything in the ritual of Priestess and Goddess can be applied to the Priest and the God and the invoking ceremony is the same (alter the words to fit, of course).

Invocations to the Gods

I present a list of invocations you can use during God rituals with tips on when to perform them. With each invocation I include the devocation (farewell) and an oil specifically meant to enhance the energy of the ritual. Anoint your forehead, wrists and heart with it. The recipes for each oil follow the devocations, instructions for blending the oils appear on page 115.

Horned Lord

Rituals to the Horned God are usually best performed outside in a wild, natural spot.

Invocation

From the veiled mists of the Grove, I call thee. Your antlers ride the sky, Horned One, and carry with them the legacy of Kingship. Come to my side, Lord of the Forests, bring Your strength and stability that are the mountains rising high. Bring Your joy and ecstasy, that we might know Your nature. Come to this ritual and be with us tonight.

Devocation

Horned One, Lover of the Goddess! You have consented to join us tonight and we thank You for that favor. Stay with us in our hearts, let us always feel the pull of Your wild forests even though we be in the midst of the city. Go if You must, stay if You will. Blesséd be.

Forest Lord Oil

¼ ounce almond oil
15 drops patchouli oil
13 drops cedarwood oil
13 drops dark musk oil
 7 drops lemongrass oil

 7 drops sandalwood oil
13 drops violet oil
   flower: patchouli
   gem: malachite

PAN

Pan rituals are usually fun and surrounded by music, feasting and laughter. Invoke Pan into your Beltane ritual, or any ritual involving sensuality.

Invocation

O Pan, come into our midsts, God of the Rut! You who play the Pipes and lead us into the Dance, come now and join our merriment. Come now and inspire our bodies and hearts. Pan, God of the Woodland, Shepherd of Wild Ones, travel from Arcadia to be with us now, Goat-Horned Lord!

Devocation

Goat God! We have danced and drunk and sung Your tunes. Even as You leave us, know that we honor and respect Your masculine strength and vigor. Be with us in the fields and the forest and the wild places of nature. Io Pan!

Pan Oil

¼ ounce olive oil
10 drops earth oil
 2 drops cinnamon oil
 8 drops patchouli oil
 3 drops sandalwood oil

 5 drops cedarwood oil
 2 drops dark musk oil
   flower: cedar
   gems: citrine, garnet

MERLIN

Merlin, like Morgana, is mentioned in Arthurian legend. However, the essence of Merlin goes back far before the mythology of Camelot. Merlin embodied the energy not only of a magician, but of a bard. He was, in essence, a remnant of the Druidic order. Merlin rituals, then, are nature rituals of song, story, and magick. You might want to incorporate a bardic circle into your Merlin rituals.

Invocation

Merlin, Old One, Grandfather Druid
Can You hear us across the mists of time?
We sing Your praises, spar with our rhymes.
Ancient Bard, Magick-Maker
Come into our midsts this darkened night,
We seek Your wisdom, Your inner sight.
Merlin, Magician, Oak Father,
This night will You be our guide?
Come forth from the cavern where You hide.

Devocation

To our circle have You come,
Teaching us Your ancient ways,
Of magick, wisdom, lines that ley.
Merlin, Wise One, return to the past
We honor and respect Your lessons
and ask You leave us with Your blessing.

Merlin Oil

¼ ounce olive oil
6 drops vetiver oil
5 drops pine oil
1 drop clove oil
2 drops cypress oil
   or cedarwood oil

2 drops rose geranium oil
5 drops green forest oil
5 drops oakmoss oil
   flowers: clove or cedar
   gem: tiger's eye

LUGH

Lugh, the Celtic Sun God, is a God of enlightenment, knowledge and to some extent, battle. Epitomizing summer and growth, Lugh Rituals are appropriate for expansion and creation. Lughnasadh, or Lammas (August 1) is the ritual celebration of His sacrifice. Lugh, as Lord of the Corn, dies that we might live through the long, cold winter. He is reborn on the Winter Solstice.

Invocation

Lugh the Long-Handed, Bright God who rises above us each morning and guides our path through the day, we call to thee. Ancient Sun, come to our circle and encourage our magick to grow. You who wed fair Blodewedd, shine Your love into our lives that we might see our true directions. Welcome to our rites, Great Lugh.

Devocation

Sun Lord, as You fade from our circle know that our honor and respect are Yours. We thank You for the strength and warmth of Your presence. As You leave us now, know we await Your rising with joy. Bléssed be.

Lugh Oil

¼ ounce apricot oil
9 drops lime oil
9 drops rose oil
6 drops sandalwood oil
6 drops dragon's blood oil

9 drops rose geranium oil
9 drops lavender oil
   flowers: Sunflowers, marigolds
   gems: citrine, carnelian

Magus Oil

This is a good general Priest oil for use in ritual.

¼ ounce almond oil
3 drops vetiver oil
12 drops lemon oil
7 drops orange oil

10 drops frankincense oil
10 drops sandalwood oil
   flower: frankincense resin
   gem: malachite

17

EARTH HEALING RITUALS

One of the things that most disturbs me about the Craft today (and perhaps this is not the case outside of my own region, in the Pacific Northwest) is the lack of focus given to Mother Earth and taking care of Her.

In this area of the country it seems like the major concerns among a number of the Pagans I meet include discussions on how to seduce this or that person; what black clothes and make-up to wear that will freak out mother, father, aunt, uncle, teacher, or anyone else; and "how much persecution I've been through because I'm a Pagan."

Perhaps I'm just hearing a vocal minority, perhaps I don't know many of the solitaries who are out there working to steward the planet. I hope this is the case.

It seems to me that the primary focus of an Earth-centric religion should be the care and feeding of the Earth. If you want to be a Witch just to make your parents angry or impress your friends, then you obviously don't have what it takes to make it in the Craft.

The Craft is for people who truly choose to worship the Earth, who have the common sense and wisdom to know when to use their magick and when not to use it (or who are willing to develop that wisdom and common sense). The Craft exists not because we are rebels to the Establishment, but because we are determined, willing to walk a lonely road, and because we believe in the forces of which we speak.

Pagans and Witches come in all flavors: lawyers, police officers, teachers, writers, computer analysts, housewives, artists, and yes . . . even politicians. Some of us wear black because we look good in it, not because it's a dark, mysterious color. Some of us also wear floral dresses, sweat pants, and three-piece suits.

My point is that if you choose to enter the Craft, please do so out of a true connection to the Earth, out of a desire and pull to learn Her ways and magick. Don't throw on a pentacle, a black cape and call yourself a Witch just to stir up controversy. We don't need people like that giving us a bad name.

HUMAN PENTACLE SPELL

This spell is designed for use by a group of five people. I originally designed it to protect a piece of land that was in danger of being developed. The land boasts beautiful maple trees, apple trees—two groves that are as magickal as they come. The developers are from another country and they hadn't even seen the land. They bought it, sight unseen, because the area is primed for expansion. Since we cast the spell in 1991, the lots across the street have been mowed down and the house next door is gone, but that five acres still stands. I hope it lasts far longer than I will.

To protect an area of land, divide the parcel into five sections, with each person assigned one section. The five ritualists walk the borders, each person spending several hours exploring the land and getting to know it. When time is up, gather a branch from a bush or tree in your area and head back to the meeting place, which should be in the center of the parcel of land, if possible.

Once in the center, clear a space and kindle a small fire. Be sure you have plenty of water on hand to put out the flames. Lay the branches down, taking care to keep them separate, and form a small circle near the fire.

Cast a circle and invoke the elements. Invoke the Earth Goddess and the Horned God.

The Priestess says:

We are here to protect this land, to set up a Guardian who will walk its borders and oversee the woodlands (prairie, etc.). *We ask the Lord and Lady to watch over this land, to protect it from harm and development. We ask that the trees stand tall, the Earth steady and that the waters flow freely.*

Now form the human pentacle (see illustration below).

The Priestess uses her right hand to grasp the left hand of Person three. Person three uses their right hand to grasp the left hand of Person five. Person five uses their right hand to grasp the left hand of Person two. Person two uses their right hand to grasp the left hand of Person four. Person four uses their right hand to grasp the left hand of the Priestess.

You might want to practice this part before the ritual, but it will work!

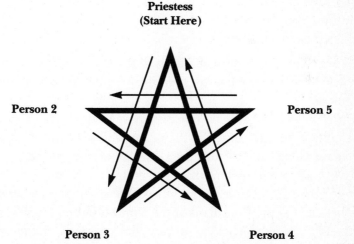

Human Pentacle Spell: Joining Hands

When all hands are clasped, the Priestess says:

We combine our wills, we combine our might
We call on the strength of day and night
Protect this land from all that harms
Magick bind with this charm.
Should any tear the land asunder
Let lightning flash, crash of thunder
Machines that rip and destroy the land
Will not the power of this charm withstand.
Developers shall overlook this place
They will always find a better space.
God and Goddess walk these trails
The spirit of Earth shall prevail!
By Flame and Earth, By Wind and Sea
As our wills combine, so mote it be!

The person with the strongest voice should begin the chant, and the Priestess will monitor the energy, building the cone of power until it peaks.

Mother of the Earth, Father of the Trees,
Protect this land, we ask of Thee!

As the chant peaks raise all hands to the sky, breaking open the pentacle to release the energy, then drop to the ground and earth the power.

Once the power has been released move to the fire and pick up your branch. In turn, describe the beauty and strength of the area which you walked and ask that the Guardian of the Land watch over it. Then cast your branch into the fire and watch it burn.

When the ritual is over do not devoke the circle or the elements. Let them rest as the Guardians of the land work their magick. This spell, of course, works best to protect your own land, but try it for endangered areas. It can only help.

ENDANGERED SPECIES RITUAL

This is a good ritual for a large group of people. A few days in advance, the entire group should meet to discuss what will happen and to practice the chants. The Priestess and her four assistants should prepare a number of paper slips (a few more than people expected for the ritual), each with the name of an endangered species written on it. You may choose to include plants and animals, or just one or the other.

You will also need:

> a large bowl or box for the paper slips
> frankincense incense
> sage smudge stick
> altar decorations
> athame
> as many 9-inch long ribbons as there are people in the ritual
>> a collage of extinct species that have died out because of human interference

Light the incense and candles if you are indoors. This is an excellent outdoor ritual, however, if you choose to work outside, use your discretion when lighting incense and candles. Everyone should gather in a circle around the Priestess and her assistants. When everyone is quiet, the Priestess says:

> *We have come together to add our protection to the Earth and Her endangered children. We gather in sorrow, we gather in hope. Each person's voice makes a difference. Together we can change the devastation, through our votes, our voices and our magick.*

Cast the circle. The four assistants call the elements. From each element, also invoke an animal spirit (good examples: Earth—wolf; Air—condor; Fire—tiger; Water—whale).

Working deosil, the first assistant carries the smudge stick around to each person. The second assistant carries the ribbons, giving one to each person except the Priestess. The third assistant carries around the collage, allowing everyone to look at it. The fourth assistant carries around the box and each participant draws a slip of paper. This will be the species they are to represent during the ritual.

The four assistants each take a ribbon and slip of paper and fade back into the circle.

The Priestess begins a low moan. She cries out:

Our children are dying, our brothers and sisters of the forest breathe their last breaths. We have stood and watched their death throes long enough. It is time to take action!

The first assistant answers:

What can we do? We are but a handful.

The Priestess then commands:

First we must speak out against the slaughter!

The participants of the ritual should now spontaneously begin shouting things like "Stop the killing," "No more slaughter," "Stop the poachers," or "Strengthen the Endangered Species Act." As the energy builds in this part, voices will layer on each other as participants shout out their ideas for protecting endangered species.

The Priestess lets this build for a while then, loud enough to be heard, shouts:

Enough! We use our tongues, but how will you act to back your words? What will you do to stop the destruction?

Since the group discussion a few days ago, each member of the ritual should have decided what they alone can do. One by one, working deosil, they should shout out their responses. These might include donating to the Audubon Society, calling governmental representatives to find out their stand on environmental issues, or volunteering at the local nature sanctuary. Participants should be aware that they will be expected to follow up on their pledges. When everyone has spoken, the Priestess asks:

What species do you stand for tonight?

One by one, deosil, each member calls out the name on their piece of paper. They say:

I stand here to protect the (animal or plant). *I send my energy to
the spirit of that species.*

The Priestess begins the chant and everyone joins in. As the chant
continues each person brings one end of their ribbon into the circle
and gives it to the Priestess. Keep hold of the other end. The circle
should look like a bicycle wheel with spokes when finished.

*We weave a web of power tonight,
A web of protection and of light.*

The Priestess begins to build the power by building the volume
of the chant. Just before it peaks she shouts:

Call out your name, you who are in danger!

Shout the name of your species as the power peaks, sending the
energy to the different groups of animals. Ground the energy by
kneeling on the Earth.

After everyone has centered themselves, serve cakes and wine
and quietly discuss the energy. Then devoke the elements and circle
and return home to follow up on the pledges made in sacred space.

NOTES ON RITUALS OF THE EARTH

There are so many problems today that it can sometimes seem overwhelming. Where do we start? What can we do? How can we combat such incredible forces?

I think we are asking the wrong questions. In fact, there is no
question. Only the truth that we must act. We must do what we can
even when it seems insignificant. Do you recycle? That makes a difference. Do you compost your leftovers? That makes a difference.
Do you pick up the beer cans on the trail when you're out walking
in the park? You're making a difference. Do you drive a fuel-efficient car? Good for you and good for the environment!

Among the most important things we can do are to vote and to
make ourselves heard. You don't like a bill in Congress? Let your
representatives know. They can't gauge how angry the public is
unless they hear from us.

We don't have a perfect system but we can use it for all we're worth. Every time I hear about some political act that makes me cringe or one that makes me happy, I call and let the politicians know. If one person does it, it might not seem like much. A thousand calls will catch their ear. Ten thousand calls can change a vote. We still have a beautiful country. Let's keep it that way.

May the Lord and Lady be with you on all your magickal journeys, and may They guard over you. Blesséd be.

Resource Guide

Most, if not all, of the shops listed here offer mail-order service and catalogs. Be aware, however, that retail shops go in and out of business with alarming frequency—some of those listed may not be in service when you write to them. Still others will have sprung up since this book was written.

As far as finding local suppliers, look for candles in drug stores, stationery stores, grocery stores and gift shops; flowers at grocery stores and florists, as well as your friends' gardens. You can sometimes find essential oils in gift shops or perfume shops, and crystals can be located in gift shops and rock shops. For herbs, gather them wild, purchase them through grocery stores or food co-ops, herb shops, and local plant nurseries for the plant itself.

Look for unusual altar pieces at local import supply stores and secondhand stores. Altar cloths are easy—go to your favorite fabric shop and buy a piece of cloth large enough to cover your altar table.

Finally, don't overlook the Yellow Pages. Look under such headings as Metaphysical, Herbs, Books (bookstores often carry far more than books), Lapidary Supplies, and Jewelry.

Five Corners, the local Witchcraft/Pagan shop owned by my friends Tony and Daniela (they don't do mail-order!), is listed under "Metaphysical" in our local directory. Small businesses need our support—don't overlook the shops in your home town. They may be hiding under obscure titles!

MAGICKAL SUPPLIES

Abyss   *jaynegreen. com.*
48-NWL Chester Road
Chester, MA 01011-9735
Abyss has a wonderful selection of items and their catalogs often feature advertisements from other shops.

White Light Pentacles/Sacred Spirit Products
P.O. Box 8163
Salem, MA 01971-8163
White Light Pentacles carries some of the loveliest jewelry I've ever owned.

Serpentine Music Productions
P.O. Box 2564-L1
Sebastopol, CA 95473
Wide variety of hard-to-find pagan music.

Eden Within
P.O. Box 667
Jamestown, NY 14702
Wide variety of magickal supplies.

Gypsy Heaven
115 S. Main St.
New Hope, PA 18938
catalog costs $3.00 (they say it's refundable through purchase—money orders only). Tarot decks, books, crystal balls, jewelry, etc.

MoonScents and Magickal Blends
P.O. Box 3811588-LL
Cambridge, MA 02238   *1-800-368-7417*
Wide variety of magickal supplies.

free catalog

PAGAN AND MAGICKAL JOURNALS AND MAGAZINES

New Moon Rising
3916 Southeast Harrison Street
Milwaukie, OR 97222

Green Egg
P.O. Box 488
Laytonville, CA 95454

SageWoman
P.O. Box 641LL
Point Arena, CA 95648

Shaman's Drum
P.O. Box 430
Willits, CA 95490-0430

Open Ways
P.O. Box 14415
Portland, OR 97293-0415

The Beltane Papers
P.O. Box 29694
Bellingham, WA 98228-1694

Suggested Music for Ritual

The following list consists of albums that I use in many of my ritual workings. I have found many of them quite effective for helping to create an appropriate mood.

• indicates one of my personal favorites

† indicates artists whose work can usually be purchased directly at a mainstream music store or special ordered through their distributors.

Alan, Todd
 Carry Me Home •
 Earth Magick
Barratt and Smith
 Aeolus
 Music of the Rolling World •
The Chieftans†
 A Chieftan's Celebration •
Dead Can Dance †
 Aion
 Into The Labyrinth •
 The Serpent's Egg
Deuter †
 Call of the Unknown
 Land of Enchantment •
Earth Tribe Rhythms
 A Total Drum Experience
Gabriel, Peter †
 Passion, Music from The Last Temptation of Christ
 Passion—Sources
Granger, Victoria
 Neandir, Lady of the Flame
 Starmony
Gwydion
 The Faerie Shaman
 Songs from the Old Religion

Holst †
 Planets, The
James, Tamarra
 Libation •
Jethro Tull †
 Heavy Horses •
 Songs from the Wood •
Kenny and Tzipora
 Branches
 Dreamer's Web
 Fairy Queen
Lady Isadora
 Queen of Earth and Sky •
 The Witching Hour
Oldfield, Todd †
 Tubular Bells
Roth, Gabrielle †
 Bones
 Initiation •
 Ritual
 Totem •
 Waves
Tangerine Dream †
 Force Majure
 Le Park
 Ricochet •
 Stratosphere

Tempest
  Bootleg •
  Serrated Edge •
  Sunken Treasures •
Tempest's work can be ordered directly from:
Tempest
2155 Park Blvd., Suite 1
Oakland, CA, 94606
Telephone: (510) 452-5048.
Call for prices first.

Some of the more obscure, Pagan-oriented music can be difficult to find. I suggest looking in *Circle Network News* or ordering through a distributor (Abyss sells music through its catalogs).

GLOSSARY

Amulet: a magickally charged object, often used to deflect negative energy.

Asperge: to sprinkle with water during or preceding ritual, to purify with sprinkled water.

Athame: a double-edged dagger for ritual use.

Aura: the energy field existing around all living things.

Balefire: a fire lit for magickal purpose. Traditional fires were lit on hills during Beltane and Samhain.

Bane: that which is dangerous or destructive.

Beltane: May 1 Sabbat celebration of life and sexuality.

Besom: a magickal broom.

Bolline: a white-handled knife for practical purposes, used by many traditional Witches during ritual.

Book of Shadows: a book of magickal spells, rituals, and lore.

Censer: an incense burner.

Centering, to Center: to find an internal point of balance.

Chalice: a ritual goblet.

Charge: to infuse an object or person with energy; also an oath or instruction.

Circle: a sphere created by a Witch, constructed of energy. Sacred space.

Cleansing, to Cleanse: to remove negative energy, to purify.

Coven: a group of Witches who come together to practice magick and celebrate the Sabbats.

Craft, the: Witchcraft, natural magick.

Deosil: clockwise (sunwise).

Deva: a powerful Faerie, land, plant, or mineral spirit; a collective oversoul.

Devoke; Devocation: a formal farewell in ritual, usually to the Gods or elements.

Divination: magickal art of discovering the unknown through use of cards, runes, stones, crystals balls, and other oracular tools.

Divine Marriage: (see Hieros Gamos).

Elements: the four building blocks of the universe. Earth, Air, Fire, Water. Major forces used in natural magick.

Equinox, Autumnal: The point during autumn when the Sun crosses the celestial equator; day and night are of equal length (see Mabon).

Equinox, Spring: (see Equinox, Vernal) (see Ostara).

Equinox, Vernal: The point during spring when the Sun crosses the celestial equator; day and night are of equal length (see Ostara).

Evocation: calling up spirits or other non-physical entities either to visible or invisible attendance.

Faerie: one of many nature spirits that inhabit a realm or dimension next to our own.

Faerie Kingdom: the realm of Faerie.

Fey: to be like or of the Faerie.

Futhark: the Norse Rune system/alphabet.

Grimoire: a magickal workbook.

Grounding, to Ground: to root one's self firmly in the physical world in preparation for magickal and metaphysical work.

Handfasting: a Witch, Wiccan, Pagan or Gypsy wedding.

Herbalist: one who works with herbs.

Hieros Gamos: the sacred mating of the God and Goddess.

Hunt: the Wild Hunt led by various Gods or Goddesses.

Hunter: the Horned God of the Witches.

Imbolc: festival of the Goddess Brid; Sabbat celebrated on February 2 each year.

Immolg: literally means "in milk." Name for Imbolc.

Initiation: a process of formally introducing or admitting the self or someone else into a Coven, religion, or other group.

Invoke, Invocation: an appeal or petition to a God or Goddess, element or energy.

Kelpie: Scottish water Faerie that lures men to their death.

Litha: (see Solstice, Summer). Sabbat festival honoring the Oak King and the Goddess in Their prime.

Lughnasadh: festival of the God Lugh; Sabbat celebrated on August 1 each year.

Mabon: (see Equinox, Autumnal). Sabbat festival honoring the harvest. A Pagan Thanksgiving.

Magick: the manipulation of natural forces and psychic energy to bring about desired changes.

Meditation: a state of reflection, contemplation.

Metsanhaltija: the Finnish wood nymphs and dryads under the rule of Mielikki, Goddess of the Hunt and of Faerie.

Midsummer's Eve: the night preceding the Summer Solstice. Often celebrated for its connections with the Faerie Kingdom.

Naiad: Grecian water nymph (water Faerie).

Nymph: Grecian woodland spirit (forest Faerie).

Ogham: the Celtic Rune system/alphabet.

Old Religion: Paganism, in all its myriad forms. A religion pre-dating the Judeo-Christian religions.

Ostara: (see Equinox, Vernal). Sabbat festival celebrating the Goddess Eostre and the advent of Spring.

Pagan, Paganism: (a follower of) one of many ancient (or modern revivals) Earth-centric/eco-centric religions.

Pentacle: a ritual object or piece of jewelry with a pentagram inscribed or woven into it.

Pentagram: Five-pointed star.

Phoenix: Egyptian bird that was consumed by fire every 500 years and rose, renewed from the ashes.

Polarity: the concept of equal, opposite energies.

Poppet: a figurine made of cloth, clay, wax or wood used in magick to represent a specific person.

Reincarnation: the doctrine of rebirth. Most Pagans and Witches accept this as a fact and see it as a part of the Wheel of Life.

Ritual: ceremony.

Ritualist: one who takes part in ritual.

Runes: symbols carved onto rocks, crystals, clay, or other surface, which embody powerful energies to be used during magick. Also: symbols used in early alphabets.

Sabbat: one of the eight Pagan holidays which comprise the Wheel of the Year.

Samhain: Sabbat festival celebrated every November 1, to honor and remember our ancestors and the dead.

Scry: to gaze into or at an object while in trance, to open oneself to visions from the future; to discern hidden motives and energies behind an event or situation.

Shaman: a man or woman who has attained a high degree of knowledge concerning altered states of consciousness. Usually an honored title associated with a structured form of study in what are generally regarded as Primitive or aboriginal religions.

Shamanism: the practice of Shamans.

Sidhe (Daoine Sidhe): children of the goddess Danu. The Celtic Faerie-Folk.

Skyclad: to practice magick and ritual in the nude; naked.

Solstice, Summer: when the sun is at its zenith over the Tropic of Cancer, during the month of June. The longest day of the year (see Litha).

Solstice, Winter: when the Sun is at its zenith over the Tropic of Capricorn, during the month of December. The shortest day of the year (see Yule).

Spell: a magickal ritual used to produce certain results in the physical world.

Sylphs: Faerie spirits of the air.

Talisman: a magickally charged object used to attract a specific force or energy to its bearer.

Tradition: a specific subgroup of Pagans, Witches, Wiccans or magick-workers.

Underworld: the realm of the spirit; realm of the dead.

Undines: Faerie spirits of the water.

Unicorn: a magickal horned horse.

Virgin: a woman who is not controlled by a man.

Visualization: the process of forming mental images.

Wicca, Wiccan: (a participant of) a modern revival of ancient Earth-centric religions focusing on the God and Goddess of Nature.

Widdershins: counterclockwise.

Will o' the Wisp: Faerie lights or energy beings that can and will lead humans astray in swamps, marshes, moors and the forest.

Witch, Witchcraft: (a practitioner of) the craft of magick (usually also a member of a Pagan religion).

Yule: (see Solstice, Winter). Midwinter Sabbat festival celebrating the rebirth of the Oak/Sun King.

BIBLIOGRAPHY

Andrews, Ted. *Enchantment of the Faerie Realm.* St. Paul, MN: Llewellyn, 1993.

———. *Animal-Speak.* St. Paul, MN: Llewellyn, 1995.

Anderson, William. *Green Man.* San Francisco: HarperSanFrancisco, 1990.

Cabot, Laurie. *Power of the Witch.* New York: Delacorte, 1989.

Campanelli, Pauline. *Ancient Ways.* St. Paul, MN: Llewellyn, 1991.

Conway, D. J. *The Ancient and Shining Ones.* St. Paul, MN: Llewellyn, 1993.

———. *Celtic Magic.* St. Paul, MN: Llewellyn, 1991.

Cunningham, Scott. *Earth, Air, Fire and Water.* St. Paul, MN: Llewellyn, 1992.

———. *Earth Power.* St. Paul, MN: Llewellyn, 1983.

———. *The Complete Book of Incenses, Oils and Brews.* St. Paul, MN: Llewellyn, 1989.

———. *The Magickal Household.* St. Paul, MN: Llewellyn, 1987.

Farrar, Janet and Stewart. *The Witches' Goddess: The Feminine Principle of Divinity.* Custer, WA: Phoenix, 1989.

———. *The Witches' God: The Masculine Principle of Divinity.* Custer, WA: Phoenix, 1989.

———. *Life and Times of a Modern Witch.* Custer, WA: Phoenix, 1987.

Fitch, Ed. *Magical Rites from the Crystal Well.* St. Paul, MN: Llewellyn, 1984.

Frazier, Sir James George. *The Golden Bough.* New York: Criterion Books, Inc., 1959.

Froud, Brian, and Alan Lee. *Faeries.* New York: Bantam, 1978.

Gadon, Elinor. *The Once and Future Goddess.* New York: Harper and Row, 1989.

Galenorn, Yasmine. *Trancing the Witch's Wheel.* St. Paul, MN: Llewellyn, 1997.

Kane, Herb Kawainui. *Pele, Goddess of Hawai'i's Volcanoes.* Captain Cook, HI: Kawainui Press, 1987.

Koppana, K. M. *Snakefat and Knotted Threads.* Finland: Mandragora Dimensions, 1990.

MacCana, Proinsias. *Celtic Mythology.* Bedrick Books, 1985.

Medicini, Marina. *Good Magic.* New York: Prentice Hall, 1989.

Murray, Liz and Colin. *The Celtic Tree Oracle.* New York: St. Martin's Press, 1988.

Pennick, Nigel. *Practical Magic in the Northern Tradition.* Wellingboro, England: Aquarian Press, 1989.

Peschel, Lisa. *A Practical Guide to the Runes.* St. Paul, MN: Llewellyn, 1991.

Starhawk. *The Spiral Dance.* New York: Harper and Row, 1979.

Teish, Louisa. *Jambalaya.* New York: HarperCollins, 1985.

Thorsson, Edred. *The Book of Ogham.* St. Paul, MN: Llewellyn, 1992.

INDEX

☾ Look For The Crescent Moon

Llewellyn publishes hundreds of books on your favorite subjects! To get these exciting books, including the ones on the following pages, check your local bookstore or order them directly from Llewellyn.

Order By Phone
- Call toll-free within the U.S. and Canada, 1-800-THE MOON
- In Minnesota, call (612) 291-1970
- We accept VISA, MasterCard, and American Express

Order By Mail
- Send the full price of your order (MN residents add 7% sales tax) in U.S. funds, plus postage & handling to:

  Llewellyn Worldwide
  P.O. Box 64383, Dept. K-304-2
  St. Paul, MN 55164–0383, U.S.A.

Postage & Handling
(For the U.S., Canada, and Mexico)
- $4.00 for orders $15.00 and under
- $5.00 for orders over $15.00
- No charge for orders over $100.00

We ship UPS in the continental United States. We ship standard mail to P.O. boxes. Orders shipped to Alaska, Hawaii, The Virgin Islands, and Puerto Rico are sent first-class mail. Orders shipped to Canada and Mexico are sent surface mail.

International orders: Airmail—add freight equal to price of each book to the total price of order, plus $5.00 for each non-book item (audio tapes, etc.).

Surface mail—Add $1.00 per item.

Allow 4–6 weeks for delivery on all orders.
Postage and handling rates subject to change.

Discounts
We offer a 20% discount to group leaders or agents. You must order a minimum of 5 copies of the same book to get our special quantity price.

Free Catalog

Get a free copy of our color catalog, *New Worlds of Mind and Spirit*. Subscribe for just $10.00 in the United States and Canada ($30.00 overseas, airmail). Many bookstores carry *New Worlds*— ask for it!

Visit our web site at www.llewellyn.com for more information.

Trancing the Witch's Wheel

A Guide to Magickal Meditations

Yasmine Galenorn

Meet the Wind and the Queen of Air; stand watch as the Sun King is reborn on Yuletide day; cross the barren lava fields with Pele, and learn to shapeshift like Gwion in his flight from Cerridwen.

In *Trancing the Witch's Wheel,* you will find twenty intricate and beautiful guided meditations, written to lead you into the very heart of the seasons, the elements, and the nature of the Divine. This book offers beginning and advanced students a guide as they journey through the cycles of the Pagan year.

Discover how to hone your sense of focus and clearly envision what you want to create in your life. The meditations in *Trancing the Witch's Wheel* are designed for both solitary and group work, and each chapter includes an overview of the subject and suggested exercises to help you in your explorations.

1-56718-303-4, 6 x 9, 224 pp., softcover $12.95

To order, call 1–800–THE MOON

Prices subject to change without notice

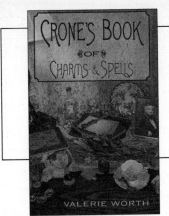

Crone's Book of
Charms & Spells

Valerie Worth

Here is a charming little grimoire of magical practices and rituals that reads as if it were written in an earlier century. In a style that is poetic and appealing to the imagination, this book will give you practical directions for carrying out numerous spells, charms, recipes, or rituals—all of which take their inspiration from nature and folklore.

Concoct herb brews for mental vigor and to strengthen passion. Inscribe talismans and amulets to gain wealth, eternal youth, or relief from pain. Practice spells to drive away evil, procure your heart's desire, warm the affections of another, or break a troublesome habit. Conduct twelve symbolic rites to honor the ceremonies of the year.

In a world where nature is so often slighted or ignored, this book serves to heighten your awareness of the magic lying beneath the surface, and the powerful ties that exist between mind and matter, even in modern times.

1-56718-811-7, 208 pp., 5 ³⁄₁₆ x 8, illus., softcover $6.95

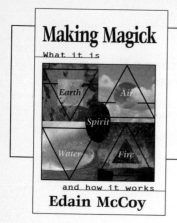

Making Magick

What It Is and How It Works

Edain McCoy

How do I raise and send energy? What happens if I make a mistake in casting a spell? What is sex magick all about? What is the Moon's role in magick? Which magickal tools do I need the most?

Making Magick is a complete course in natural magick that answers these and hundreds of other questions. Through exercises designed to develop basic skills, *Making Magick* lays a firm foundation of elemental magickal wisdom. The first chapters begin with an introduction to magick and how it works. You will study Craft tools, learn to connect with the elements—the building blocks of magick—and delve into the intricacies of spell construction and timing. The last half of the book will take you into the advanced magickal arts, which rely on highly honed skills of meditation, astral projection, visualization, and sustaining of creative energy. A special chapter on the tattwas will show you how to use these ancient Hindu symbols as gateways into the astral worlds.

1-56718-670-X, 6 x 9, 336 pp., illus., photos $14.95

The Complete Book of Incense, Oils and Brews

Scott Cunningham

For centuries the composition of incenses, the blending of oils, and the mixing of herbs have been used by people to create positive changes in their lives. With this book, the curtains of secrecy have been drawn back, providing you with practical, easy-to-understand information that will allow you to practice these methods of magical cookery.

Scott Cunningham, world-famous expert on magical herbalism, first published *The Magic of Incense, Oils and Brews* in 1986. *The Complete Book of Incense, Oils and Brews* is a revised and expanded version of that book. Scott took readers' suggestions from the first edition and added more than 100 new formulas. Every page has been clarified and rewritten, and new chapters have been added.

There is no special, costly equipment to buy, and ingredients are usually easy to find. The book includes detailed information on a wide variety of herbs, sources for purchasing ingredients, substitutions for hard-to-find herbs, a glossary, and a chapter on creating your own magical recipes.

0-87542-128-8, 288 pp., 6 x 9, illus., softcover $12.95

Moon Magick

Myth & Magic, Crafts & Recipes, Rituals & Spells

D.J. Conway

No creature on this planet is unaffected by the power of the Moon. Its effects range from making us feel energetic or adventurous to tense and despondent. By putting excess Moon energy to work for you, you can learn to plan projects, work and travel at the optimum times.

Moon Magick explains how each of the 13 lunar months is directly connected with a different type of seasonal energy flow and provides modern rituals and spells for tapping this energy and celebrating the Moon phases. Each chapter describes new Pagan rituals—79 in all—related to that particular Moon, plus related Moon lore, ancient holidays, spells, meditations and suggestions for foods, drinks and decorations to accompany your Moon rituals. This book includes two thorough dictionaries of Moon deities and symbols.

By moving through the year according to the 13 lunar months, you can become more attuned to the seasons, the Earth and your inner self. *Moon Magick* will show you how to let your life flow with the power and rhythms of the Moon to benefit your physical, emotional and spiritual well-being.

1-56718-167-8, 7 x 10, 320 pp., illus., softcover $16.95

The Magical Household

Empower Your Home with Love,
Protection, Health and Happiness

Scott Cunningham and
David Harrington

Whether your home is a small apartment or a palatial mansion, you want it to be something special. Now it can be with *The Magical Household*. Learn how to make your home more than just a place to live. Turn it into a place of security, life, fun and magic. Here you will not find the complex magic of the ceremonial magician. Rather, you will learn simple, quick and effective magical spells that use nothing more than common items in your house: furniture, windows, doors, carpet, pets, etc. You will learn to take advantage of the intrinsic power and energy that is already in your home, waiting to be tapped. You will learn to make magic a part of your life. The result is a home that is safeguarded from harm and a place which will bring you happiness, health and more.

0-87542-124-5, 208 pp., 5¼ x 8, illus., softcover $9.95

A Victorian Grimoire

Romance • Enchantment • Magic

Patricia Telesco

Like a special opportunity to rummage through your grandmother's attic, *A Victorian Grimoire* offers you a personal invitation to discover a storehouse of magical treasures. Enhance every aspect of your daily life as you begin to reclaim the romance, simplicity and "know-how" of the Victorian era—that exceptional period of American history when people's lives and times were shaped by their love of the land, of home and family, and by their simple acceptance of magic as part of everyday life.

More and more, people are searching for ways to create peace and beauty in this increasingly chaotic world. This special handbook—Grimoire—shows you how to recreate that peace and beauty with simple, down-to-earth "Victorian Enchantments" that turn every mundane act into an act of magic . . . from doing the dishes . . . to making beauty-care products . . . to creating games for children. This book is a handy reference when you need a specific spell, ritual, recipe or tincture for any purpose. What's more, *A Victorian Grimoire* is a captivating study of the turn of the century and a comprehensive repository of common-sense knowledge. Learn how to relieve a backache, dry and store herbs, help children get over fears of the dark, treat pets with first aid, and much, much more.

0-87542-784-7, 384 pgs., 7 x 10, illus., softcover $14.95

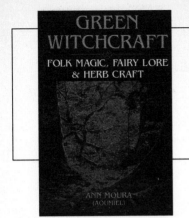

Green Witchcraft

Folk Magic, Fairy Lore & Herb Craft

Aoumiel

Very little has been written about traditional family practices of the Old Religion simply because such information has not been offered for popular consumption. If you have no contacts with these traditions, *Green Witchcraft* will meet your need for a practice based in family and natural Witchcraft traditions.

Green Witchcraft describes the worship of nature and the use of herbs that have been part of human culture from the earliest times. It relates to the Lord & Lady of Greenwood, the Primal Father and Mother, and to the Earth Spirits called Faeries.

Green Witchcraft traces the historic and folk background of this path and teaches its practical techniques. Learn the basics of Witchcraft from a third-generation, traditional family Green Witch who openly shares from her own experiences. Through a how-to format you'll learn rites of passage, activities for Sabbats and Esbats, Fairy lore, self-dedication, self-initiation, spellwork, herbcraft and divination.

This practical handbook is an invitation to explore, identify and adapt the Green elements of Witchcraft that work for you, today.

1-56718-690-4, 6 x 9, 288 pp., illus. $14.95